HTML 5 and CSS 3

Made Simple

IVAN BAYROSS

www.bpbonline.com

REPRINT 2026

First Edition 2011

ISBN: 978-81-8333-441-9

Distributors:

BPB PUBLICATIONS
20, Ansari Road, Darya Ganj
New Delhi-110002
Ph: 23254990/23254991

DECCAN AGENCIES
4-3-329, Bank Street,
Hyderabad-500195
Ph: 24756967/24756400

MICRO MEDIA
Shop No. 5, Mahendra Chambers,
150 DN Rd. Next to Capital Cinema,
V.T. (C.S.T.) Station, MUMBAI-400 001
Ph: 22078296/22078297

Published by Manish Jain for BPB Publications, 20 Ansari Road, Darya Ganj, New Delhi-110002 and Printed by him at Manipal Technologies, Manipal

www.bpbonline.com

Foreword

All programmers know that programming for the Internet is a great place to be. This employment window is constantly renewing itself and is ever evolving. Coding in it will retain its fascination for a long long time.

The Internet is a huge number of heterogeneous computers with heterogeneous operating systems and programming environments all working together in complete harmony hence this difference.

The traditional **U**ser **I**nterface programming environment for the Internet is HTML and CSS.

Today HTML**5** and CSS**3** are actively supported in several modern Browsers. The combination of HTML5 and CSS3 empowers programmers to deliver a rich and extraordinary site visitor experience when creating any website's, User Interface (U.I.).

There are not too many books written that cover these environments, here is what makes this book different.

It's written in such a way that you will**:**

- Rapidly start using HTML5
- Rapidly start using CSS3 for marking up the HTML5 elements
- Deliver a rich and extraordinary site visitor experience via the UI that you create

By the end of working through the examples in this book you will have acquired all the skills you need to create great, dynamic, interactive Web Sites using HTML5 elements and CSS3 attributes. Growth beyond this is by surfing the web and trying to figure out how specific functionality was brought to a website using this combination.

There are a number of web sites that have excellent HTML5 and CSS3 tutorials that are mapped to real world examples. Most offer such material for free. I strongly recommend you Google for these tutorial sites. Do subscribe to a few that make sense to you. This will really make you fly.

Concepts are built using simple language. Examples have easily understood logic. Once these are grasped the skill gained will allow any commercial application developer to create a rich site visitor experience quickly, confidently and successfully

The enclosed CD-ROM has the code examples used in the book and several useful goodies. I've also added several web site snippets, which would help give you a direction when you are creating you're a web site for the first time.

Additionally, the CD-ROM contains Apache, PHP and MySQL executables that will help you setup the framework on any computer.

I must add that the very best way to create great, User Interfaces is by surfing the Internet constantly and checking out the web site's that interest you. Try and figure how the web site was coded to provide the functionally that it actually has.

My approach, (where possible) right click on an interesting web page and 'View Source'. This will give you an unparalleled insight into the coding techniques used by others to create the web site.

This foreword will not be complete without my thanking the many people who encouraged me and put up with the many revisions and updations of the manuscript with patience and tolerance.

My sincere **THANKS** go to**:**

- My publisher Mr. Manish Jain. He has brought enormous changes in my life. This is a debt of gratitude I will never be able to pay in full.
- Ms. Meher Bala and Ms. Kavita Mavani who carefully checked and rechecked the manuscript until all the errors of Coding and English Grammar and formatting were corrected (*as humanly possible*). Thank you for being so meticulous.
- The many programmers who read this material, without you all I would not be an author. I welcome both your brickbats and bouquets. You can contact me via BpB, New Delhi, else you could check out my web site appropriately named www.opensourcevarsity.com.
- Finally, my wife Cynthia who has always encouraged me whenever I thought that I'd never get a manuscript ready for publishing. You have always helped to keep my feet firmly on the ground, in you I am truly blessed.

Ivan N. Bayross

TABLE OF CONTENTS

SECTION I – HTML5

SECTION II – CSS3

OTHER TITLES OF INTEREST

Building Production-ready **Web Apps** with **Node.js**
ISBN: 9789391392338

Modern Web Development with **Deno**
ISBN: 9789355510969

Building Modern Web Applications with **ASP.NET Core Blazor**
ISBN: 9789355518798

Building Modern Serverless **Web APIs**
ISBN: 9789390684786

Exploring Web Components
ISBN: 9789389423976

Web Designing & **Development** Training Guide
ISBN: 9788183335799

Building Modern Web Applications with **Jakarta EE, NoSQL Databases...**
ISBN: 9789389423341

Advanced Web Development with **React**
ISBN: 9789389423594

Web Data Mining with **Python**
ISBN: 9789355513632

Web Testing with **Cypress**
ISBN: 9789355510280

Web Development Toolkit for **Java Developers**
ISBN: 9789355510341

Java for **Web Development**
ISBN: 9789355511430

A Python Guide for Web Scraping
ISBN: 9789390684991

D3: Modern Web Visualization
ISBN: 9789355511010

Building Dynamic Web Experiences with **PHP**
ISBN: 9789355516596

JavaScript for **Modern Web Development**
ISBN: 9789389328721

Section 1

HTML5

1. An Introduction To HTML5

A short while ago, let's say six months or so, it seemed like everyone is talking about HTML5. The discussions were pretty widely spread and seldom provided any specific HTML5 background. There also was a lot of argument on whether HTML5 was really ready for prime time use or not.

In this material I'd like to:

- Provide a little history
- Explain what HTML5 is
- What HTML5 covers
- Work through a few code examples

Finally, with reference to the above try and figure out whether HTML5 is ready for prime time use or not.

A Little Bit Of Background

HTML5 emerged from within the **W**eb **H**ypertext **A**pplication **T**echnology **W**orking **G**roup (WHATWG). Their singular focus is the development of HTML and APIs for web applications.

In 1999 the specifications of HTML 4 was completed by W3C. Next W3C, the organization responsible for HTML, CSS, and numerous other, web standards began work on XHTML, which was then the new direction for web content markup.

Many (if not most) HTML coders will have used XHTML version 1 codespec. XHTML version 1 is compatible with older browsers, and older versions of HTML.

The XHTML version 2 specifications, however, were far less compatible. Many professional web developers openly criticized several aspects of XHTML version 2. W3C continued on this specification, which had little relevance to the "real" world of web development.

Starting in 2004, Apple, Mozilla and Opera, began worrying about the direction W3C were taking with XHTML. It appeared there was no clear focus in the XHTML2 specifications on the real-life needs for web developers.

In 2004, to address the seeming growing difference between the work of W3C and the needs of web and Browser developers, the W3C held a Web Applications workshop. There were huge disagreements between various stake holders in the Web Applications workshop.

The **W**eb **H**ypertext **A**pplication **T**echnology **W**orking **G**roup (WHAT-WG) was formed almost immediately, by employees of Opera Software, Mozilla Foundation (developers of Firefox) and Apple. The WHAT-WG began work on its own future version of HTML. They called this version Web Applications 1.0.

In 2007, W3C began work once more on versions of HTML that were not based on XML technologies, with the WHAT-WG work as its foundation. This became known as HTML5. In July 2009, W3C announced that XHTML version 2 would be cancelled in favor of HTML5.

Cancelling XHTML version 2 and favoring HTML means that the only way forward for HTML is in the form of HTML5. Hence, it appears that HTML5 really is the future.

HTML5 is the correct way to spell the word. HTML5 is written exactly like that, i.e. no space between the L and the number 5. This way of spelling HTML5 has now been totally adopted by both WHATWG and W3CWG.

The WHAT-WG's version is a superset of the W3C HTML5 specification. The WHAT-WG's version includes technologies that are not yet (and may never be) part of HTML5 as published by the W3C. In this material what will be covered is all that is part of the W3C's - HTML5 specification.

What Is HTML5?

HTML5 is a specification defined to help web developers by extending HTML/XHTML with new:

- Semantically rich elements
- Deprecating specific attributes
- Introducing new attributes
- Altering some old element and their attributes

Additionally, there is the possibility of using HTML5 attributes to create web pages that are **W**eb **A**ccessibility **I**nitiative - **A**ccessible **R**ich **I**nternet **A**pplications (WAI-ARIA) enabled. This refers to make web pages a whole lot more accessible to people with various disabilities.

HTML5 also introduces a number of APIs which helps making it easy to create web applications, such as:

- 2D drawing API with the canvas element
- API for playing of video and audio (with the video and audio elements)
- API that allows a Web application to register itself for certain protocols or media types
- Editing API in combination with a new global content editable attribute
- Drag & drop API in combination with a draggable attribute
- API that exposes Browser history and allows pages to add to it to prevent breaking the back button
- Cross-document messaging with postMessage

HTML5 seems to have two main areas of focus. Markup of webpage content, which is focused on the look and feel of web sites and their pages. API (***A****pplication* ***P****rogramming* ***I****nterface*), which is focused on building web driven commercial applications. In both these two areas HTML5 delivers of a lot of brand new syntax, semantics and technology.

Hence the term HTML5 is used by a lot of web developers to imply that they are using new state-of-the-art technologies to create a web site or an Internet driven application. In reality this may just be HTML with some new semantic enhancements or it could be a complex block of code that uses several new API's and JavaScript to display Internet driven magic in a requesting Browser.

Backwards Compatibility & Progressive Enhancement

HTML5 set out to be backwards compatible. Hence, it has been widely adopted. HTML5 works with the latest versions of web Browsers available today as well as several older versions of the same Browsers.

HTML5 has defined a number of new elements that do not have a particular look or behavior attached to them. These new elements offer a semantic richness to HTML codespec that simply did not exist before. The best is that these elements can be styled as desired using CSS.

Since HTML5 is backward compatible, when it is executed in Browsers that can correctly interpret its syntax it will deliver a richer user experience than when HTML5 is executed in Browsers that cannot interpret its new syntax.

HTML5 degrades gracefully and thus delivers default content in Browsers that cannot handle its new codespec (i.e. perhaps older versions of a Browser that currently can).

There are multiple new input types defined in HTML5, for example:

tel	search	url	email
datetime	month	week	Time
datetime-local	number	range	color

So far, Webkit (an open source Browser engine) and Opera are the early adopter Browsers. Their rendering engines can implement some of these new input types. This is especially true because of the really great work that Opera is doing to support WebForms 2.0.

In other web Browsers, wherever these new input types have not been defined, they will gracefully degrade to input type="text".

This means that the input type = "search" will give subtle, but a better user experience in the latest versions of Webkit, Opera, Safari and Google Chrome, (where the rendering engine recognizes the new input types) but will still remain fully functional in all other (perhaps older version) Browsers.

HTML5 is a huge specification, far from complete, and very far from being completely supported in modern web Browsers. This material will focus on those parts of the HTML5 specification that are supported in modern web Browsers.

This means that this material will be of:

- Immediate use and value to developers
- Particularly relevant to semantic and structural markup
- Useful in a wide range of modern browsers
- Where not supported there exist workarounds

Hence, all the Browsers widely used today, should interpret the HTML5 codespec used in this book hopefully without breaking the web page.

This material will focus on the following HTML5 aspects (there are a lot more, but these are the most relevant, currently supported and useful futures)

- New structural and semantic markup - such as the header, footer and nav elements
- The new canvas element, for creating web based bitmap graphics using JavaScript
- New native audio and video elements
- Related elements and attributes for embedding multimedia
- Content that Browsers can play without plugins

Most of which will be covered in some detail in this material.

Today most modern Browsers actually support HTML5. Hence within the HTML programming community there is quite a bit of excitement about HTML5 with most websites and portals crafted today using HTML5 to add both glitz and functionality.

HTML5, the new Web standard has been adopted by:

- Apple
- Google
- And many others

HTML5 allows Web developers to embed advanced graphics, typography, animation and transitions effortlessly into their webpages.

A ton of newspapers around the world have started writing about HTML5 on the first page, that's when you know for sure that there's something big happening with HTML5.

The term HTML5 is increasingly being used as a mark for some really interesting stuff being displayed in webpages. This interesting stuff that is happening on webpages is specifically bound to the technologies that are defined in the HTML 5 specification. Using the new Tags, whose functionality is defined in HTML specification is a good thing as it makes the Web a better place for Web users.

Offline Web Application Support

For web application to work successfully they have to be connected to the web. With HTML5 that's no longer the case. HTML5 supports offline web applications in a number of ways

By enabling resources like HTML, CSS and JavaScript to be cached, so that if a user goes offline, the browser will have kept these resources, and the application can still be used, or even installed locally on say a mobile device

By sending events to a web application when a user goes on and offline

These two requirements are very much part of the HTML5 specification.

Web Storage which is not part of the official W3C specification, enables the persistent storage of data on a client device between sessions (*you can imagine this to be something like cookies, but much more sophisticated*).

Data stored this way is stored using simple key value pairs. Based on SQL there is also a partially complete specification for a much more sophisticated storage mechanism. For rather complicated reasons, this partially completed specification is unlikely to be completed as it stands.

Threaded JavaScript

To date, JavaScript has not easily allowed multiple processes to run in parallel.

This means that scripts which take a long time to execute can bring most Browsers to a halt, unless web developers have done considerable coding that ensures processes which may take a long time to complete their execution, pause what they are doing and hand control back to the Browser - frequently.

Standardized Communication Between Browsers And Web Servers

Communication between Browsers and Web servers for a long time has been less than ideal.

The websockets API (*an HTML5 specification from W3C*)

And

The websockets protocol (*being developed by the IETF*)

Facilitates two way communications between a Browser and a Web server. Currently web sockets is supported by Firefox, Safari and Chrome.

Communicating between a Browser and a Web server has long been a relatively complicated process.

Before the introduction of XMLHttpRequest DOM object it was only possible to communicate whole pages at a time between a Browser and Web server.

The introduction of XMLHttpRequest DOM object which has been widely adopted by most browsers enables web pages and applications to communicate with a Web server, but browsers must still explicitly request data from the Web server.

There have been relatively complicated techniques, which collectively go by the name of **Comet** which enables a Web server to send data without a Browser explicitly requesting for this information.

Web Sockets are a standardized approach (*in both the Browser, and on the Web server*) to genuine bi-directional communication between Browsers and Web servers (*i.e. either the Browser or the Web server can independently send messages to one another*).

Richer Forms Support

As its original WHAT-WG name implies, HTML5 started life focusing on Web applications.

One area in which this was particularly evident was in Web Forms. Web Forms are now officially part of the HTML5 specification.

Web Forms include many new possible, commonly used input element types, like:

- Sliders
- Date pickers
- Attributes like - required
- Placeholder text

And more

We will cover some of the most useful and widely supported, or backwards compatible aspects of Web Forms later in this material. As we've just seen, HTML5 is a very diverse. Some aspects of HTML5 are nonexistent in any Browser, some aspects are very patchily supported. Other HTML5 features are wither widely supported, or work, or can be made to work in ways that are compatible with all commonly used Browsers.

For the moment, let's look Browser by Browser at their support for the major aspects of HTML5. In this material we will focus on IE6 and up, as well as the latest versions of Safari (4 and 5), Firefox (3.6) and Opera (10.6), as users of these browsers tend to upgrade far more quickly than many IE users.

New Structural And Semantic Markup

HTML Elements

Most Browsers for quite some time now have handled the inclusion of HTML elements and attributes they don't recognize gracefully. Internet Explorer (*until version 8*) did not allow the styling of unrecognized HTML elements (*though Firefox, Opera and Safari have permitted this for a long time now*)

This means that in a sense, the new structural and semantic elements of HTML5 are **not compatible** with IE 7 or older – which is still a sizeable (*if reducing*) share of the Browser market.

CSS Attributes

For attributes, rather than elements, things are a bit better. From IE7 on, as well as other modern Browsers, you can use CSS attribute selectors to style known and even unknown elements contained within the HTML codespec.

For example:

```
section {color: blue}
```

Will color the text of the following element blue in IE 8 and 9, as well as Firefox, Safari and Opera,

But

Not in IE6 or 7

```
<section>It was a dark and stormy night</section>
```

But, this CSS

```
[section] {color: blue}
<section section="true">It was a dark and stormy night</section>
```

Will color the text blue in the following element, in IE7 and up, as well as Firefox, Safari and Opera.

Strange but true.

Video And Audio

At present, as we'll see in, Safari, Firefox and Opera, as well as version 9 of Internet Explorer, support the video and audio elements of HTML5. But there are some complexities.

Firstly, these elements are designed so that we can gracefully fallback to the object element if they aren't supported. Which is good.

The not quite so good bit is that even when the `video` and `audio` element are supported in Browsers, because different Browsers support different audio and vides codecs natively, we still have to encode our audio and video in multiple ways , before our audio or video files play in all Browsers.

Canvas

Introduced in Safari way back in version 1.3, the HTML5 Canvas element is now supported in Firefox, Opera, and IE 9. It is however not supported in versions 8 and older of IE.

Geolocation

The Geolocation API that allows a web site or an application to ask the Browser where the user is located. This includes longitude, latitude and altitude. This also potentially can include the direction the user faces when travelling and their speed of travel. Of course, if the user wants to share this information or not is at their own discretion.

Geolocation is not and has never really been a part of the HTML 5 specification but, it can be reasonably considered part of practical HTML5, i.e. HTML5 codespec used and recognized by most modern Browsers.

Safari 5, Safari on the iPad and iPhone, Opera 10.6, Firefox 3.5, and many mobile devices, support the Geolocation API. However it is not supported in Internet Explorer 9 preview releases, and is rumored at the time of creating this material that the Geolocation API will not be supported by Internet Explorer.

For anyone who is proficient in JavaScript, and the JavaScript DOM, using the Geolocation API is really pretty straightforward.

A new `geolocation` object, a child of the document object exposes a number of methods, including, (*as in this example*), the ability to watch the users location.

```
navigator.geolocation.watchPosition(function(position) {
  showLocation(position.coords.latitude,
position.coords.longitude,
      position.coords.altitude);
}
```

To locate the user it may take some time and hence the Geolocation API works asynchronously. We have to pass the `geolocation` object a callback function `showLocation` which we define elsewhere, and when the position is known, the callback function is executed. It is very straightforward technology to start working with.

Developers have long been able to roughly determine where a user is located from the user Browser's IP.

With the rise of the mobile web, and devices with support for GPS and compasses, mobile devices can now locate their users within a few meters anywhere on this earth. Hence, the question arises, would this be useful for developers of web sites and web driven applications? Indeed it is.

While the W3C Geolocation API is only moderately well supported on the desktop (Opera 10.6 introduced it, as did Safari 5, while Firefox 3.5 introduced Geo API support, but even the latest preview versions of IE9 don't support it).

However, where geolocation is very well supported is in mobile devices. iOS based devices version 3 and up (*iPod Touch, iPad and iPhone 3G*) support the Geo API, as do Android 2.0 devices, among others.

For Browsers which do not support the GeoAPI, there are JavaScript based approaches to looking up the location of a user from the IP address that their browser reports.

Offline Support

As was mentioned earlier, there are three HTML5 features which when used together help create web applications that work offline as well as they do online.

- Explicit caching of web based resources using a manifest file
- Persistent storage of data on the client
- The ability to determine whether the device is currently online or offline

Together, these HTML5 features give web developers the ability to create applications that can be effectively installed on a client device, and run even if the device is not connected to the web. When the device does connect to the web, it can easily synchronize its content with a Web server if required.

Caching is supported on all modern web enabled devices, as well as all modern Browsers with the exception of IE. However, persistent data storage, and the ability to determine whether a browser is connected are supported on all modern browsers and devices, including IE8 and up.

Web Workers

Web Workers is supported in all modern browsers with the exception of IE.

Web Sockets

Web Sockets are currently supported in Firefox, Safari and Chrome.

Web Forms

HTML5's extensions to forms, are not widely supported in current Browsers, but several features, such as new input element types like `tel`, `url`, `email` and `search` can be widely used, because when required all current Browsers gracefully degrade these elements to the type `text`.

So, when web developers use input element types of tel, url, search and so on as applicable, where a plain text field is also an appropriate form control, they are future proofing their form based applications.

By doing this, web developers add a little extra sophistication to their web site for visitors whose Browsers currently support these new input element types.

For example, Safari on the iPhone will present different keyboard layouts to users depending on whether the input element that the form cursor is focused on is of type tel or email.

So, what HTML5 elements can be used right now?

This answer really depends on various factors. For some HTML5 features, there is already widespread support. With web forms HTML5 input element types, Browsers graceful degrade to text where the element type is not supported.

For some HTML5 features, there are JavaScript libraries which provide the missing features for Browsers which do not support them.

If you are specifically tailoring a web site or a web driven application for example modern mobile devices, where HTML5 features are widely supported, it's possible to use many of W3C's new HTML features/specifications.

And when experimenting for your own professional development, and the problems of patchy support are not an issue, of course then by all means use HTML5.

In any case with the current momentum of HTML5 adoption in Browsers, (*including in IE9*), these HTML5 features will become increasingly mainstream.

Chrome Frame And Google Gears

For some years, Google has developed a Browser plug-in for most browsers (*including IE6 and up*) that provides offline storage, geolocation services, background JavaScript execution, and other HTML5-like features. If any site visitor has this plugin placed within their Browser, web developers can use HTML5 features in their sites and applications.

Google has discontinued this project in favor of Chrome Frame (*as well as of course native HTML5 features in Google Chrome*), a plug-in specifically created for Internet Explorer (6 and up), that web developers may opt into using.

If any website HTML document includes the following meta element within <head></head>

```
<meta http-equiv="X-UA-Compatible" content="chrome=1" />
```

then, where Chrome Frame is installed, developers can use many more HTML5 features than are supported natively in Internet Explorer. This is because for pages where developers opt in, Chrome Frame in fact *uses Google Chrome to render the page*, and provides these features.

To Round Up And Conclude

The HTML4 specification has been with us for quite a while now. Approximately about ten years. HTML4 has not really has any major update.

The XHTML specification did little more than make coding slightly stricter, forcing programmers to write better quality code if they were concerned with compliance.

HTML5 does much more than XHTML. HTML5 adds a few new features. Not a huge amount, but the ones that it does add are very useful.

Very Quickly – Here's what's new?

<canvas> </canvas>

The <canvas> tag is a 2D (*at the moment – the third dimension may come later*) drawing area controlled by JavaScript.

Canvas can use it for doing a wide variety of things in a webpage - Graphs, Games, Presentations and more.

Because Canvas is controlled by JavaScript, you can use simple JavaScript codespec to interact with it very easily.

<video></video>

The <video> tag makes it pretty simple to embed video clips with web pages.

The <video> tag has attributes like src, autoplay, and loop.

The <video> tag can contain additional markup describing the video, perhaps, the full transcript of the video.

<audio></audio>

The <audio> tag is very similar to the <video> in functionality, but is used for audio files.

Context Menus

HTML5 provides a method for defining context menus. This makes using Context Menus remarkably simple in web applications.

Using Context menus may not be of vital importance when creating websites or portals, but when creating applications driven via the Internet context menus provide a lot of options without taking up space within the User Interface

New Structural Elements

HTML is largely unstructured. Hence in HTML5 a few new elements have been introduced to try and rectify this weakness.

The HTML5 Structure based elements are:

Element	Explanation
<section>	A section with web page content, or section of a chapter of a text within a book
<header>	The <header> element can be used to describe the web page header section. This is not the same as the <head> element
<footer>	The <footer> element can be used to describe the web page footer section
<nav>	The <nav> element can be used to encompass web page links. The websites menu items can be bound within these elements
<article>	The <article> element can be used to encapsule a blog article
<aside>	The <aside> element can be used to provide extra information for a block of text. Much like sidebar material in books.
<figure>	The <figure> element can be used to annotate main text with diagrams

New Inline Elements

HTML5 has introduced several new elements to help encapsule such content as Time or Numbers with a webpage.

The new inline elements are:

<mark>	The <mark> element indicates that a specific section of text is marked up in some way. You could, for example, use this to mark search terms in a list of results
<time>	The <time> element is used to represent Time or a Date within a block of text
<meter>	The <meter> element can be used to enclose a figure of some sort. It has multiple attributes such as: value, min, max, low, high, and optimum
<progress>	The <progress> element can be used to show a progress bar of some sort on the webpage. It has a couple of attributes such as: value and max

New Form Input Types

In HTML4 there was just a single Input element type named TextBox, HTML5 now has several new Input element types, such as:

- datetime
- datetime-local
- date
- month
- week
- time
- number
- range
- email
- url

Some of these new input types are already commonly used when creating desktop User Interfaces. Regretfully not a lot of these new Input elements have been implemented by Browsers, but luckily all Browsers gracefully degrade the new Input element type to Text.

Hence, all forms created using the new HTML5 Input elements will still work perfectly well and will be future proof when Browsers start supporting the new HTML5 input types.

Dropped Elements

The following elements have been dropped or replaced in HTML5:

- acronym
- applet
- basefont
- big
- center
- dir
- font
- frame
- frameset
- isindex
- noframes
- noscript
- s
- strike
- tt
- u

Character Encoding Syntax

The character encoding syntax for an HTML5 document is now: <meta charset="UTF-8">.

New Interactive Elements

Here are some of the new HTML5 elements that will help make building websites and web applications, a lot easier.

<details>	The <details> element can be used to provide further information about something specific. For example, it could be implemented by Browsers to display information as tooltips. This tag can have an open attribute which dictates whether the content is initially shown to the user or not.
<datagrid>	The <datagrid> element, unlike traditional tables (*which are designed to be static*), can be used to provide a set of user data with has some degree of interactivity. For example, a user can select rows or columns, edit data, sort data, and generally interact with data in the Browser, when the data is enclosed within the <datagrid> element
<menu>	<menu> is a deprecated element but the <menu> element is back in HTML5 with a new meaning. The <menu> element can contain <command> elements which cause a particular action to happen. For example, the <menu> element which encloses the <command> element can be used to provide a toolbar, or a context menu. It can have label and icon attributes. These can be nested to provide multiple levels of menus.

New DTD

HTML5 has a new, much simpler DTD. <!doctype html>.

This is so much simpler than the HTML4 DTD and far simpler to remember.

The Async Attribute

This indicates that a block of script must be executed asynchronously this will cause the script to execute without blocking the rest of the webpage until it's finished its execution.

To Sum Up:

HTML5 could actually be the HTML update that everyone has been waiting for. It provides multiple useful additions to the scripting language that make building web based applications a whole lot easier, work a whole lot more efficiently, while making the codespec a lot simpler.

As is usual in the Internet domain, all Browsers do not support everything significantly MS IE, but over time this is bound to change.

Most Browsers already support some of the HTML5 specifications. Some Browsers have done so for quite a while now. For example the <canvas> element is supported by Firefox, Opera, Chrome, and Safari. Browser manufacturers are rapidly and comprehensively adopting HTML5 into building this their HTML interpreters.

Interesting Websites Created Using HTML 5

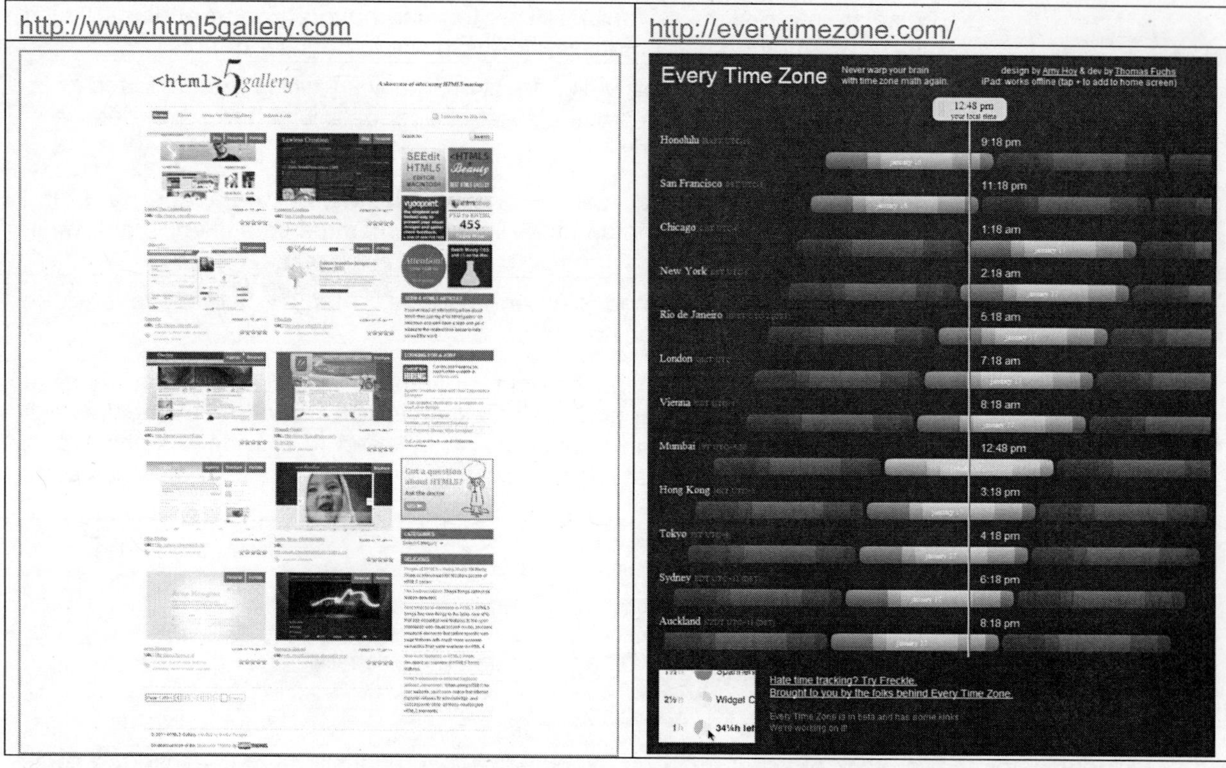

If you're keen to read more, here are some great websites that I visit regularly to keep abreast with HTML5 features, Browser support, as well as to gather knowledge to play around with HTML5 features. These include:

- http://caniuse.com, To know when to can use modern browser features
- http://html5demos.com from Remy Sharp,

  http://www.html5doctor.com from Bruce Lawson
- http://www.html5rocks.com from Google
- http://www.quirksmode.org/dom/html5.html which covers HTML5 browser compatibility

Perhaps the biggest question about HTML5 right now is, "is it ready for prime time".

At the time of creating this material there is definitely a feeling among many HTML5 developers that HTML5 is interesting, hot, but perhaps not well enough supported across Browsers yet, to use HTML5 in production website work.

On the other hand several HTML thought leaders are already adopting HTML5 on their production website so that as soon as Browser support catches up, their websites will be the first to be fully HTML5 compliant.

Eventually, it is the HTML5 coding professionals will have to learn where and when to use HTML5 on production websites.

What better time than now than to learn to use HTML5 confidently?

Self Review Questions

Fill In The Blanks

1. The ________________ tag is a 2D drawing area controlled by JavaScript.
2. ____________________ is compatible with older browsers, and older versions of HTML.
3. ___________________is largely unstructured.
4. HTML5 attributes creates webpages that are ____________________________enabled.
5. HTML5 allows Web developers to embed _____________, _______________, _______________, and _______________effortlessly into their webpages.
6. HTML5, the new Web standard has been adopted by ____________and ___________
7. The ____________ element can be used to provide extra information for a block of text.
8. Before the introduction of ___________________________object it was only possible to communicate whole pages at a time between a Browser and Web server.
9. ________________are now officially part of the HTML5 specification.
10. The ________________API that allows a web site or an application to ask the Browser where the user is located.
11. In ______________there was just a single Input element type named TextBox
12. The <article> element can be used to encapsule a ______________
13. For anyone who is proficient in ______________, and the_____________________, using the Geolocation API is really pretty straightforward.
14. The ____________ element can be used to annotate main text with diagrams
15. Many professional web developers openly criticized several aspects of _____________
16. The <nav> element can be used to encompass__________________.
17. Geolocation is not and has never really been a part of the _________________ specification
18. The ________________ tag has attributes like src, autoplay, and loop.
19. ______________________provides a method for defining context menus.

20. HTML5 emerged from within the ________________________.
21. The ____________ element can be used to describe the web page header section.
22. For some HTML5 features, there are _____________libraries which provide the missing features for Browsers which do not support them.
23. The ____________ tag is very similar to the ___________ in functionality, but is used for audio files.

True Or False

24. XHTML version 1 is not compatible with older browsers, and older versions of HTML.
25. The specifications of HTML 4 were completed by W3C.
26. The XHTML version 2 specifications, however, were far more compatible.
27. Many professional web developers openly criticized several aspects of XHTML version 2.
28. Starting in 2004, Apple, Mozilla and Opera, began worrying about the direction W3C were taking with XHTML.
29. It appeared there was clear focus in the XHTML2 specifications on the real-life needs for web developers.
30. The WHAT-WG's version is a superset of the W3C HTML5 specification.
31. In HTML4 there was multiple Input element type named TextBox.
32. HTML5 features, there are JavaScript libraries which provide the missing features for Browsers which do not support them.
33. HTML5's new elements offer a semantic richness to HTML codespec that simply did not exist before.
34. API does not allow a web application to register itself for protocols or media types.
35. HTML5 is useful in wide range of modern browsers.
36. HTMLS support the web application only when the user is online.
37. Web storage is a part of official w3c specifications.
38. Before the introduction of XMLHttp request DOM object it was only possible to communicate whole pages at a time between a browser & web server.
39. Comet disables a Web server to send data without a Browser explicitly requesting for the information.
40. HTMLS5 features have JavaScript libraries which provide the missing features for browsers which does not supports them.

2. The HTML4 Doctype Declaration

All HTML4 codespec starts with a doctype declaration, this is written even before <html> start tag. The code snippet below is a typical doctype declaration.

```
<!DOCTYPE html PUBLIC "-//W3C//DTD XHTML 1.0 Strict//EN"
 "http://www.w3.org/TR/xhtml1/DTD/xhtml1-strict.dtd">
```

The use of the doctype declaration came into existence when developers at Microsoft, who were working on Internet Explorer 5, found themselves with a very surprising problem. Internet Explorer 5, had improved its HTML standards support so much that older webpages no longer rendered properly in Internet Explorer 5.

Actually, the pages rendered properly, according to the HTML specifications but people expected them to render *improperly*. This is because web pages that were coded before IE5, were coded to exploit the quirks of the dominant Browsers of those days and render great looking pages. Once Browsers started to conform more and more to standards these great looking pages began to break in the Browsers and look perhaps terrible. Internet Explorer 5 was apparently *so standards compliant* that it actually broke to web.

Microsoft then came up with what they thought was a great solution. Before rendering any HTML page IE5 looked for a doctype declaration which was placed immediately before the opening <html> tag. Older HTML pages, that relied on their rendering based on the quirks of older browsers generally did not have a doctype declaration at all. IE5 attempted to render those pages exactly as the older Browsers did.

In order to "activate" and use the new web standards support in IE5, web page authors had to specifically opt in for this by supplying the right doctype declaration before the opening <html> tag.

This approach seemed to catch the fancy of web developers. Very soon all major Browsers (*Firefox, Opera, Safari and others*) had two modes of operation: *quirks mode* and *standards mode*.

With this approach and rapid changes happening in Browser creation things quickly got completely out of control. When Mozilla (i.e. *The Firefox Browser*) tried to ship version 1.1 of Firefox, they discovered that all pages that were rendering in *standards mode* within Firefox were being rendered, actually relying on a specific *single Browser quirk* to render correctly.

When Mozilla fixed its HTML rendering engine within Firefox, thousands of pages broke all at once with Firefox. Thus was created – and this is the absolute truth – *almost standards mode* - for the rendering of HTML based web pages in Browsers.

To Quickly Simplify All Of This:

Quirks Mode

In the Quirks mode, Browsers actually violate Web format specifications in order to avoid the breaking of HTML pages authored according to practices that were prevalent in the late 1990s.

Standards Mode

In Standards mode, Browsers that had specification obedient HTML rendering engines built into them tried their best to give specification conforming HTML documents the correct treatment when being rendered to the extent that these standards were implemented in the particular Browser's HTML rendering engine. HTML5 calls this mode the *no quirks mode*.

Almost Standards Mode

Firefox, Safari, Chrome, Opera (since 7.5) and IE8 also have a mode known as "Almost Standards mode," that implements the vertical sizing of table cells traditionally and not rigorously according to the CSS2 specification. HTML5 calls this mode of Browser operation the *limited quirks mode*.

To round off the doctype declaration was being discussed here is *one* of 15 doctype declarations that trigger *standards mode* in all modern browsers.

```
<!DOCTYPE html PUBLIC "-//W3C//DTD XHTML 1.0 Strict//EN"
 "http://www.w3.org/TR/xhtml1/DTD/xhtml1-strict.dtd">
```

You can use this doctype declaration if you like or you can use the HTML5 doctype declaration to trigger *standards mode* in all modern browsers, which is:

```
<!DOCTYPE html>
```

Take your pick, I much rather use the HTML5 doctype declaration when I'm coding HTML.

The HTML5 Doctype Element

HTML5 is designed to be backwards compatible with both HTML4 and XHTML1. The difference between HTML4 and HTML5 is purely syntactical. The rules for marking up an XHTML document however are slightly more rigid than those for HTML4.

Because HTML5 is designed to be backwards compatible, most HTML4 and XHTML1 documents can effectively also be HTML5 documents. The syntactical rules of the languages are unchanged, meaning if your HTML4 or XHTML1 documents conform to the syntactical rules of those languages, they also automatically conform to syntactically to HTML5.

Hence, in order for any HTML4 or XHTML1 document to convert to an HTML5 document, only a single change needs to be carried out. The HTML5 doctype declaration must replace the current doctype declaration in use.

HTML5 specification states that HTML5 requires a DOCTYPE to be specified to ensure that any Browser renders the HTML5 document page in standards mode. The DOCTYPE declaration has no other purpose.

The doctype declaration for any HTML5 document is simply <!DOCTYPE html>

Simply use this doctype declaration at the start of any HTML4 or XHTML1 document, and any Browser will recognize it to be an HTML5 document and try to render the HTML document in *standards mode*.

How Browsers Handle Unknown Elements

Every browser has to know exactly what to do when its HTML interpreter encounters HTML elements. All Browsers have a master list of HTML elements that are supported by its HTML interpreter.

Mozilla Firefox's list is stored in nsElementTable.cpp. HTML elements which are not on this list and encountered by the Firefox's HTML interpreter are treated as *unknown elements*. Hence, there are some issues that have to be tackled when a non HTML5 compliant Browser has to interpret and render a web page marked up using HTML5. This is largely due to the fact that the Browser will encounter HTML elements within the web page that are unknown elements.

Here are a couple of fundamental Issues that a Browser must deal with regard to - unknown elements:

1) How should the element be styled?

For example the HTML element:

<p> has a pre-defined spacing on the top and bottom

<blockquote> is indented with a pre-defined left margin

<h1> is displayed in a pre-defined larger font when compared to the font used for <p>

2) What should the unknown element's DOM look like?

Mozilla's nsElementTable.cpp includes information about what kinds of other elements each element can contain.

If you include markup like, <p></p> the second paragraph element implicitly closes the first one, so the elements end up as siblings, not parent and child.

On the other hand if <p> contains the </span> element, the <span> element does not close the <p> element, because Firefox knows that <p> is a block element that can contain the inline <span> element so <span> ends up as a child of <p> in the DOM.

Regretfully, different Browsers answer these questions in different ways. Of the major browsers, Microsoft's Internet Explorer's answer to both questions is the most problematic.

For Browser manufacturers the first question should be relatively simple to deal with. The Browser should not give any special styling to unknown elements. The unknown element should inherit whatever CSS properties have been defined wherever the unknown element appears in the web page. This lets the HTML coder (*i.e. web page author*) specify all unknown element styling using CSS.

Unfortunately for HTML programmers Internet Explorer (*prior to Version 9*) will not allow unknown elements to inherit styling. For example if you wrote the following code snippet and executed it in all versions of IE prior to IE9:

```
<style type="text/css"> article { display: block; border: 2px solid green } </style>
<article>
<h1>Welcome to Initech</h1>
<p>This is your <span>first day</span>.</p>
</article>
```

Code snippet 1

Internet Explorer (*up to and including IE 8*) <u>will not</u> put a solid, 2 pixel, green border around the content enclosed within the unknown element <article></article>.

Note: *Microsoft has stated (and HTML coders have verified) that Internet Explorer 9 does not have this problem.*

The second problem is the DOM that browsers create when they encounter unknown elements. The most problematic Browser is Internet Explorer. If IE doesn't explicitly recognize the element name (*i.e. an unknown element*), it will insert the element into the DOM as an empty node with no children.

Hence with IE, any/all HTML elements that may have been used within the unknown element, and are therefore expected to be children of the unknown element, will actually be inserted in the DOM as siblings instead.

To illustrate this take a look at the DOM trees below (*shown as ASCII*) that showcases these differences.

This is the DOM that is created in all versions of IE (*other than IE 9*) when the HTML5 code (*identified in code snippet 2*) below is executed.

```
<style type="text/css"> article { display: block; border: 2px solid green } </style>
<article>
    <h1>Welcome to Initech</h1>
    <p>This is your <span>first day</span>.</p>
</article>
```

Code snippet 2

<table>
<tr><th>The DOM created when the HTML 5 code snippet 2 was executed:</th><th>The DOM expected when the HTML 5 code snippet 2 was executed:</th></tr>
<tr><td>article (no children)
|
h1 (sibling of article)
|
+ text node "Welcome to Initech
|
p (sibling of h1)
|
+ text node "This is your "
|
+ span
    |
    + text node "first day"
|
+ text node "."</td><td>article
|
+--h1 (child of article)
| |
| +--text node "Welcome to Initech"
|
+--p (child of article, sibling of h1)
|
+--text node "This is your "
|
+--span
| |
| +--text node "first day"
|
+--text node</td></tr>
</table>

Table 1.

There is a really simple way to work around this problem in IE. Create a dummy <article> element using Javascript within the <head></head> section of the HTML5 codespec. Since the <article> element is being created within <head></head> i.e. before it is accessed / used within <body></body> like magic, Internet Explorer will recognize the <article> element and permit it to be styled using CSS.

Hence, simply creating the <article> element once (*per page*) using Javascript is enough to get all versions of IE prior to IE9 to permit CSS based styling to be applied to unknown element.

For example:

```
<html>
<head>
    <style> article { display: block; border: 1px solid red } </style>
    <script>document.createElement("article");</script>
    </head>
    <body>
<article>
<h1>Welcome to Initech</h1>
<p>This is your <span>first day</span>.</p>
</article>
</body>
</html>
```

Now let's take this idea and expand it a little bit so that HTML5 codespec can be styled perfectly using CSS in all the non HTML5 compliant Browsers.

Here is a simple example:

```
<!--[if lt IE 9]>
<script>
    var e = ("abbr,article,aside,audio,canvas,datalist,details," +
    "figure,footer,header,hgroup,mark,menu,meter,nav,output," +
    "progress,section,time,video").split(',');
    for (var i = 0; i < e.length; i++)
    {
    document.createElement(e[i]);
    }
</script>
<![endif]-->
```

The <!--[if lt IE 9]> and <![endif]--> codespec are conditional comments. Internet Explorer interprets them like an if statement. i.e. If the current browser is a version of Internet Explorer less than Version 9, then the code block gets executed."

Every other browser will treat the entire block as an HTML comment. The net result is that Internet Explorer (up to and including Version 8) will execute this script happily, but other browsers will simply ignore it altogether. This makes your page load faster in browsers that do not need this hack.

The JavaScript code itself is relatively straightforward. The variable e ends up as an array of strings like "abbr", "article", "aside", and so on.

Then this array is looped through and each of he named elements are created by calling document.createElement(), but since we ignore the return value, the elements are never inserted into the DOM.

Still, this is enough to get Internet Explorer to treat these elements the way we want them when we actually use them later in the page. That "later" bit is important.

This script needs to be at the top of your page, preferably in the <head> element not at the bottom of your page. That way, Internet Explorer will execute the script before it parses the HTML5 elements and attributes within the webpage codespec.

If you put this script at the bottom of your page, it will be too late. Internet Explorer will have already misinterpreted the new HTML5 markup elements and constructed the wrong DOM. Regretfully IE will not go back and adjust the DOM it created just because of encountering this codespec.

This is a fairly universal approach used for instructing all non HTML5 compliant Browsers to recognize the new HTML5 elements and permit these *Browser Unknown Elements* to be styled via CSS. This ensures that programmers can create *future proof* web pages, using HTML5 for markup, today.

Declaring Character Encodings in HTML5

When you sit down and visualize how textual content will be displayed on a webpage, it's very likely that you think of characters and symbols that are displayed on the computer's VDU when it renders HTML code to display a web page.

Regretfully, computers do not deal with the characters and symbols that human being understand. Computers have each of the characters and symbols humans understand stored within particular character and symbol encoding.

There is actually a lot of such character and symbol encoding that is stored in and accessed by a computer when required. Different encoding sets are used for different languages, such Russian, Chinese, English and so on. Broadly speaking, character encoding provides the computer a way to map what you see on its screen, *i.e. what is rendered as web page content*, and the coding patterns that the computer stores within its memory and on its hard disk that it uses to render the web page.

In reality, it's a ton more complicated than that. The very same character or symbol might appear in more than one encoding, but each encoding may use a completely different sequence of bytes to actually store the character or symbol in its memory or on its hard disk. Perhaps if you visualized character encoding as a kind of decryption key for text it would help.

Hence, if the computer is given a sequence of bytes and informed that it is text, it would need to know exactly what encoding to use to correctly decode the sequence of bytes and display the correct character or symbol on its VDU.

So now the question arises, How does your Browser actually determine the character encoding used by the Web server when it delivers web page content to it? Without the Browser determining the character encoding correctly it's more than possible that the content displayed on the VDU will be erroneous.

Now it's quite possible that you've seen the following information contained with the HTTP header:

Content-Type: text/html; charset="utf-8"

Briefly, this is the Web server's way of saying that it thinks that it's sending you an HTML document and that it thinks that the document uses UTF-8 encoding. Unfortunately, very few web page creators have any kind of control on their Web server; hence HTML4 provided a way that the page creators could specify the character encoding within the HTML document itself.

It's quite possible you have seen the following codespec as well.

```
<meta http-equiv="Content-Type" content="text/html; charset=utf-8">
```

This is the way that the webpage creator informs the Browser that they authored the HTML document using the UTF-8 character encoding. Both of the techniques explained above (i.e. *HTTP headers sent by a Web server and the meta tag attributes*) still work in HTML5. The HTTP header is the preferred method. The HTTP header overrides the <meta> tag if present, but because not everyone can set HTTP headers, the <meta> tag and its attributes is still around. In HTML5 this is the syntax:

```
<meta charset="utf-8" />
```

The rule of thumb is as follows, those who create web page in languages that are entirely based on the Roman character set (*such as English*) can normally get away with not really having to bother about character encodings as most operating systems and Browsers typically treat the Roman character set as their default character set, but ideally all web developers should clearly identify which character encoding was used to create the web page either via the Web server's HTTP header or via the meta tag within the HTML document.

Character encoding is complicated. This situation has not been made easier because of the years and years of poorly written HTML codespec (*the copy–and–paste programmers are the biggest culprits*). Every HTML coder should always specify character encoding in every HTML document. Remember you can do this via the HTTP Content-Type header or the meta tag and its attributes.

The Root Element

HTML codespec interpreted by a Browser to produce a webpage is actually a series of nested elements. The entire structure of a webpage is like a tree. Some of the elements in the HTML codespec are *siblings*. These HTML elements can be visualized as multiple branches that extend from the same tree trunk.

Other HTML elements are *children* of other HTML elements. There are HTML elements that can have no *children* these are called *leaf* nodes.

The outermost element, which is the ancestor of all the other elements in the HTML codespec, is called the *root element*. The root element of HTML codespec is always *<html>*.

In most HTML codespec the root element is always coded as follows:

```
<html xmlns="http://www.w3.org/1999/xhtml" lang="en" xml:lang="en">
```

This code snippet is perfectly okay, it is valid HTML5, but parts of this code snippet are no longer necessary in HTML5, a few bytes of unnecessary HTML code can be saved by removing them.

Let's take a quick look at the following HTML codespec:

```
<html xmlns="http://www.w3.org/1999/xhtml" lang="en" xml:lang="en">
```

The first *attribute* to the opening *<html* is *xmlns*. This attribute is drawn from XHTML 1.0. The value passed to this attribute indicates that all the elements contained within the codespec are in the XHTML namespace, http://www.w3.org/1999/xhtml.

Elements that belong to HTML5 are *always in this namespace*, so there is longer a need to declare it explicitly. The HTML5 codespec will work exactly the same in all Browsers, whether this attribute is present or not.

Dropping the *xmlns* attribute leaves the root element with only the following attributes:

```
<html lang="en" xml:lang="en">
```

The two attributes, *lang* and *xml:lang*, both define the language of the HTML web page. These are remnants of XHTML. However, only the *lang* attribute has any effect in HTML5. Hence keep the *xml:lang* attribute, but ensure that it contains the same value as the *lang* attribute.

That leaves the HTML5 *root* element as: <html lang="en">

The <head> Element

The *first child* of the root element is usually the *<head>* element. The <head> element in the HTML codespec is used to contain metadata which is important technical information about the web page.

The <head> element itself has not changed in any way in HTML5. Important technical information about the web page is what is placed inside the <head></head> elements.

Here is a small example:

```
<head>
<meta http-equiv="Content-Type" content="text/html; charset=utf-8" />
<title>My Weblog</title>
<link rel="stylesheet" type="text/css" href="style-original.css" />
<link rel="alternate" type="application/atom+xml" title="My Weblog feed" href="/feed/" />
<link rel="search" type="application/opensearchdescription+xml" title="My Weblog search"
href="opensearch.xml" />
<link rel="shortcut icon" href="/favicon.ico" />
</head>
```

Code Sample 1

HTML5 breaks link relations into two categories:

1) Links to external resources.

These links point to specific resources that are external to the HTML codespec, but contain specific information that will be used to augment the current HTML document in some way.

2) Hyperlinks to other HTML documents.

In the code snippet contained in Code Sample 1, only the first *link* which has the attribute *rel="stylesheet"* is a link that points to an external resource. The rest are actually *hyperlinks* to other documents. These specific links really do not add any specific value to the current web page at all.

Expanding the very first link relation in Code Sample 1.

```
<link rel="stylesheet" href="style-original.css" type="text/css" />
```

Perhaps this is the most frequently used link relation when coding in HTML. <link rel="stylesheet"> is used for pointing to CSS rules that are stored in a separate file named style-original.css. In HTML5 the *type* attribute can be dropped. There really is only one stylesheet language for the web, CSS, hence that is always taken as the default value for the type attribute and hence need not be specifically declared. This works in all browsers.

Hence in HTNL5 a link to an external style sheet can be coded as follows:

```
<link rel="stylesheet" href="style-original.css" />
```

The *rel="alternate"* Attribute Used With *Link*

```
<link rel="alternate" type="application/atom+xml" title="My Weblog feed" href="/feed/" />
```

This link relation is also quite common in HTML codespec. <link rel="alternate">, combined with either the RSS or Atom media type in the type attribute, enables something called "*feed autodiscovery.*"

This permits syndicated feed readers, like Google Reader, to discover that a site has a news feed of the latest its articles. Most browsers also support feed autodiscovery by displaying a special icon next to the URL.

The rel="alternate" link relation definition in HTML5, has been clarified and extended to more accurately describe existing web content. For example, using *rel="alternate"* in conjunction with *type=application/atom+xml* indicates an Atom feed for the current page. The *rel="alternate"* can also be used in conjunction with other type attributes to indicate the content in another format, like PDF.

Here is a brief listing of various *rel* attributes that can be used in HTML5. This is by no means an exhaustive listing but is meant to be indicative only.

rel="archives"

This indicates that the referenced document describes a collection of records, documents, or other materials of historical interest. An excellent example is a Blogs index page which could link to an index of the blogs past posts using *rel="archives"* relation.

rel="author"

Can be used to link author information to a web page. This could be a *mailto: address*, though it doesn't have to be. It could simply be a link to a *contact form* or an *about the author* page.

rel="external"

Indicates that the link is going to lead to material that is not part of the current document. This was made popular by WordPress, which uses it on links left by commenters.

rel="first"

rel="next"

rel="prev"

rel="last"

HTML5 includes *rel="first"*. This is the most common way of saying *first page in a series*. HTML5 also includes *rel="prev"* and *rel="next"*, as well as *rel="last"*.

rel="icon"

Is in all likely hood the second most popular link relation, after *rel="stylesheet"*. It is usually found together with shortcut, as described below:

```
<link rel="shortcut icon" href="/favicon.ico">
```

All Browsers support this usage and associate a small icon with the web page. The icon is usually displayed in the Browser's location bar adjacent to the web page URL, or in the browser tab, or both. In HTML5 the height and width attributes can be used as well to indicate the size of the referenced icon if so desired.

rel="nofollow"

This indicates that the link to which it is bound is not endorsed by the original author or publisher of the web page. This link attribute was invented by Google.

WordPress for example automatically adds *rel="nofollow"* to any links added by commenters to Blog posts or articles. The thinking is that if *nofollow* links did not pass on PageRank to the commenters, spammers would give up trying to post spam comments on weblogs.

rel="pingback"

This attribute is used to specify the address of a *pingback* server. The pingback system is a way for a Blog to be automatically notified when any other Web site links to it. Most blogging systems, notably WordPress, implement the pingback mechanism to notify Blog authors that others have linked to them when creating a new Blog post on their Blogs.

rel="prefetch"

This attribute indicates that preemptively fetching and caching the specified resource is likely to be beneficial to the reader of the current web page, as it is very likely that the reader will require this resource.

Search engines sometimes add *<link rel="prefetch" href="URL of top search result">* to the search results page if they feel that the top result is much much more popular than any other.

The Structural And Semantic Aspects Of HTML5

Well for now most of the basic housekeeping aspects of an HTML5 document are out of the way. It is now time to get involved with the structural and semantic aspects of HTML5.

The *header* element

A very common section of most web page layouts is a header section. This section typically contains one or more headings for the web page.

Often web page developers using HTML4 or XHTML1 would place such content within:

<div class="header"> *Web Page header content placed here* </div>

Because this is such a common practice, HTML5 has defined an element expressly for this purpose, i.e. the *header element* (please do not confuse this with the *head* element).

The HTML5 *header* element is intended to define the start and end of a webpage's header section. Multiple blocks of page content can be place in the header section such as:

- A company Logo and Name
- A web site search sub system
- A website Login In / Register sub system

And so on.

Just remember that having a header section in a web page is completely optional.

What is interesting is that HTML5 *header* elements are not restricted to being used only at the top of a webpage.

The HTML5 *header* element can be used within page content as well, for example - Blog post titles. The *header* element may contain h1, h2 other such elements, but this is mandatory. The *header* element may also contain any kind of content. The only restriction is that *header* elements may not contain *header* or *footer* elements.

As mentioned earlier it's not mandatory that all HTML5 documents have an *header* element, so, for example, if the web page simply begins with an *h1* element, there is no need to enclose the *h1* element within a *header* element.

The *hgroup* Element

In addition to the *header* element, HTML5 also has an *hgroup* element. The *header* element may contain most kinds of content (except *section* and *footer* elements), the *hgroups* element must contain only headings. The *hgroups* element helps the sectioning (or outlining) algorithm of HTML5 work successfully.

This material will not explore what the sectioning (or outlining) algorithm of HTML5 really is because this is really more relevant to Browser developers than web page developers. Just to touch the subject HTML5 has an *explicit* outline, model, as well as an *implicit* one, while traditionally HTML has only had an *implicit* outline model.

One could visualize sectioning as the table of contents in a book typically, heading levels define where new sections start and end.

Such an outline is *implicit*, because headings imply the beginning of a new section. HTML5 goes one step further, by having an explicit outlining model. Where ever a new section of a web page is required use the *section* element, which will contain the content (i.e. *mark the start and end*) of that specific section. Anyway this will be covered in more detail in later material.

The sectioning approach of HTML5 does throw up a challenge. Since web page content outlines can be either created implicitly by heading levels, or explicitly with section elements a secondary heading within a section will be included in the implicit outline of a web page, even if that's not what's desired. Very common *header* codespec will be marked up as follows:

```
<header>
  <h1>Amped</h1>
  <h2>A Hack Day Like no Other</h2>
</header>
```

In this case, the codespec contained within the *header* section is implicitly is part of the outline, the h1 element creates an implicit section, and the h2 element an implicit subsection.

In situations like this, if only one heading from the codespec must be part of the web page outline, enclose that heading within the *hgroup* element. Then only that will be part of the web page outline when it is being interpreted by the Browser's built in HTML5 interpreter.

Now the code snippet will be as follows:

```
<header>
  <hgroup>
    <h1>Amped</h1>
    <h2>A Hack Day Like no Other</h2>
  </hgroup>
</header>
```

This is happily not something that one has to pay a great deal of attention to right now, simply because at present no Browser has actually implemented the HTML5's outlining algorithm within their HTML5 interpreters, but to future proof the HTML5 markup one can group headings like using the *hgroup* element.

The *nav* Element

HTML5 has defined a *nav* element used for marking up page or site navigation. According to the HTML5 specification - The *nav* element represents a section of a page that links to other pages or to parts within same page.

To use the *nav* element first identify the codespec of the web page used for navigation. Then markup these navigational links (*which are very commonly enclosed within <ul> <li> elements*) within a *nav* element.

According to HTML5 the *nav* element should be used to enclose links to content within a web page itself, or other pages contained within the website.

Hence, (*by the above definition*) links on a web page, which point to any kind of resource on other websites (i.e. *other webs pages, images, .pdf file and so on*) are not considered as navigational links in HTML5 and as such should not be enclosed within the *nav* element. It's really not every link or group of links on a web page that must be enclosed within the HTML5 *nav* element.

For example, the *nav* element is most likely not the most appropriate markup element to use to enclose links to privacy policies and terms and conditions linked to within the footer of a web page.

However, if a link points to contact details and other significant parts of a site these can be enclosed within the *nav* element.

The *footer* Element

Just as many HTML web pages have header sections, another common web page section is the *footer* section.

Typically up to today HTML coders marked up the web page content as follows:

```
<div class="footer"> Web Page footer content placed here </footer>
```

Just as HTML5 has defined the *header* element, it also defines a *footer* element, which can be used instead of placing web page footer content within a div whose id="footer" as shown below:

```
<footer> Web Page footer content placed here </footer>
```

Just as with the *header* element, there may be more than one *footer* element in a web page. Each specific section of the web page may have its own footer.

If this idea seems a little strange, consider the example of a Blog post. Each Blog post may have a *header* containing a title, author information and so on, as well as a *footer* which might have the Blog posts date time stamp, as well as various "share this" style links.

The *header* and *footer* elements of HTML5 are just perfect for marking up this kind of web page content.

Now that several new HTML5 elements have been explained, the very best thing to do is to create an HTML file and implement what has been explained. This will go a long way in remembering the new HTML5 elements and understanding how to use them in real world situations.

Whatever is being built through the hands on examples which follow will not be particularly stylish (*because there's no CSS, hence only default browser styling is applied*). The hands on exercise will be a rich, valid, HTML5 document, using many of the new HTML5 markup features.

To create an HTML page open any ASCII Editor of your choice.

First we declare the HTML5 doctype to trigger *standards mode* in all modern browsers.

```
<!DOCTYPE html>
```

After declaring the doctype, the root element has to be declared that contains the rest of the HTML5 document. In HTML5 the root element is <html> closed by </html>.

Next the character set of the document has to be declared. Character set of the document will always be declared inside the <head></head> section of the HTML5 document.

```
<head>
    <meta charset="utf-8" >
</head>
```

All web page content will be declared within the <body></body> element. Now let's look at what can be placed within the web page <body></body> element.

The content within the <body></body> elements can be further sectioned using HTML5 elements. Let's call the topmost content displayed within the web page as the web page's - *header section*.

Now declare the *<header></header>* section right at the top of and within the <body></body> section of the web page. This *<header></header>* section contains the:

- Name of the website
- Its tagline
- A call to action

And

- The top navigation menu bar

The name of the website (*or website logo*) can be within *<h1></h1>* elements.

```
    <h1>Ivan Bayross</h1>
```

The website's tagline cab be written in *<h2></h2>* elements.

```
    <h2>Technical Author, Mentor and Friend</h2>
```

The HTML5 *hgroups* element must contain only headings, so wrap the name of the website and its tagline within *<hgroups></hgroups>* element. The code snippet for this web page's *hgroups* element is:

```
<hgroup>
    <h1>Ivan Bayross</h1>
    <h2>Technical Author, Mentor and Friend</h2>
</hgroup>
```

A *call to action* can be specified within the paragraph *<p></p>* element. A call to action normally is information that the website visitor needs to act upon. In this

1) Register with the website
2) Chat with Ivan Bayros

```
<p>Register now and get our regular newsletter. Chat with Ivan Bayross</p>
```

A HTML5 *nav* element is used for wrapping, website menu items used to navigated to various pages contained by the site. Here is how the <nav></nav> element can be used:

Web site navigational links themselves are enclosed within a set of <ul> <li></li> </ul> elements, which are contained within the <nav></nav> element as shown below:

```
<nav>
  <ul>
   <li>Home</li>
   <li>About</li>
   <li>Free Tutorials</li>
   <li>Tech Tips</li>
   <li>Site Map</li>
   <li>Register now!</li>
  </ul>
<nav>
```

This just about wraps up a web page's *header* section expressed within the <body></body> tags.

The Complete Codespec:

```
<!DOCTYPE html>
<html>
<head>
   <meta charset="utf-8">
</head>
<body>
<header>
  <hgroup>
     <h1>Ivan Bayross</h1>
     <h2>Technical Author, Mentor and Friend</h2>
  </hgroup>
```

```
    <p>December 7th, 2010</p>
  <p>Mumbai, India</p>
  <p>Register now and get our regular newsletter. Chat with Ivan Bayross</p>
   <nav>
      <ul>
         <li>Home</li>
         <li>About</li>
         <li>Free Tutorials</li>
         <li>Tech Tips</li>
         <li>Site Map</li>
         <li>Register now!</li>
      </ul>
    <nav>
</header>
Hottest Mobile OS
Presenter: Ivan Bayross
What's the hottest mobile operating system (OS)? The one that customers desire the most and plan to upgrade to next? Practically a tie between iPhone (iOS) and Android. In the analytics firm's latest mobile report, it found that 30% of users will choose iPhone (iOS) while 28% of users will buy an Android device.
SEARCH
STAY IN TOUCH
     Email Id: ivan@ivanbayross.com
     Twitter: ivanbayross

<footer>

  <h3>ABOUT IVAN BAYROSS</h3>
  <p>Ivan Bayross is an Indian Technical Author. <br /><br />
  To date, he has written and published 75 books focused on commercial application development using various software tools and technologies and still writing. <br /><br />Some of his books have been adopted as standard reference material for students who aspire to a degree in Computer Science and Engineering, by M.I.T, Singapore University and a few Indian Universities.</p>
```

```
    <h3>SUBSCRIBE TO OUR DAILY NEWSLETTER</h3>
    Subscribe to our monthly newsletter to stay up-to date with the new technologies
    Name:
    Email Id:
    <h3>SUBSCRIBE</h3>
    <p>&copy; Ivan Bayross Inc. All rights reserved. <br />
    Terms and Conditions | Privacy Policy</p>
</footer>
</body>
</html>
```

When this code is executed in any HTML5 compliant Browser the output will be as shown in diagram 2.1, diagram 2.2, diagram 2.3 and diagram 2.4 below.

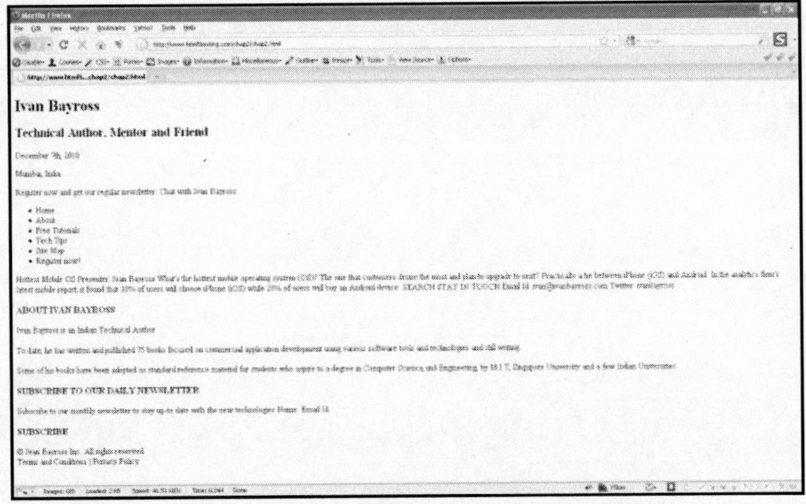

Diagram 2.1 - Firefox (version 3.6.13)

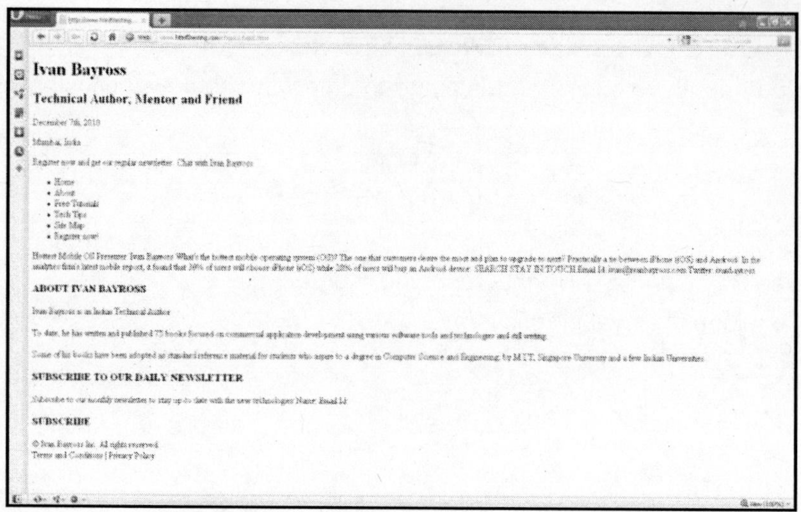

Diagram 2.2 - Opera (version 11.00.00)

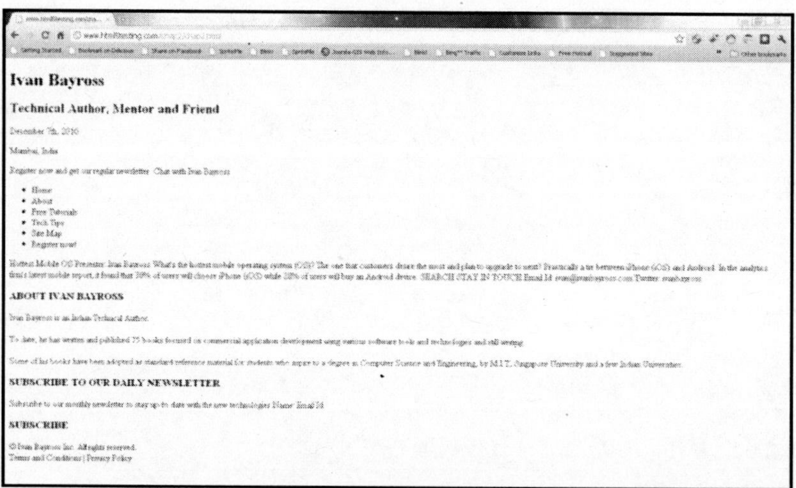

Diagram 2.3 - Google Chrome (version 8.0.552)

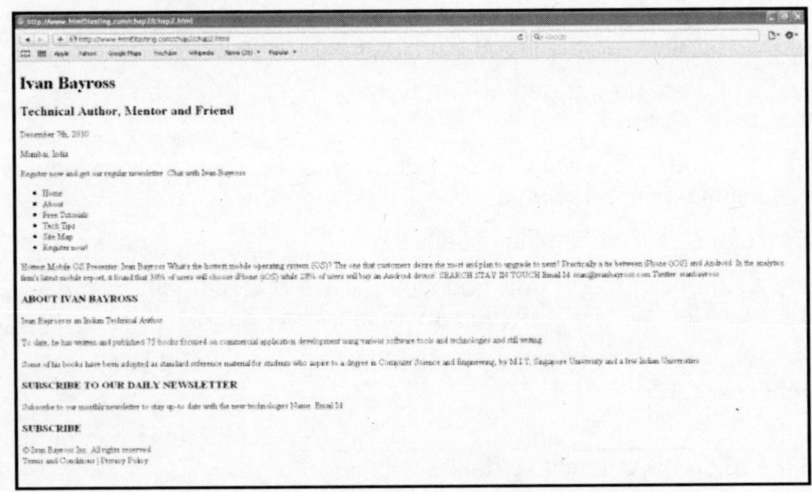

Diagram 2.4 - Safari (version 5.0.2)

Self Review Questions

Fill In The Blanks

1. The _______________declaration must replace the current doctype declaration in use.
2. Some of the elements in the HTML codespec are _______________.
3. ___________________ indicates that the referenced document describes a collection of records, documents, or other materials of historical interest.
4. rel="pingback" attribute is used to specify the address of a ________________ server.
5. The rules for marking up an ______________ document however are slightly more rigid than those for HTML4.
6. In HTML5 the _________________ attribute can be dropped.
7. rel="author" Can be used to link ________________ information to a web page.
8. All HTML4 codespec starts with a doctype declaration, this is written even before ___________ start tag.
9. You can use the HTML5 doctype declaration to trigger ________________________ in all modern browsers, which is <!DOCTYPE html>
10. HTML5 is designed to be backwards compatible with both _________ and ___________.
11. The difference between HTML4 and HTML5 is purely ______________.
12. In order for any HTML4 or XHTML1 document to convert to an _________________ document, only a single change needs to be carried out.

13. The doctype declaration for any HTML5 document is simply ____________________
14. Regretfully, computers do not deal with the ________________ and ________________ that human being understand.
15. ______________ codespec when interpreted by a Browser to produce a webpage is actually a series of nested elements.
16. The *first child* of the root element is usually the ________________ element.
17. The <head> element in the HTML codespec is used to contain ____________________ which is important technical information about the web page.
18. ______________________ Indicates that the link is going to lead to material that is not part of the current document.
19. In HTML5 the ____________ and __________________ attributes can be used to indicate the size of the referenced icon if so desired.
20. ______________________ indicates that the link to which it is bound is not endorsed by the original author or publisher of the web page.
21. rel="nofollow" link attribute was invented by _________________.

True Or False

22. According to the HTML5 specification - The *nav* element represents a section of a page that links to other pages or to parts within same page.
23. In addition to the *header* element, HTML5 also has an *hgroup* element.
24. The pingback system is a way for a Blog to be automatically notified when any other Web site links to it.
25. HTML5 specification states that HTML5 does not require a DOCTYPE to be specified to ensure that any Browser renders the HTML5 document page in standards mode.
26. If your HTML4 or XHTML1 documents conform to the syntactical rules of the languages, they also automatically conform to syntactically to HTML5.
27. Most blogging systems, do not implement the pingback mechanism to notify Blog authors that others have linked to them when creating a new Blog post on their Blogs.
28. A very common section of most web page layouts is a header section.
29. It's mandatory that all HTML5 documents have an *header* element.
30. HTML5 has defined a *nav* element used for marking up page or site navigation.
31. HTML5 has an *explicit* outline, model, as well as an *implicit* one.
32. According to HTML5 the *nav* element should be used to enclose links to content within a web page itself, or other pages contained within the website.

33. rel="prefetch" attribute indicates that preemptively fetching and caching the specified resource is likely to be non-beneficial to the reader of the current web page.

34. The HTML5 *nav* element is intended to define the start and end of a webpage's header section.

35. The *hgroups* element helps the sectioning (or outlining) algorithm of HTML5 work successfully.

36. Traditionally HTML has only had an *explicit* outline model.

Hands-On Exercise

1. Write the HTML 5 code spec which makes use of following information.
   Please use all the HTML5 elements that have been learned in this chapter.
   Output of this exercise is shown in diagram 2.5

Website Name	Lorem Ipsum
Website Tagline	Come learn how to use lorem ipsum
Date	1st January 2011
Page Menu	• Home | • About | • Demo | • Affiliates | • Contact Us
Contents of the Website	Lorem Ipsum Presenter: John Lorem Ipsum is simply dummy text of the printing and typesetting industry. Lorem Ipsum has been the industry's standard dummy text ever since the 1500s, when an unknown printer took a galley of type and scrambled it to make a type specimen book. It has survived not only five centuries, but also the leap into electronic typesetting, remaining essentially unchanged. It was popularized in the 1960s with the release of Letraset sheets containing Lorem Ipsum passages, and more recently with desktop publishing software like Aldus PageMaker including versions of Lorem Ipsum.

Copyright	©2011. All Right Reserved.
Footer Menu	Terms and Conditions | Privacy Policy

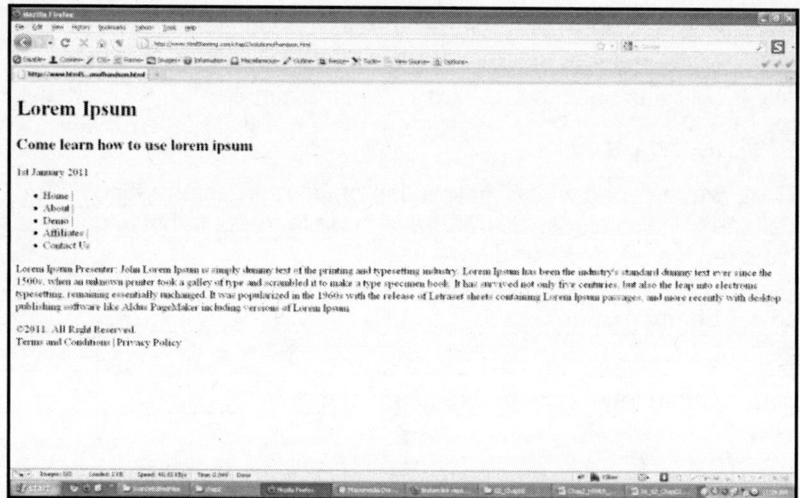

Diagram 2.5: Output of Hands on Exercise

Note: *The Codespec for the Hands-On-Exercise is given in the CD.*

3. HTML5 Is Open To Interpretation

All languages, natural ones such as English, and artificial ones like HTML have two kinds of rules, Syntactical and Semantic. Syntactic rules, describe exactly how the language elements are put together. Semantic rules, describes how meaning emerges from sentences constructed using the syntactical rules.

Syntactical rules are cut and dried, particularly in artificial languages like HTML. It's relatively easy to determine whether syntactical rules have been obeyed when constructing a particular sentence and hence whether the sentence is valid or invalid.

Semantic rules on the other hand are more open to interpretation. This is where the power of literature comes from—a single sentence or phrase written in English may be open to many interpretations, and many shades of meaning.

HTML is definitely not as expressive as a natural language, but as with all languages (*which are used to communicate - in this case between web developer and Browser*), it is open to interpretation.

HTML4 has been in existence for a while now, hence has been subject to developers thinking about how to use it meaningfully. HTML5, particularly its new language elements, has yet to be fully really scrutinized, discussed and implemented by both web developers and Browser manufacturers.

In these early times, HTML5 specifications act as a guide. Over time, conventions for use will emerge, just as they did for HTML4 hence currently this is not hard-and-fast answers to questions about the most appropriate HTML5 element to use when constructing a specific portion of any web page. All this will be answered, over time, simply by the way web developers begin to use the new elements defined in HTML5.

The Web Page Sectioning Algorithm In HTML5

HTML4 has a single, *implicit* outlining model that helped describe the structure of a webpage to the HTML interpreter within a supporting Browser. HTML5 has two outlining models, an implicit as well as an explicit model. The explicit model being based on the use of *section* and *article* elements. Here's a brief explanation of how HTML5 explicit model works.

In HTML5 codespec each *section* element as well as *article* element starts a section of the document outline. The first *heading* in a *section* or *article* is associated with that specific section in the HTML5 document (i.e. web page) outline.

All subsequent *heading* elements used within a section will start *implicit* sections of the document (i.e. web page) provided they are not contained within nested *section* elements themselves.

If this is sounding a little confusing, hang on to the belief that like much in web page development, what sounds complicated is really just common sense, hence HTML5 rules follow a common-sense approach to structuring web page content and you will begin to feel a lot less insecure.

The one minor complication is where it's necessary to have a second heading as part of a content section which really has nothing to do with web page document structure. Here is where the use of the *hgroup* element, effectively hides all but the first heading in the group from being part of the web page document outline.

In HTML4 a web page should begin with a single *h1* element (*required for **S**earch **E**ngine **O**ptimization* - SEO), then subsequently have *h2*, *h3,* and other heading levels as appropriate for the web page which determines the webpage outline to the HTML interpreter within Browsers.

If the explicit outline mechanism of HTML5 is used to communicate the web page outline to a Browser, then the use of h1, h2, h3 heading levels are not required to create the web page outline it is the *section* and *article* elements of HTML5 that do it for us.

Logically, this means that HTML5 web page can have multiple *section* and/or *article* elements used within it to describe web page structure, which in turn can have an h1 element and then subsequent implicit sections are possibly created with h2, h3, to implicitly describe the hierarchy of that *section* and/or *article* to a Browser.

In essence therefore, each *section* and/or *article* of a web page document can have its own document outline, starting with h1. This way, it's possible to have an infinite number of headings in our web page outline.

However, as usual, there's a catch. Commonly screen-reader users (i.e. *used by a visually impaired site visitor*) need headings as a navigational tool. To date, screen readers that provide this functionality rely on implicit sectioning and heading levels. Hence, if we use HTML5 approach to creating web page sections, the accessibility of the website for people using screen readers will be seriously compromised.

As such, from an visitor / website accessibility point of view, the best practice is to use heading levels to create the web page document outline. This need not stop programmers from using HTML5 *section* and *article* elements, but it is important for the implicit and explicit outline models of any web page to be in synch that the heading levels used within sections and/or article matches the level of that section within the overall document outline, which, again, is mostly common sense.

Sectioning In HTML5

If anyone takes a close look at the contents of any web page, one can see that it is organized into chunks, or sections. For example if the web page represents a newspaper this will definitely contain sections such as sports, news, business, articles, and so on simply because these are the sections that all newspapers contain. Similarly if the webpage is part of an E-Book it would contain chapters, appendices, and such like.

Although a ton of web page content is written as chunks or sections of information neither HTML4 nor XHTML1 ever provided any explicit markup elements that could be used to creating such discrete web page chunks or sections.

One may ask, what about the HTML *div* element? Well, a div is just a generic container in which to place web page content. The *div* element can be visualized as a catch all bucket for web page content, which must be marked up by a host of other HTML4 or XHTML elements. The *div* element has no explicit meaning of its own. Wrapping web page content within a *div* element is great for managing code complexity. It provides programmers a mechanism for placing web page content within a *div* and styling such content using CSS, but there is no specific semantics associated with a *div*.

All web page content sections in an HTML4 document are *implicit*. Headings begin new sections of a document. This is not in any way relevant to most normal web users, but is a very important feature for vision impaired site visitors who use screen readers. These site visitors frequently rely upon headings in a web page as a means of navigating through it.

HTML5 introduces an *explicit* sectioning model. There are a number of new structural elements, (*some have been already touched on*), which can be used to section web page content.

Here are the new sectioning HTML5 elements with brief descriptions from the HTML5 specification:

The *section* Element

The HTML5 *section* element represents a generic chunk of content within a web page or web application. The HTML5 *section* element represents a thematic grouping of web page or web application content, typically with a heading.

The *article* Element

The HTML5 *article* element represents a self-contained block of web page content in an HTML5 web page or web application. The *article* element is intended to be independently distributable or reusable, for example in data syndication. The *article* element can be used to enclose:

- A forum post
- A magazine or newspaper feature story
- A blog entry
- A user-submitted comment

- An interactive widget or gadget

OR

- Any other independent block of content

The *nav* Element

The HTML5 *nav* element, represents a section of a page that links to other pages or to parts within the same page. It is a section of web page content with navigation links.

The *aside* Element

The HTML5 *aside* element represents a section of page content which is tangentially related to the main content of the web page. The web page content enclosed with the *aside* element can be considered separate from main page content. In the print world such content is often represented in the sidebar of the printed page.

Now let's explore the usage of these new HTML5 elements which will really help in understanding them and using them in crafting future proof web pages.

<section>

The HTML5 *section* element is used for grouping *related content* within the body of any web page. The *section* element can be nested, i.e. *<section></section>* may contain other *<section></section>*.

Some web developers ask where does this leave the *div* element? Well, a *div* need not be used to segregate web page content any more. The web page content placed within a single *<div></div>* can be segregated using *<section></section>*. Further segregation of the same web page content can be achieved by nesting *<section></section>* within another *<section></section>*. The *<div></div>* elements can often be converted to *<section></section>* in a web page crafted using HTML5.

Here is a simple example of what web page content should be enclosed within a *<div></div>* and not a *<section></section>*.

Think of a very common web page, design pattern. The web page will have a header content, a main page content with two adjacent columns—one column which could be devoted affiliate links displayed as affiliate banners and the other column could be used to display web site navigation links, a blog rolls, a login sub-system and so on, followed by web page footer content as shown in diagram 3.1.

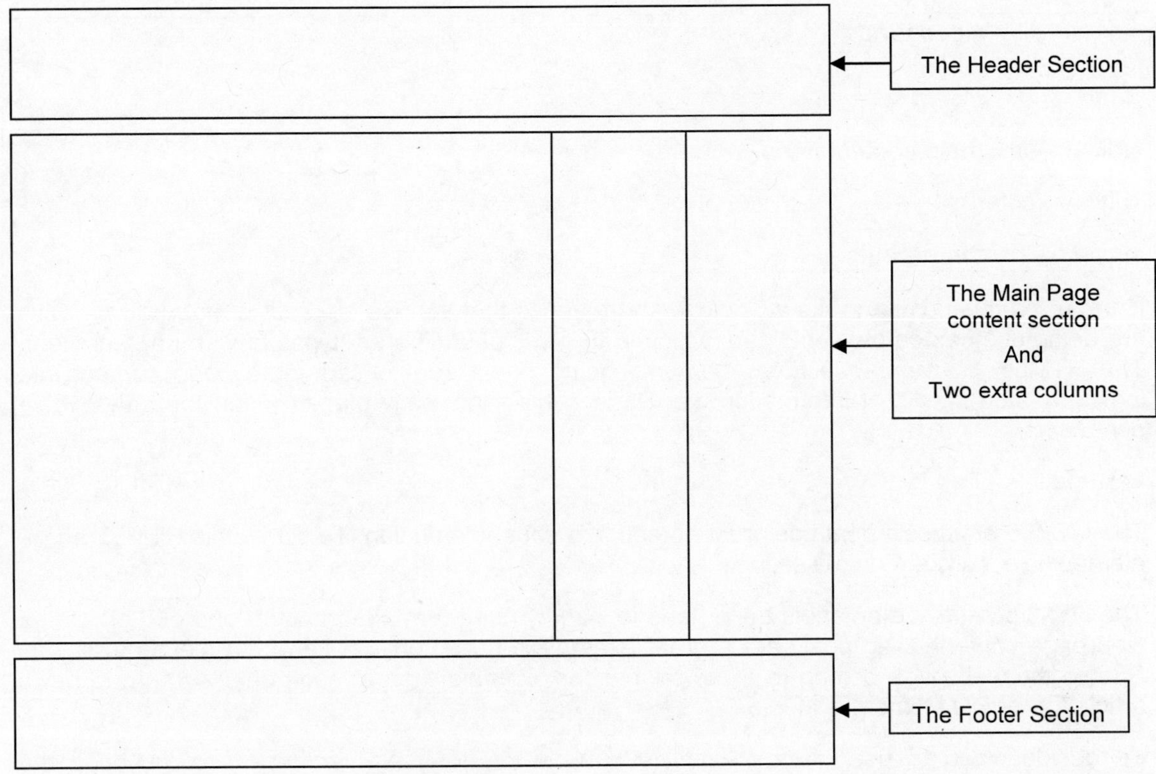

Diagram 3.1.

Web page coders will always craft such an empty shell (i.e. page template) as shown in diagram 3.1 above as a set of *<div></div>* elements. Take a look at the code snippet below:

```
<div id="header">

</div><!—div header Ends -->

<div id="main-content">
      <div id="posts-content">
            ...
      </div>

      <div id="sidebar-affiliate">
            ...
      </div>
```

```
    <div id="sidebar-nav">
        ...
    </div>
</div><!—div main-content Ends -->
<div id="footer">
</div><!—div footer Ends -->
```

Here, using nested divs make a whole lot more sense that the use of *<section></section>*. Divs are being used as empty containers which in turn will hold different types of web page content. The HTML5 *<section></section>* elements being best used to segregate *page content* into logical related blocks of information. i.e. Page content normally placed within the <div></div> container.

<article>

The HTML5 *article* element has great potential to cause confusion. To clarify this HTML5 *article* element is a *special kind* of *section*.

The HTML5 *section* element is quite generic, simply used to make the start and end of related web page content. Blog posts are a great example for the correct use of the element *section*. Should the web page belong to a newspaper for example then to segregate and group news article the *article* element is ideal.

To decide when to use *<article></article>* and when to use *<section></section>,* use the HTML5 element *<section></section>* to enclose any block of web page information that can stand separately / independently within the rest of the web page content.

When writing Blog posts, a Blogger often writes each Blog post in such a way that each post's content is in some way linked with the one immediately above or below. This kind of web page content is ideally enclosed using *<section></section>*.

Anyway, if ever you are puzzled and are wondering whether to use *<section></section>* or *<article></article>* to enclose specific web page content (*please do not over think this*) simply use *<section></section>* and all should work just fine.

<aside>

I think the HTML5 element *aside* is poorly named, but that's the element name that the HTML5 developers have chosen so I guess we will just have to live with it.

Enclose web page content that is tangentially related to the rest of the web page content within the *<aside></aside>* elements in the web page.

Do remember that there are no hard and fast rules associated with using HTML5 elements, hence simply use these elements using common sense and the HTML5 codespec will be interpreted correctly by most HTML5 compliant Browsers.

Headers, Footers And Sections In Segregating Content

As touched upon briefly in chapter two, web pages can have quite a complex structure. For example, a blog post may contain a *header* that includes:

The title of the post

The author name

And so on.

The *footer* might contain:

A publication date and time stamp

Share this information - mapped to specific icons for social networks

And so on.

As mentioned earlier, sections may also contain other sections. Sections may contain articles, as well as articles may contain sections, and on and on.

The key is for using such markup elements to reflect the *logical structure of the web page*.

Never let an obsession with perfect markup get in the way of web page content itself. Just use good judgment and commonsense and all will be well.

A really great way to sort out all of this information is by creating a web page that actually uses these elements. Exactly such page codespec is comes next.

```
<!DOCTYPE html>
<html>
<head>
    <meta charset="utf-8">
    <title>Personal Profile Professional Profile</title>
</head>
<body>
<header>
```

```
    <hgroup>
        <h1>Ivan Bayross</h1>
        <h2>Technical Author, Mentor and Friend</h2>
    </hgroup><!-- hgroup  ENDS -->
    <p>December 7th, 2010</p>
    <p>Mumbai, India</p>
    <nav>
        <ul>
            <li>Skip to the content</li>
            <li>Home</li>
            <li>About</li>
            <li>Free Tutorials</li>
            <li>Tech Tips</li>
            <li>Register now!</li>
        </ul>
    <nav><!-- nav  ENDS -->
</header><!-- header  ENDS -->
<div id="divMainContent">
    <section class="track">
        <article>
            <header>
                <hgroup>
                    <h3>Hottest Mobile OS</h3>
                </hgroup>
                <figure>
                    <img src="" alt="" >
                    <figcaption>Presenter: Ivan Bayross</figcaption>
                </figure>
            </header>
```

```
        <p>What's the hottest mobile operating system (OS)? The one that customers desire the
most and plan to upgrade to next? Practically a tie between iPhone (iOS) and Android.
        In the analytics firm's latest mobile report, it found that 30% of users will choose iPhone
(iOS) while 28% of users will buy an Android device.</p>

        </article>

        <article>

            <header>
                <hgroup>
                    <h3>Video for iPad</h3>
                </hgroup>

                <figure>
                    <img src="" alt="">
                    <figcaption>Presenter: Kavita Mavani</figcaption>
                </figure>
            </header>
            <p>iPad can only play limited format of video files, include QuickTime .mov file, MP4
file in h264 codec or MPEG4 codec file. Many other format of videos, include .AVI file, .MPG
file, .RMVB file, .WMV file, .ASF file, and .FLV file that download from video sharing website like
YouTube.</p>
            <p>Even a video file already in .mov or .mp4 format, not means it can play with iPad:
if the file&acute;s properties like size or bitrate not fit iPad&acute;s limit, when you syncing it to
iPad through iTunes, you will get an error message like this: &quot;blablabla&quot; was not
copied to the iPad &quot;your iPad name&quot; because it cannot be played on this iPad, or
just cannot import it to iTunes library.</p>

        </article>

        <article>

            <header>
                <hgroup>
                    <h3>Set The IP Address</h3>
                </hgroup>

                <figure>
                    <img src="" alt="">
```

```
            <figcaption>Presenter: Meher Bala </figcaption>
        </figure>
    </header>
    <p>An IP address has to be correctly entered in your desktop computer or notebook, in order to browse the internet. It is a four number that can be between 0 and 255.  It contains 4 octets and is separated by dot (.). You can collect your this address number from your LAN service provider. Some time the IP address gets vanished
from the computer and hence you will not be able to connect to the internet. In such cases you need to re-setup it.</p>

  </article>

  <article>

    <header>
        <hgroup>
            <h3>E Commerce Development is Beneficial for Masses</h3>
        </hgroup>

        <figure>
            <img src="" alt="">
            <figcaption>Presenter: Prerna Gupta</figcaption>
        </figure>
    </header>
    <p>The present day companies involved in IT technology are well skilled in software developments. They adopt a single point stratagem to analyze and understand the client's requirement, so that they can offer a truly distinctive and effective solution. These software development companies have developed expertise with various kinds of technologies which helps them to work with all kinds of client's business and professional needs.</p>

  </article>

</section> <!-- track-->

<aside id="divSidebar">

<form>SEARCH</form>
```

```
    <section>
        <h3>STAY IN TOUCH</h3>
        <ul>
            <li>Email Id: ivan@ivanbayross.com</li>
            <li>Twitter: ivanbayross</li>
        </ul>
    </section>

    <section>
        <h3>DOWNLOAD OUR ONE-PAGER</h3>

        <p>Need to convince the person who writes the checks? Grab our ready to print one-
pager.</p>
    </section>

    <section id="divBrought2uBy">

        <h3>BROUGHT TO YOU BY</h3>

        <section id="divSponsors">
            <h4>OUR SPONSORS</h4>
        </section> <!-- divSponsors ENDS -->

        <section id="divPartners">
            <h4>OUR PARTNERS</h4>
        </section> <!-- divPartners ENDS -->

    </section> <!-- divBrought2uBy ENDS -->

    </aside> <!-- divSidebar ENDS -->

</div> <!-- divMainContent  ENDS -->

<footer>

    <h3>ABOUT IVAN BAYROSS</h3>

    <p>Ivan Bayross is an Indian Technical Author.</p>

    <p>To date, he has written and published 75 books focused on commercial application
development using various software tools and technologies and still writing.</p>

    <p>Some of his books have been adopted as standard reference material for students who
aspire to a degree in Computer Science and Engineering, by M.I.T,
```

```
    Singapore University and a few Indian Universities.</p>

    <section>
    <h3>SUBSCRIBE TO OUR DAILY NEWSLETTER</h3>
    <p>Subscribe to our monthly newsletter to stay up-to date with the new technologies</p>

    <form>
        <label>Name:</label>
        <label>Email Id:</label>
        <input type="button" value="SUBSCRIBE" />
    </form>
    </section>

    <p>&copy; Ivan Bayross Inc. All rights reserved.
    Terms and Conditions | Privacy Policy</p>

</footer><!-- footer  ENDS -->

</body>
</html>
```

When this code is executed in any HTML5 compliant Browser the output will be as shown in diagram 3.2, diagram 3.3, diagram 3.4 and diagram 3.5 below.

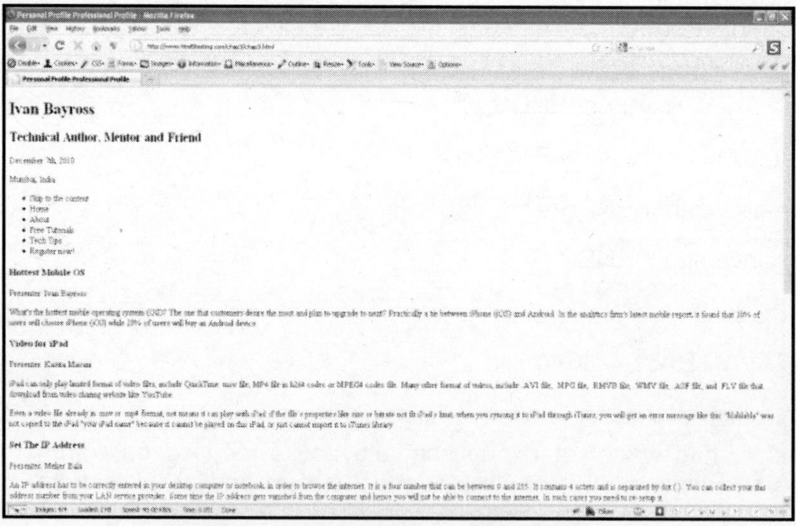

Diagram 3.2 - Firefox (version 3.6.13)

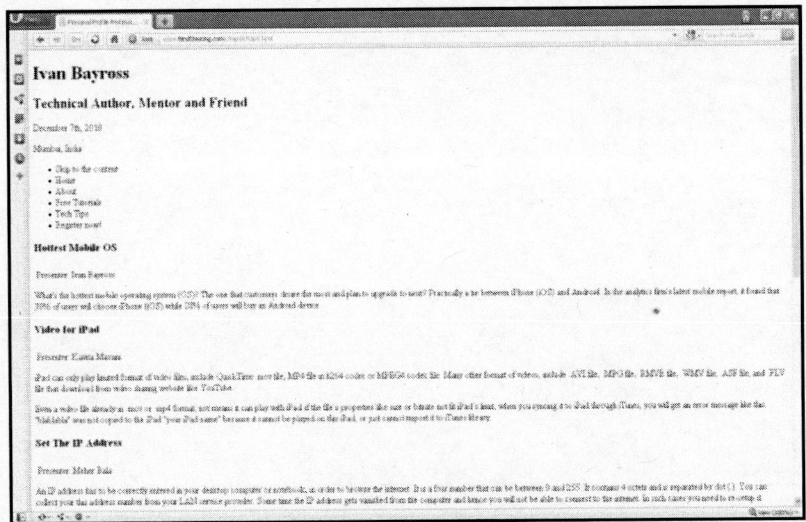

Diagram 3.3 - Opera (version 11.00.00)

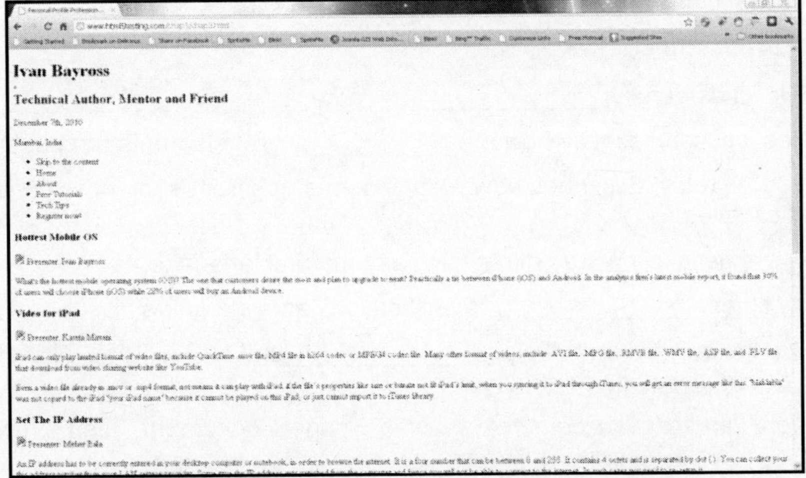

Diagram 3.4 Google Chrome (version 8.0.552)

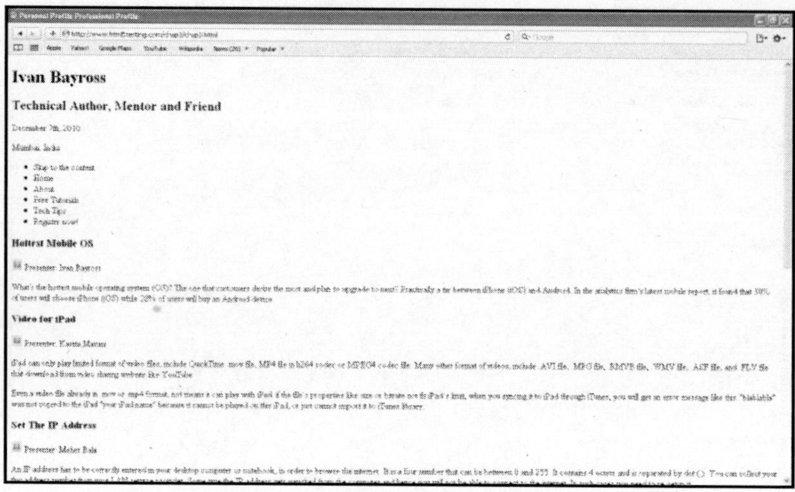

Diagram 3.5 - Safari (version 5.0.2)

Self Review Questions

Fill In The Blanks

1. HTML has two kinds of rules,________________ and ______________________.
2. Syntactic rules, describe exactly how the ________________elements are put together.
3. ________________rules, describes how meaning emerges from sentences constructed using the syntactical rules.
4. _____________is definitely not as expressive as a natural language.
5. In these early times, _______________ specifications act as a guide.
6. HTML5 web page can have multiple _______________and/or _____________elements used within it to describe web page structure
7. Each *section* and/or *article* of a web page document can have its own document____________, starting with h1.
8. The HTML5 ____________element has a great potential to cause confusion.
9. The HTML5 ____________element is to be used for grouping related content within the body of any web page.
10. The HTML5 ____________element represents a section of page content which is tangentially related to the main content of the web page.
11. _______________are a great example for the correct use of the element *section*.
12. The __________element is intended to be independently distributable or reusable

13. HTML5 introduces an ______________ sectioning model.
14. All web page content sections in an HTML4 document are______________.
15. ______________ begin new sections of a document.
16. The ______________ element has no explicit meaning of its own.

True Or False

17. The HTML5 *nav* element is a section of web page content with navigation links.
18. The *div* element has explicit meaning of its own.
19. HTML is as expressive as a natural language.
20. HTML4 has a single, *implicit* outlining model that helped describe the structure of a webpage to the HTML interpreter within a supporting Browser.
21. Syntactic rules, describes how meaning emerges from sentences constructed using the syntactical rules.
22. All web page content sections in an HTML4 document are *implicit*.
23. Th*e article* element is not intended to be independently distributable or reusable.
24. HTML5 introduces an *explicit* sectioning model.
25. The web page content enclosed with the *aside* element can be considered separate from main page content.
26. Semantic rules, describe exactly how the language elements are put together.

Hands-on Exercise

1. Write the HTML 5 code spec which makes use of following information.
   Please use all the HTML5 elements that have been learned in this chapter.
   Output of this exercise is shown in diagram 3.6

Website Name	Lorem Ipsum
Website Tagline	Come learn how to use lorem ipsum
Date	1st January 2011
Page Menu	• Home | • About | • Demo | • Affiliates | • Contact Us

<table>
<tr>
<td>Contents of the Website</td>
<td>
Lorem Ipsum [The title of the post]

Presenter Image: [image]
Presenter: John [author name]

Lorem Ipsum is simply dummy text of the printing and typesetting industry. Lorem Ipsum has been the industry's standard dummy text ever since the 1500s, when an unknown printer took a galley of type and scrambled it to make a type specimen book. It has survived not only five centuries, but also the leap into electronic typesetting, remaining essentially unchanged.

It was popularized in the 1960s with the release of Letraset sheets containing Lorem Ipsum passages, and more recently with desktop publishing software like Aldus PageMaker including versions of Lorem Ipsum. There are many variations of passages of Lorem Ipsum available, but the majority have suffered alteration in some form, by injected humour, or randomized words which don't look even slightly believable.

Google v/s Microsoft: The game becomes filthier [The title of the post]

Presenter Image: [image]
Presenter: Vidya [author name]

Google is enjoying its dominance in the search arena, which is challenged by Microsoft Corp, the software giant, which had updated its search engine with a new Decision Engine, called Bing in June last year. While, Microsoft leads in operating system, enterprise applications and web browsers market, Google holds the lead in search arena.

Meanwhile, the search giant is gearing up in various fields like operating system, web based apps and web browser, to compete with the software giant. But, besides healthy competition, the two biggies are also trying other ways out to beat each other in various fields.

Essential add-ons for Twitter and FaceBook [The title of the post]

Presenter Image: [image]
Presenter: Sneha [author name]

FaceBook is the world's number one social networking website with over 400 million active users worldwide. Similarly, Twitter is a leading micro-blogging social website, where users can send and read messages called as tweets, consists of upto 140 characters. Recently, Twitter has achieved yet another milestone by reaching 10 billion "tweets."
</td>
</tr>
</table>

	Today, people are actively using these mediums to connect socially with their friends, reaching new markets and also for promoting their business profiles. Users love to play games on the FaceBook like FarmVille, Mafia Wars, and also create their company's social profile to promote or make the followers on its home page.
Create a Side Bar: a) Form --------------------- b) Show Sponsors & Partners Name	Search --- BROUGHT TO YOU BY OUR SPONSORS OUR PARTNERS
Users Registration --------------------- Fields in the Registration form are:	REGISTER WITH OUR SITE --- User Name: Password: Confirm Password: Email Id: Register button
Copyright	©2011. All Right Reserved.
Footer Menu	Terms and Conditions | Privacy Policy

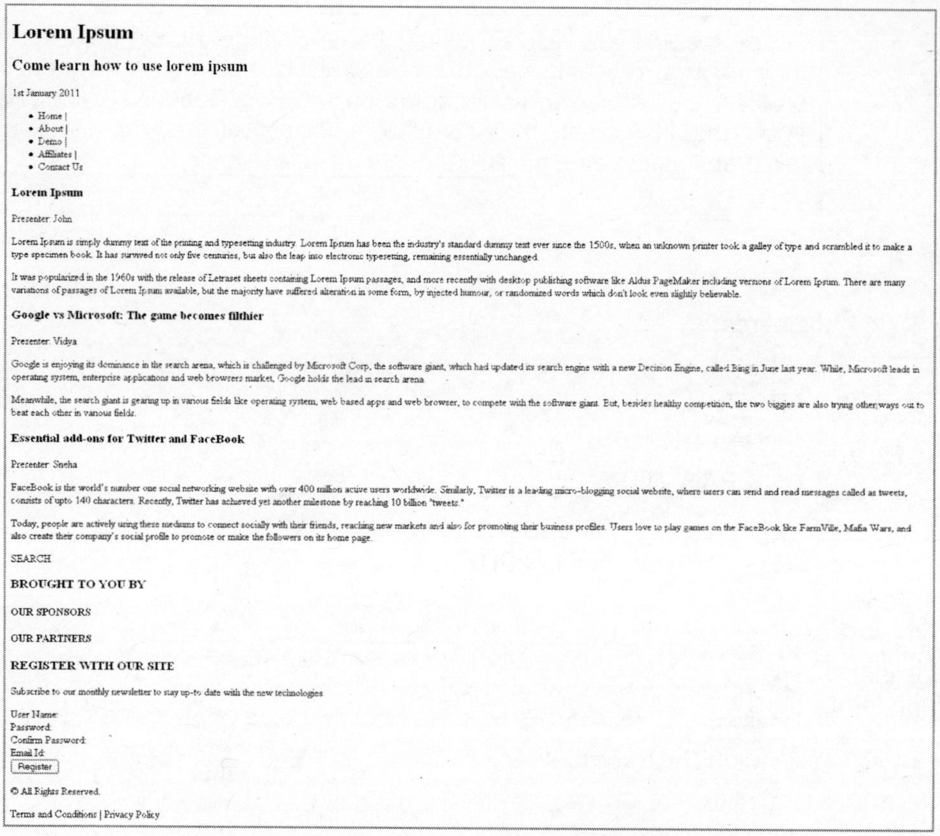

Lorem Ipsum

Come learn how to use lorem ipsum

1st January 2011

- Home |
- About |
- Demo |
- Affiliates |
- Contact Us

Lorem Ipsum

Presenter: John

Lorem Ipsum is simply dummy text of the printing and typesetting industry. Lorem Ipsum has been the industry's standard dummy text ever since the 1500s, when an unknown printer took a galley of type and scrambled it to make a type specimen book. It has survived not only five centuries, but also the leap into electronic typesetting, remaining essentially unchanged.

It was popularized in the 1960s with the release of Letraset sheets containing Lorem Ipsum passages, and more recently with desktop publishing software like Aldus PageMaker including versions of Lorem Ipsum. There are many variations of passages of Lorem Ipsum available, but the majority have suffered alteration in some form, by injected humour, or randomized words which don't look even slightly believable.

Google vs Microsoft: The game becomes filthier

Presenter: Vidya

Google is enjoying its dominance in the search arena, which is challenged by Microsoft Corp, the software giant, which had updated its search engine with a new Decision Engine, called Bing in June last year. While, Microsoft leads in operating system, enterprise applications and web browsers market, Google holds the lead in search arena.

Meanwhile, the search giant is gearing up in various fields like operating system, web based apps and web browser, to compete with the software giant. But, besides healthy competition, the two biggies are also trying other ways out to beat each other in various fields.

Essential add-ons for Twitter and FaceBook

Presenter: Sneha

FaceBook is the world's number one social networking website with over 400 million active users worldwide. Similarly, Twitter is a leading micro-blogging social website, where users can send and read messages called as tweets, consists of upto 140 characters. Recently, Twitter has achieved yet another milestone by reaching 10 billion "tweets."

Today, people are actively using these mediums to connect socially with their friends, reaching new markets and also for promoting their business profiles. Users love to play games on the FaceBook like FarmVille, Mafia Wars, and also create their company's social profile to promote or make the followers on its home page.

SEARCH

BROUGHT TO YOU BY

OUR SPONSORS

OUR PARTNERS

REGISTER WITH OUR SITE

Subscribe to our monthly newsletter to stay up-to date with the new technologies

User Name:
Password:
Confirm Password:
Email Id:
Register

© All Rights Reserved.

Terms and Conditions | Privacy Policy

Diagram 3.6: Output of Hands on Exercise

Note: *The Codespec for the Hands-On-Exercise is given in the CD.*

4. WAI-ARIA and HTML5

W3C's **W**eb **A**ccessibility **I**nitiative's - **A**ccessible **R**ich **I**nternet **A**pplications specification is not part of HTML5. ARIA was developed independently of HTML5 but there's a lot of useful input to be gained from ARIA especially because it improves the accessibility and usability of web pages and Internet delivered applications.

ARIA is essentially designed to make web content and Internet delivered applications more accessible to people with disabilities. This need came about because web-based applications became more and more desktop-like, incorporating complex controls which are referred to in ARIA as *widgets*.

The ARIA specification defines how information about these complex controls can be conveyed to Browsers, Screen readers, and other assistive devices to make the complex controls (i.e. ARIA widgets) usable by all.

ARIA provides several mechanisms for doing this, including:

Defining roles which describe various widgets (for example, menus and sliders) can play

Defining roles for describing the structure of web pages

Properties to describe various control states; for example, whether an element is currently being clicked on

In this material, the some of the features of ARIA will be examined, which can be used in conjunction with HTML5 to extend HTML5 semantics. This definitely improves the accessibility of HTML5 based web sites and Internet delivered applications.

Using the Role Attribute

XHTML 1.1 introduced the role attribute as a new language feature. The role attribute was introduced to enable developers to describe the purpose of an element.

Developers use, the HTML4 *class* and *id* attributes for this purpose, most likely the following code has been encountered in XHTML compliant pages.

```
<div class="header"></div>
```

Unfortunately the class attribute is designed for general purpose data processing, such as binding a set of styling attributes to an HTML element. Hence, the class attribute really should not be used for conveying a specific meaning to an HTML element.

The *role* attribute can be conceptualized as being much like the *class* or *id* attribute, but expressly for used for *describing* or *annotating*, an element's purpose in a document.

The role specification defines a number of role attribute values, which include:

`banner`

This *banner* role attribute value is used to identify a web page region that holds the heading or internal title of the page. The content placed within *banner* would be site-oriented, rather than being page-specific.

Site-oriented content typically includes web page elements as a logo, a main heading for the web page, and a website search tool. This typically appears at the top of the page, and normally spans the full width of the page.

`complementary`

The *complimentary* role attribute value can be used to identify any section of the web page content that supports the main content of the page but can be separated from the main content. Such a block of web age information is semantically meaningful on its own.

Several different types of web page content conform to this role. For example, in the case of a portal the complimentary attribute can be used to separate show times, current weather, related articles, or stocks to watch from the main page content.

The content thus separated should is always relevant to the main content on the webpage. Remember if such content can stand entirely on its own, (i.e. *it is completely separable from the main content of the web page*), a more general role attribute could be used.

`contentinfo`

The *contentinfo* role attribute value is used to identify / describe meta information about the content on the web page. For example, footnotes, copyrights, links to privacy statements, and other such content blocks can be enclosed within this role attribute on the web page.

`main`

The *main* role attribute value is used to identify the main content displayed within a web page. It marks the start of the content that is directly related to the central topic of the web page.

`navigation`

The *navigation* role attribute value is used to identify the collection of website navigation links used for navigating through the web page or between related web pages.

note

The *note* role attribute is used to identify web page content that is ancillary to the main content of contained within the web page.

search

The *search* role attribute is used to identify a text box or a form used to submit search requests to the web site or to a more general internet search service like a search engine.

If one step back and takes a good look at many of the new HTML5 elements, one will notice a definite overlap, for example:

- The *banner* role attribute value and the header element
- The *complementary* role attribute value and the aside element
- The *navigation* role attribute value and the nav element
- The *complementary* and *note* role attribute values in combination cover the purpose of the *aside* element

All seem to overlap in functionality.

Apparently the *main* role attribute value describes a functionality for web page content for which HTML5 does not have an element (i.e. *the main content information block of a web page*).

Unlike with *class* or *id*, the values accepted by role are not usually user defined. While it is possible to define role attribute values formally, this will be of little or no practical use as browsers and other software will not have any idea of what to do with these values.

ARIA does define a number of additional values in addition to the standard role values defined in XHTML 1.1. ARIA roles can be quite complex, hence here we will focus on some of the most immediately useful ones.

> **Note:** *Simply adding a role attribute value to an HTML5 element (for example, role="button" to let's say a span element) does not make that element a button. A role attribute and its associated values is for describing the purpose for which an HTML element is being used. It's the really up to the web page coder to make the span behave like a button if required.*

ARIA defines several types of roles. Among these are widget roles. ARIA calls controls -> widgets. Some of the roles defined are:

Landmark roles

i.e. Regions of the page intended as navigational landmarks

Document structure roles

i.e. structures that organize content in a page.

Here is a quick overview of the most common ARIA roles:

Widget (control based) Roles include:	Landmark Roles include:	Document Structure Roles include:
alert	banner	article
alertdialog	complementary	group
button	contentinfo	heading
checkbox	main	list
combobox	navigation	listitem
dialog	search	note
marquee		presentation
menuitem		separator
menuitemcheckbox		
menuitemradio		
option		
progressbar		
radio		
scrollbar		
slider		
spinbutton		
status		
tab		
tabpanel		
textbox		
timer		
tooltip		
treeitem		

Table 1. ARIA –Roles

Using Roles

The attribute *role* must be used just as any other attribute would be used such as *class* or *id* within HTML codespec. For example, the HTML5 header element could be marked up as:

```
<header role="banner">
```

The question then arises as to why this would be done? Well HTML5 has a header element, HTML4 doesn't. So in HTML4, our equivalent might be:

```
<div role="banner">
```

Regretfully even in HTML5, not all the types of role attributes that ARIA defines are provided by HTML5 within elements.

So we could mark up the main content block of a web page as follows:

```
<div id="main-content">
```

This can be annotated with a role attribute as follows:

```
<div id="main-content" role="main">
```

Where HTML5 does provide an element which has a role attribute/value, here is a good reason to use the role attribute/value.

Presently, support for ARIA roles in various screen readers is reasonably good. (i.e. *A screen reader is software that is used by visually challenged people to visit websites*), Roles are an older, more stable specification, support for the role attribute and its values should improve over time and quite possibly remain richer than HTML5 support in screen readers. Additionally, having a role bound to an HTML5 element also enables the element to be styled in browsers from IE7 onwards

Hence, where there's a role attribute and an appropriate value that matches the element being used, whether it's an HTML5 element or HTML4 element, its good programming practice to use it.

Now, here is an exercise to which will help put all of this into practice.

```
<!DOCTYPE html>
<html>
<head>
    <meta charset="utf-8">
    <title>Personal Profile Professional Profile</title>
</head>
<body>
<header role="banner">
    <hgroup role="heading">
        <h1>Ivan Bayross</h1>
        <h2>Technical Author, Mentor and Friend</h2>
    </hgroup><!-- hgroup  ENDS -->
```

```
    <p>December 7th, 2010</p>
    <p>Mumbai, India</p>
    <nav role="navigation">
        <ul>
            <li>Skip to the content</li>
            <li>Home</li>
            <li>About</li>
            <li>Free Tutorials</li>
            <li>Tech Tips</li>
            <li>Register now!</li>
        </ul>
    <nav><!-- nav  ENDS -->
</header><!-- header  ENDS -->
<div id="divMainContent">
    <section class="track">
        <article>
            <header>
                <hgroup>
                    <h3>Hottest Mobile OS</h3>
                </hgroup>
                <figure>
                    <img src="" alt="" >
                    <figcaption>Presenter: Ivan Bayross</figcaption>
                </figure>
            </header>
            <p>What's the hottest mobile operating system (OS)? The one that customers desire
the most and plan to upgrade to next? Practically a tie between iPhone (iOS) and Android. In
the analytics firm's latest mobile report, it found that 30% of users will choose iPhone (iOS)
while 28% of users will buy an Android device.</p>
        </article>
```

```
<article>
    <header>
        <hgroup>
            <h3>Video for iPad</h3>
        </hgroup>
        <figure>
            <img src="" alt="">
            <figcaption>Presenter: Kavita Mavani</figcaption>
        </figure>
    </header>
    <p>iPad can only play limited format of video files, include QuickTime .mov file, MP4 file in h264 codec or MPEG4 codec file. Many other format of videos, include .AVI file, .MPG file, .RMVB file, .WMV file, .ASF file, and .FLV file that download from video sharing website like YouTube.</p>
    <p>Even a video file already in .mov or .mp4 format, not means it can play with iPad: if the file&acute;s properties like size or bitrate not fit iPad&acute;s limit, when you syncing it to iPad through iTunes, you will get an error message like this: &quot;blablabla&quot; was not copied to the iPad &quot;your iPad name&quot; because it cannot be played on this iPad, or just cannot import it to iTunes library.</p>
</article>
<article>
    <header>
        <hgroup>
            <h3>Set The IP Address</h3>
        </hgroup>
        <figure>
            <img src="" alt="">
            <figcaption>Presenter: Meher Bala </figcaption>
        </figure>
    </header>
```

```
        <p>An IP address has to be correctly entered in your desktop computer or notebook, in order to browse the internet. It is a four number that can be between 0 and 255. It contains 4 octets and is separated by dot (.). You can collect your this address number from your LAN service provider. Some time the IP address gets vanished from the computer and hence you will not be able to connect to the internet. In such cases you need to re-setup it.</p>
    </article>
    <article>
        <header>
            <hgroup>
                <h3>E Commerce Development is Beneficial for Masses</h3>
            </hgroup>
            <figure>
                <img src="" alt="">
                <figcaption>Presenter: Prerna Gupta</figcaption>
            </figure>
        </header>
        <p>The present day companies involved in IT technology are well skilled in software developments. They adopt a single point stratagem to analyze and understand the client's requirement, so that they can offer a truly distinctive and effective solution. These software development companies have developed expertise with various kinds of technologies which helps them to work with all kinds of client's business and professional needs.</p>
    </article>
</section> <!-- track-->
<aside id="divSidebar" role="complementary">
<form>SEARCH</form>
<section>
    <h3>STAY IN TOUCH</h3>
    <ul>
        <li>Email Id: ivan@ivanbayross.com</li>
        <li>Twitter: ivanbayross</li>
    </ul>
</section>
```

```
    <section>
        <h3>DOWNLOAD OUR ONE-PAGER</h3>
        <p>Need to convince the person who writes the checks? Grab our ready to print one-pager.</p>
    </section>
    <section id="divBrought2uBy">
        <h3>BROUGHT TO YOU BY</h3>
        <section id="divSponsors">
            <h4>OUR SPONSORS</h4>
        </section> <!-- divSponsors ENDS -->
        <section id="divPartners">
            <h4>OUR PARTNERS</h4>
        </section> <!-- divPartners ENDS -->
    </section> <!-- divBrought2uBy ENDS -->
    </aside> <!-- divSidebar ENDS -->
</div> <!-- divMainContent  ENDS -->
<footer>
    <h3>ABOUT IVAN BAYROSS</h3>
    <p>Ivan Bayross is an Indian Technical Author.</p>
    <p>To date, he has written and published 75 books focused on commercial application development using various software tools and technologies and still writing.</p>
    <p>Some of his books have been adopted as standard reference material for students who aspire to a degree in Computer Science and Engineering, by M.I.T, Singapore University and a few Indian Universities.</p>
    <section>
    <h3>SUBSCRIBE TO OUR DAILY NEWSLETTER</h3>
    <p>Subscribe to our monthly newsletter to stay up-to date with the new technologies</p>
    <form>
        <label>Name:</label>
        <label>Email Id:</label>
```

```
        <input type="button" value="SUBSCRIBE" />
    </form>
    </section>

    <p role="contentinfo">&copy; Ivan Bayross Inc. All rights reserved.
    Terms and Conditions | Privacy Policy</p>

</footer><!-- footer  ENDS -->

</body>
</html>
```

When this code is executed in any HTML5 compliant Browser the output will be as shown in diagram 4.1, diagram 4.2, diagram 4.3 and diagram 4.4. below.

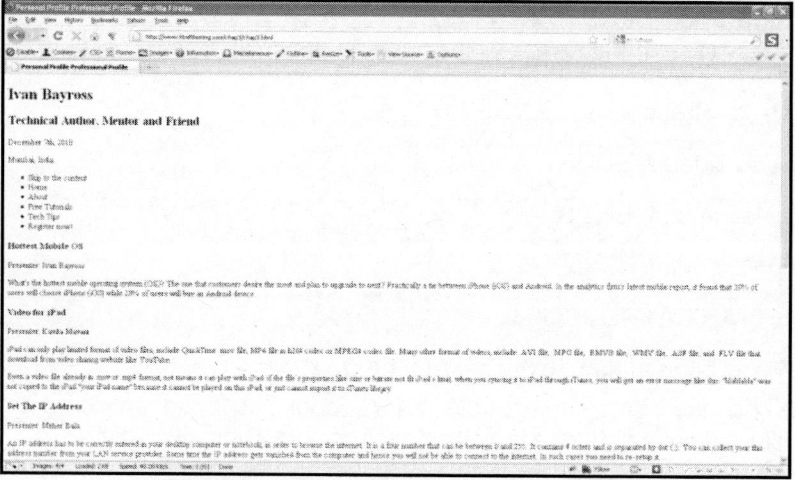

Diagram 4.1 - Firefox (version 3.6.13)

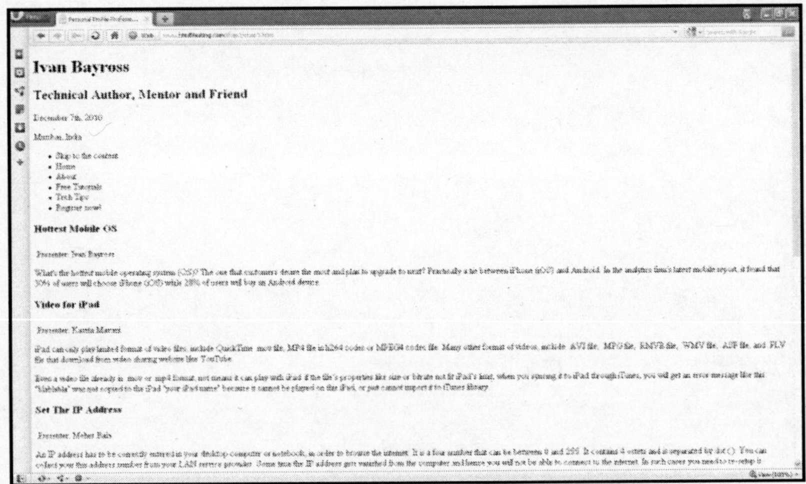

Diagram 4.2 - Opera (version 11.00.00)

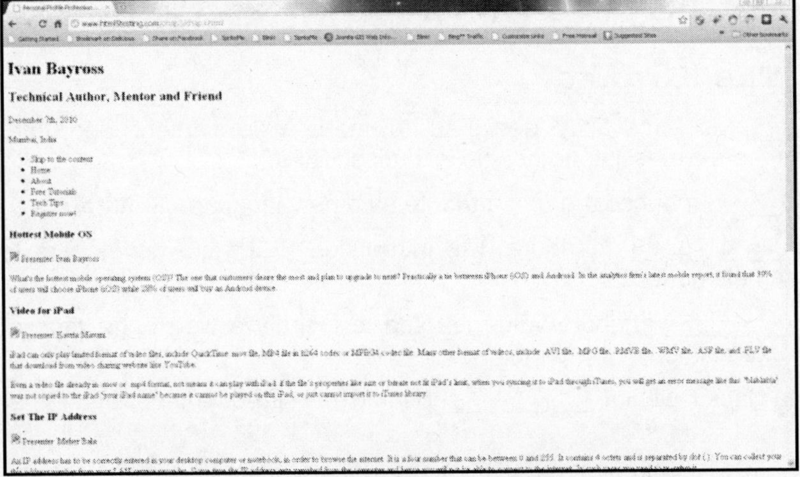

Diagram 4.3 - Google Chrome (version 8.0.552)

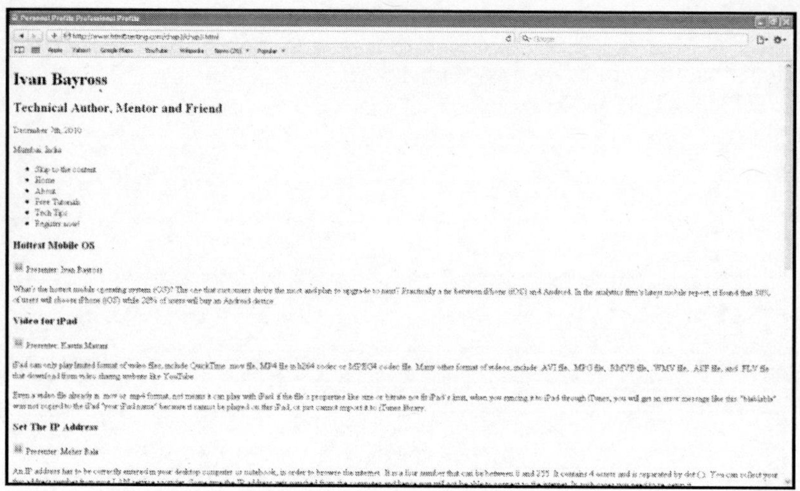

Diagram 4.4 - Safari (version 5.0.2)

Self Review Questions

Fill In The Blanks

1. _____________ is essentially designed to make web content and Internet delivered applications more accessible to people with disabilities.
2. _____________ introduced the role attribute as a new language feature.
3. The _________________ attribute was introduced to enable developers to describe the purpose of an element.
4. The ______________ attribute value is used to identify a web page region that holds the heading or internal title of the page.
5. The content placed within ___________ would be site-oriented, rather than being page-specific.
6. The _____________ role attribute value is used to identify / describe meta information about the content on the web page.
7. The ______________ role attribute value is used to identify the main content displayed within a web page.
8. The ____________ role attribute value is used to identify the collection of website navigation links used for navigating through the web page or between related web pages.
9. The _____________ role attribute is used to identify web page content that is ancillary to the main content of contained within the web page.
10. The __________role attribute is used to identify a text box or a form used to submit search requests to the web site or to a more general internet search service like a search engine.

True Or False

11. Apparently the *banner* role attribute value describes functionality for web page content for which HTML5 does not have an element.
12. Unlike with *class* or *id*, the values accepted by role are usually user defined.
13. The class attribute is designed for general purpose data processing, such as binding a set of styling attributes to an HTML element.
14. ARIA does not define a number of additional values in addition to the standard role values defined in XHTML 1.1.
15. The class attribute really should not be used for conveying a specific meaning to an HTML element.
16. The content placed within *banner* would be site-oriented, rather than being page-specific.
17. The attribute *role* must not be used just as any other attribute would be used such as *class* or *id* within HTML codespec.
18. Simply adding a role attribute value to an HTML5 element makes that element a button.
19. A role attribute and its associated values is for describing the purpose for which an HTML element is being used.

Hands-on Exercise

1. Write the HTML 5 code spec which makes use of following information.
   Define appropriate role for each element.
   Please use all the HTML5 elements that have been learned in this chapter.
   Output of this exercise is shown in diagram 4.5

Website Name	Lorem Ipsum
Website Tagline	Come learn how to use lorem ipsum
Date	1st January 2011
Page Menu	• Home | • About | • Demo | • Affiliates | • Contact Us

<table>
<tr><td>Contents of the Website</td><td>Lorem Ipsum [The title of the post]

Presenter Image: [image]
Presenter: John [author name]

Lorem Ipsum is simply dummy text of the printing and typesetting industry. Lorem Ipsum has been the industry's standard dummy text ever since the 1500s, when an unknown printer took a galley of type and scrambled it to make a type specimen book. It has survived not only five centuries, but also the leap into electronic typesetting, remaining essentially unchanged.

It was popularized in the 1960s with the release of Letraset sheets containing Lorem Ipsum passages, and more recently with desktop publishing software like Aldus PageMaker including versions of Lorem Ipsum. There are many variations of passages of Lorem Ipsum available, but the majority have suffered alteration in some form, by injected humour, or randomized words which don't look even slightly believable.

Google v/s Microsoft: The game becomes filthier [The title of the post]

Presenter Image: [image]
Presenter: Sneha [author name]

Google is enjoying its dominance in the search arena, which is challenged by Microsoft Corp, the software giant, which had updated its search engine with a new Decision Engine, called Bing in June last year. While, Microsoft leads in operating system, enterprise applications and web browsers market, Google holds the lead in search arena.

Meanwhile, the search giant is gearing up in various fields like operating system, web based apps and web browser, to compete with the software giant. But, besides healthy competition, the two biggies are also trying other ways out to beat each other in various fields.</td></tr>
<tr><td>Create a Sidebar:
a) Form
----
b) Show Sponsors & Partners Name</td><td>Search

BROUGHT TO YOU BY
OUR SPONSORS
OUR PARTNERS</td></tr>
<tr><td></td><td></td></tr>
</table>

Users Registration -------------------- Fields in the Registration form are:	REGISTER WITH OUR SITE -- User Name: Password: Confirm Password: Email Id: Register button
Copyright	©2011. All Right Reserved.
Footer Menu	Terms and Conditions | Privacy Policy

Lorem Ipsum

Come learn how to use lorem ipsum

1st January 2011

- Home |
- About |
- Demo |
- Affiliates |
- Contact Us

Lorem Ipsum

Presenter: John

Lorem Ipsum is simply dummy text of the printing and typesetting industry. Lorem Ipsum has been the industry's standard dummy text ever since the 1500s, when an unknown printer took a galley of type and scrambled it to make a type specimen book. It has survived not only five centuries, but also the leap into electronic typesetting, remaining essentially unchanged.

It was popularised in the 1960s with the release of Letraset sheets containing Lorem Ipsum passages, and more recently with desktop publishing software like Aldus PageMaker including versions of Lorem Ipsum. There are many variations of passages of Lorem Ipsum available, but the majority have suffered alteration in some form, by injected humour, or randomised words which don't look even slightly believable.

Google vs Microsoft: The game becomes filthier

Presenter: Vidya

Google is enjoying its dominance in the search arena, which is challenged by Microsoft Corp, the software giant, which had updated its search engine with a new Decision Engine, called Bing in June last year. While, Microsoft leads in operating system, enterprise applications and web browsers market, Google holds the lead in search arena.

Meanwhile, the search giant is gearing up in various fields like operating system, web based apps and web browser, to compete with the software giant. But, besides healthy competition, the two biggies are also trying other ways out to beat each other in various fields.

Essential add-ons for Twitter and FaceBook

Presenter: Sneha

FaceBook is the world's number one social networking website with over 400 million active users worldwide. Similarly, Twitter is a leading micro-blogging social website, where users can send and read messages called as tweets, consists of upto 140 characters. Recently, Twitter has achieved yet another milestone by reaching 10 billion "tweets."

Today, people are actively using these mediums to connect socially with their friends, reaching new markets and also for promoting their business profiles. Users love to play games on the FaceBook like FarmVille, Mafia Wars, and also create their company's social profile to promote or make the followers on its home page.

SEARCH

BROUGHT TO YOU BY

OUR SPONSORS

OUR PARTNERS

REGISTER WITH OUR SITE

Subscribe to our monthly newsletter to stay up-to-date with the new technologies

User Name:
Password:
Confirm Password:
Email Id:
Register

© All Rights Reserved.

Terms and Conditions | Privacy Policy

Diagram 4.5: Output of Hands on Exercise

Note: *The Codespec for the Hands-On-Exercise is given in the CD*

5. Drawing With The Canvas Element

The HTML5 Canvas element is used to display graphics in web pages. The HTML5 syntax for creating such an element within a webpage is pretty simple and is as follows:

```
<canvas width="xxxpixels" height="yyypixels"></canvas>
```

Once the <canvas></canvas> elements have been used to define an area within a webpage, Javascript is used to draw graphic images within the area defined.

Here is the specification of the Canvas element in HTML5:

Element:	<canvas>
Start tag required:	Yes
End tag required:	Yes
Mandatory Attributes:	Height and Width – specified in pixels The value passed to either attribute is always numeric. Optionally can be qualified by the word pixels.
Browsers that support *Canvas*:	Chrome, Firefox, Opera, Safari

Once the area to work within is defined in the webpage, the real work is done using Javascript. Javascript is what draws within the area described by the canvas element in an HTML5 web page.

Using The HTML5 Element - Canvas

To learn how to use the canvas element, create a file named canvas.html with appropriate HTML5 code spec, then use Firefox as your Browser of choice and view the code spec being rendered.

Open your favorite Editor and create a file named canvas.html. canvas.html will contain the following HTML5 code spec.

```
<html>
<head>
<title>Canvas tutorial</title>
<script type="text/javascript">
function draw()
{
var canvas = document.getElementById('tutorial');
if (canvas.getContext)
{
var ctx = canvas.getContext('2d');
}
}
</script>
<style type="text/css">
canvas { border: 2px solid red; }
</style>
</head>
<body onLoad="draw();">
<canvas id="tutorial" width="175" height="175"></canvas>
</body>
</html>
```

Save the above codespec in the file named canvas.html as indicated above to any appropriate folder in your hard disk.

Here's what will happen if the codespec is executed in any HTML5 compliant Browser. When this codespec is executed the *onload* event of *body* fires when the web page is loads into the Browser.

The *onload* event invokes the Javascript function named loader(). When this function is invoked its signature is executed by the Browser's built-in Javascript interpreter.

```
var canvas = document.getElementById('canvas');
```

The variable *canvas* is loaded with the *canvas* object.

```
var canvas1 = canvas.getContext('2d');
```

The variable *canvas1* uses the getContext(); method of canvas to get access to the area defined by the canvas object's height and width attributes.

Once access to the canvas area is obtained another Javascript method can be invoke to paint a rectangle within this canvas area.

Drawing Rectangles

You can draw hollow rectangles with the strokeRect function: strokeRect(float x, float y, float w, float h);

OR

You can draw filled-in rectangles with the fillRect function: fillRect(float x, float y, float w, float h);

You pass these functions the (x, y) coordinate of the upper-left corner of the rectangle and the width and height of the rectangle you want.

> **Note:** *In a Canvas element, the upper-left corner of the Canvas corresponds to (0,0), positive x is to the left, positive y is downward, and all measurements are in pixels.*

Now let's look at filling each rectangle drawn with a user defined color.

The fill color of the rectangle is set with the fillStyle attribute. Use rgbal(), to specify a color and pass this to the fillStyle attribute of the rectangle created earlier.

rgba() requires four values:

The **R**ed, **G**reen, and **B**lue values, specified in a numeric range of 0 – 255, and a visibility factor i.e. either 0 or 1. Where 0 means the rectangle will be invisible, and 1 means it will be fully visible.

For example, to set the fill style of the *canvas1* object to *blue*: canvas1.fillStyle = "rgba(0, 0, 200, 1)";

Here's how to draw multiple rectangles filled in with different colors.

Over write the Javascript function loader(), with the following codespec. Then save canvas.html to an appropriate folder on the hard drive.

```
function loader()
{
        var canvas = document.getElementById('canvas');
    var canvas1 = canvas.getContext('2d');

    //Rectangles

    canvas1.fillStyle = "rgba(400, 50, 0, 1)";
    canvas1.fillRect(50, 50, 80, 90);
```

```
    canvas1.fillStyle = "rgba(900, 500, 0, 1)";
    canvas1.fillRect(60, 60, 80, 40);

    canvas1.fillStyle = "rgba(0, 0, 200, 1)";
    canvas1.fillRect(80, 80, 80, 40);
}
```

Execute canvas.html in Firefox. The output will be as shown in diagram 5.1 will be displayed in the Browser.

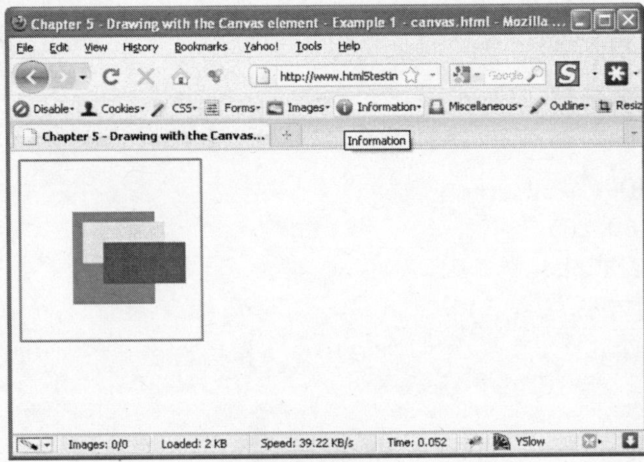

Diagram 5.1.

Drawing Line Art

You can draw line art with a Canvas element. Start with *beginPath()* to let the Canvas know that a figure is being created. Then use a combination of the *moveTo()* and *lineTo()* to position the physical drawing location and actually draw lines.

When the figure desired is drawn completely, use *closePath()* to complete the path drawn. Finally use *stroke()* to draw the result within the canvas design area.

Here is an example where three triangles are drawn using the above techniques. Additionally by passing the Canvas *strokeStyle* attribute the value red the triangles will be drawn in red.

To do this open canvas.html in your favorite editor and save it as redtriangles.html or you can copy and paste canvas.html to redtriangles.html. Next, open redtriangles.html in the editor and overwrite the Javascript codespec it holds with the following codespec.

```
function loader()
{
    var canvas = document.getElementById ('canvas');
    var canvas1 = canvas.getContext('2d');
    // Creating the stroked triangles
    canvas1.beginPath();
    canvas1.strokeStyle = 'rgba(800, 0, 0, 5)';
    canvas1.moveTo(110, 205);
    canvas1.lineTo(110, 100);
    canvas1.lineTo(30, 200);
    canvas1.closePath();
    canvas1.stroke();
    canvas1.beginPath();
    canvas1.moveTo(100, 205);
    canvas1.lineTo(100, 135);
    canvas1.lineTo(20, 205);
    canvas1.closePath();
    canvas1.stroke();
    canvas1.beginPath();
    canvas1.moveTo(150, 205);
    canvas1.lineTo(120, 145);
    canvas1.lineTo(10, 205);
    canvas1.closePath();
    canvas1.stroke();
}
```

Save redtriangles.html in an appropriate folder on the hard disk. Then execute redtriangles.html in Firefox and the output as shown in diagram 5.2 will be displayed in the Browser.

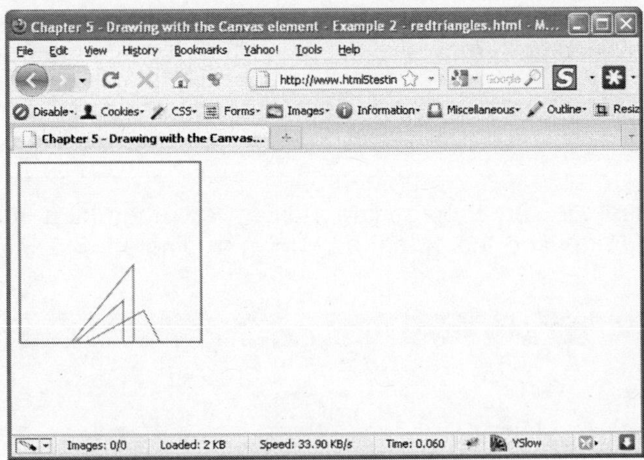

Diagram 5.2.

Filling Line Art

Line drawn figures can also be filled in with color. Here is how to draw a solid green triangle.

In this case, draw the triangle using beginPath(), moveTo(), lineTo(), and closePath(), which will in effect inform the canvas that a line drawing in about to be done within its drawing area. Now instead of using stroke() to finally draw the triangle, use fill().

fill() a figure being drawn in the canvas drawing area with the canvas's current fill color, which has been set using the fillStyle attribute and passing this attribute the color green using rgb notation as explained earlier.

Here is how to try this out. Open redtriangles.html in your favorite editor and save this as greentriangle.html OR copy redtriangles.html and paste this as greentriangle.html in the same folder on hard disk. Next, open greentriangle.html in your favorite editor and over write the Javascript loader() codespec as follows:

```
function loader()
{
   var canvas = document.getElementById('canvas');
   var canvas1 = canvas.getContext('2d');

    //Filled triangle
    canvas1.fillStyle = "rgba(0, 200, 0, 0.5)";
    canvas1.beginPath();
    canvas1.moveTo(10, 100);
    canvas1.lineTo(100, 25);
```

```
canvas1.lineTo(170, 105);
canvas1.closePath();
canvas1.fill();
}
```

Save greentriangle.html in an appropriate folder on the hard disk. Then execute greentriangle.html in Firefox and the output as shown in diagram 5.3 will be displayed in the Browser.

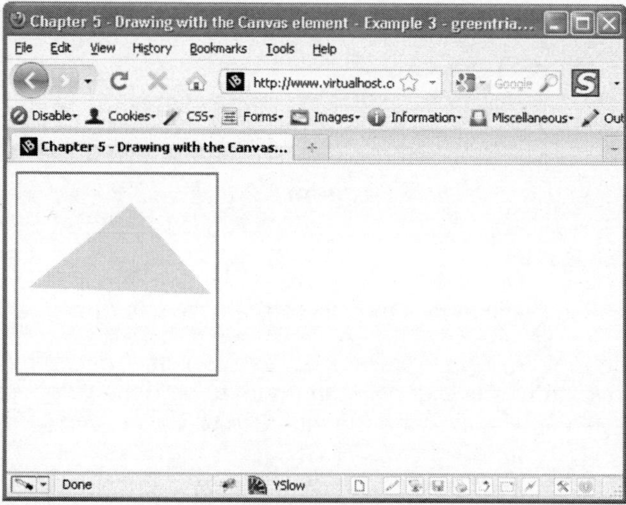

Diagram 5.3.

Drawing Arcs

Draw arcs on the canvas with arc() as follows:

Open redtriangle.html in your favorite editor and save this as arcs.html OR you can copy redtriangle.html and paste this as arcs.html in an appropriate folder on the hard disk.

Next open arcs.html and over write the Javascript loader() function with the following codespec:

```
function loader()
{
    var canvas = document.getElementById('canvas');
    var canvas1 = canvas.getContext('2d');

    // Arcs
    canvas1.beginPath();
```

```
canvas1.arc(275, 275, 50, 0, Math.PI * 2, true);
canvas1.moveTo(310, 275);
canvas1.arc(275, 275, 35, 0, 0.75 * Math.PI, false);
canvas1.moveTo(300, 255);
canvas1.arc(265, 255, 35, 0, 0.5 * Math.PI, false);
canvas1.moveTo(280, 255);
canvas1.arc(245, 255, 35, 0, 0.2 * Math.PI, false);
canvas1.closePath();
canvas1.stroke();
}
```

Save arcs.html in an appropriate folder on the hard disk. Then execute arcs.html in Firefox and the output as shown in diagram 5.4 will be displayed in the Browser.

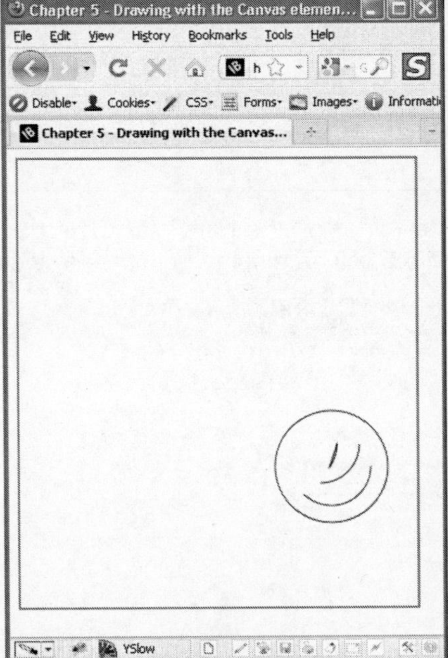

Diagram 5.4

Drawing Text

Text can also be drawn on the canvas start off by selecting a font to use by passing the Canvas control's *font* attribute a value which is a string that contains the font specification selected, as follows:

```
canvas1.font = 'italic 40px sans-serif';
```

This syntax ensure that the italic san-serif font, 40 pixels high is set as the default font for the canvas area in which Text will be written. If italics is not required, just omit *italic*.

Now open arcs.html in your favorite editor and save this as text.html OR you can copy arcs.html and paste this as text.html in an appropriate folder on the hard disk.

Next open text.html and over write the Javascript loader() function with the following codespec:

```
function loader()
{
    var canvas = document.getElementById ('canvas');
    var canvas1 = canvas.getContext('2d');

    //Setting the default canvas font
    canvas1.font = 'italic 50px sans-serif';
    //Writing text to the canvas
    canvas1.strokeText("Hello!", 20, 100);
}
```

Save text.html in an appropriate folder on the hard disk. Then execute text.html in Firefox and the output as shown in diagram 5.5 will be displayed in the Browser.

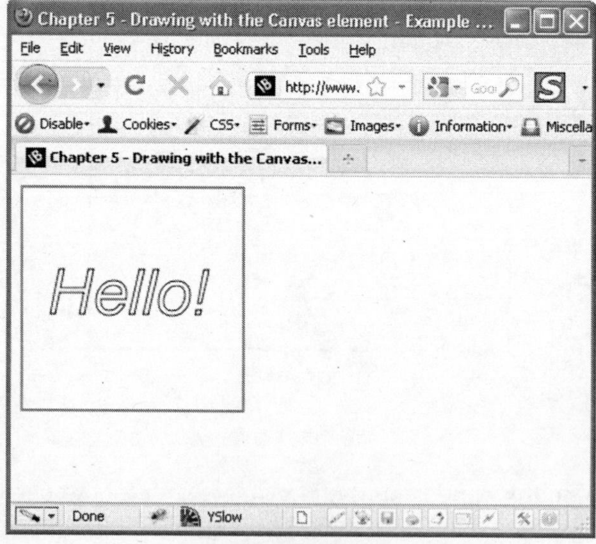

Diagram 5.5.

Drawing with Bezier Curves

A canvas element is not limited to drawing lines, or arcs or text.

Bezier curves can be drawn within the canvas element using the function: bezierCurveTo();

The generic syntax is as follows:

```
bezierCurveTo(float cp1x, float cp1y, float cp2x, float cp2y, float x, float y);
```

Here's an example that draws a red heart using bezierCurveTo();

Now open text.html in your favorite editor and save this as curves.html OR you can copy text.html and paste this as curves.html in an appropriate folder on the hard disk.

Next open curves.html and over write the Javascript loader() function with the following codespec:

```
function loader()
{
   var canvas = document.getElementById('canvas');
   var canvas1 = canvas.getContext('2d');

   // Heart
   canvas1.fillStyle = "rgba(200, 0, 0, 0.5)";
   canvas1.beginPath();

   //Drawing on the Canvas Element
   canvas1.moveTo(75, 250);
   canvas1.bezierCurveTo(75, 247, 70, 235, 50, 235);
   canvas1.bezierCurveTo(20, 235, 20, 272.5, 20, 272);
   canvas1.bezierCurveTo(20, 290, 40, 312, 75, 330);
   canvas1.bezierCurveTo(110, 312, 130, 290, 130, 272);
   canvas1.bezierCurveTo(130, 272.5, 130, 235, 100, 235);
   canvas1.bezierCurveTo(85, 235, 75, 247, 75, 250);
   canvas1.closePath();
   canvas1.fill();
}
```

Save curves.html in an appropriate folder on the hard disk. Then execute curves.html in Firefox and the output as shown in diagram 5.6 will be displayed in the Browser.

Diagram 5.6.

Drawing with Quadratic Curves

Besides Bezier curves quadratic curves can be used to draw within a canvas element by using the function: quadraticCurveTo();

The generic syntax is as follows:

```
quadraticCurveTo(float cpx, float cpy, float x, float y);
```

Here's an example that draws a simple irregular shape in the canvas element using quadraticCurveTo();

Now open curves.html in your favorite editor and save this as quad.html OR you can copy curves.html and paste this as quad.html in an appropriate folder on the hard disk.

Next open quad.html and over write the Javascript loader() function with the following codespec:

```
function loader()
{
    var canvas = document.getElementById('canvas');
    var canvas1 = canvas.getContext('2d');
    //Quadratic curves
```

```
canvas1.strokeStyle = "rgba(0, 0, 0, 1)";
canvas1.beginPath();
canvas1.moveTo(275, 125);
canvas1.quadraticCurveTo(225, 125, 225, 162);
canvas1.quadraticCurveTo(260, 200, 265, 200);
canvas1.quadraticCurveTo(325, 200, 325, 162);
canvas1.quadraticCurveTo(325, 125, 275, 125);
canvas1.closePath();
canvas1.stroke();
}
```

Save quad.html in an appropriate folder on the hard disk. Then execute quad.html in Firefox and the output as shown in diagram 5.7 will be displayed in the Browser.

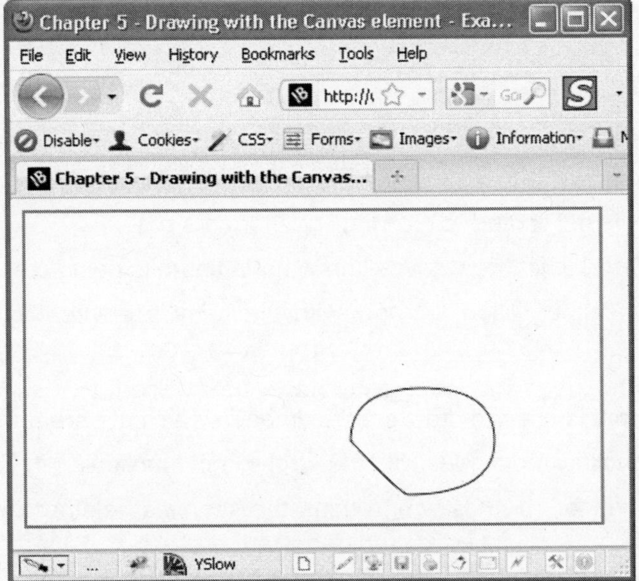

Diagram 5.7

Self Review Questions

Fill In The Blanks

1. The HTML5 ____________ element is used to display graphics in web pages.
2. Quadratic curves can be used to draw within a canvas element by using the function ____________________
3. Once the <canvas></canvas> elements have been used to define an area within a webpage, ______________ is used to draw graphic images within the area defined.
4. You can draw hollow rectangles with the __________________ function
5. You can draw ____________ with a Canvas element.
6. Start with ___________ to let the Canvas know that a figure is being created.
7. A canvas element is not limited to drawing __________, or ___________ or ___________.
8. Bezier curves can be drawn within the canvas element using the function ______________
9. You can draw _________________ with the fillRect function

True Or False

10. You cannot draw line art with a Canvas element.
11. A canvas element is not limited to drawing lines, or arcs or text.
12. Start with *beginPath()* to let the Canvas know that a figure is being created.
13. Quadratic curves can be used to draw within a canvas element by using the function: bezierCurveTo();
14. Once the <canvas></canvas> elements have been used to define an area within a webpage, JavaScript is used to draw graphic images within the area defined.
15. You cannot draw hollow rectangles with the strokeRect function
16. Bezier curves cannot be drawn within the canvas element using the function bezierCurveTo();
17. You can draw filled-in rectangles with the fillRect function
18. The HTML5 Canvas element is used to display graphics in web pages.

Hands-on Exercise

1. Create a "No Parking" sign using the HTML5 elements that have been learned in this chapter. Output of this exercise is shown in diagram 5.8

Diagram 5.8

2. Create a "Warning Sign" using the HTML5 elements that have been learned in this chapter. Output of this exercise is shown in diagram 5.9

Diagram 5.9

6. Video On The Web

YouTube.com has over the past several years admirably demonstrated that video can be embedded in a webpage. Prior to HTML5 there was no standard way of doing this.

All the video content delivered via the web and displayed in a Browser were played through a third party plugin that had to be installed within the Browser first. Only then could video content be displayed within the Browser.

If unfortunately your Browser had downloaded a video file for which the Browser did not have a suitable plugin installed, simple the video did not play. The most common video plugins for Browsers being Quick time, Real Player, Flash and so on, YouTube uses Flash for those who are interested. Today, HTML5 defines a standard way to embed any video in a web page, using the <video> element.

Support for the <video> element is still evolving, this means that the <video> element does not work correctly across all Browsers yet, but there are multiple alternatives, fallbacks and options today.

Table 1 shows which browsers support the <video> element at the time of creating this material.

IE9	Firefox 3.5 and >	Safari 3.0 and >	Chrome	Opera

Table 1.

Browser support for the <video> element itself is really just one small step in the display of video content within a Browser. Perhaps it's time to understand a little bit about video content first before attempting to display this video content in an HTML5 compliant Browser.

Many coders think of video content as *AVI files* or *MP4 files.* In reality, AVI and MP4 are container formats. Just as a ZIP file can hold any sort of file within it, a video container formats only defines how to store things within it, not what kind of data is stored within.

The actual video file usually contains multiple tracks. A video track (*without any audio*), plus one or more audio tracks (*without any video*). These tracks are usually interrelated.

The audio track will contain markers within it to help synchronize the audio with the video. Additionally, individual tracks can have metadata, such as the aspect ratio of a video track or the language of the audio track and so on.

Containers can also have metadata, such as the title of the video itself, cover art for the video, episode numbers (*for television shows*), and so on.

Video Codecs

When watching a video within a Browser, the Browser is handling a combination of one video file streaming content and one audio streaming content.

The Browser is really not handling two different files, its handling the *video* file which could be resident within an AVI or MP4 container. As explained earlier AVI or MP4 are just container formats. Just like a ZIP file they too can contain multiple kinds of files within them. The container format used actually defines how the video and audio streams are stored within in a single container file.

Just to make life interesting for the web page coder there are lots of different video container formats. Some of the most popular containers are:

MPEG-4

Files with either the .mp4 or .m4v extension are MPEG-4 video content containers. The MPEG-4 container is based on Apple's older QuickTime container (.mov).

Flash Video

Files with the .flv extension are Flash Video – video content containers. Flash Video is, owned and used by Adobe. Prior to the Flash Player 9 Update 3, .flv was the only container format that Flash supported. More recent versions of Flash also support the MPEG-4 container.

Ogg

Files with the .ogv extension are Ogg – video content containers. Ogg is an open standard that is open source friendly and is not covered by any known patents.

Firefox 3.5, Chrome 4, and Opera 10.5 offer native support, without platform-specific plug-ins for the Ogg container format. Ogg video is called *Theora*, and Ogg audio called *Vorbis.*

On the desktop, Ogg video content container is supported by all major Linux distributions. You can execute .ogg files on the Mac and Windows by installing QuickTime components or DirectShow filters It is also playable with the excellent VLC video player available today for all platforms.

When video is being watched the video player is doing several things at once:

1. Interpreting the container format to find out which video and audio tracks are available
2. Understanding how the video and audio content are stored within the file so that it can find the data it needs to decode next
3. Decoding the video stream (i.e. video content) and displaying a series of images on the VDU screen
4. Decoding the audio stream (i.e. audio content) and sending sound to the speakers

A video codec is a program by which a video stream (i.e. video content) is encoded. It is the video codec that specifies how to do #2 above.

The word *codec* is a combination of the words *coder* and *decoder*. The video player decodes the video stream (i.e. video content) according to its video codec, then displays this as a series of images, or *frames*, on the VDU screen.

Most modern video coder / decoders (i.e. codec) do their very best to minimize the amount of information required to display one video frame after the next.

For example, instead of storing each individual frame (like screenshots), they will only store the differences between frames. Most videos do not actually change all that much from one frame to the next, so this allows for high compression rates, which results in smaller file sizes, delivered as the output of the video codec.

There are lossy and lossless video codecs. Lossless video codec produces output video files that are much too big to be useful on the Web. Hence, the focus here is always on lossy codecs.

When a lossy video codec is used to process a video file (*obtained perhaps directly from a video camera*) video information is permanently lost during encoding. Hence, every time video content is encoded, the source video content loses information and the video source degrades in quality.

Video content re-re-re-encoded look blocky, especially during scenes where there is a lot of movement. This can also happen if the original video source is encoded using a poor quality encoder. Having said that lossy video codec offer some amazing compression rates, and multiple ways to smooth over the blockiness during playback to make the loss of video source detail less noticeable to the human eye.

There are a large number of video codecs available today, the most relevant seem to be H.264, Theora, and VP8.

H.264

The H.264 codec is also known as *MPEG-4 part 10*, or *MPEG-4 AVC*, which is an acronym for MPEG-4 Advanced Video Coding."

H.264 was developed by the MPEG group and standardized in 2003. What is most interesting about the H.264 is that strives to provide a single codec for low-bandwidth, low-CPU devices (*such as cell phones*), high-bandwidth, high-CPU devices (*such as modern desktop computers*), and everything in between.

The H.264 standard is split into multiple *profiles.* Each profile defining a set of optional features that trade complexity for file size. Higher profiles use more optional features, offer better visual quality at smaller file sizes, take longer to encode, and require more CPU power to decode in real time.

Here is a broad idea of the range of H.264 profiles:

- The iPhone supports the Baseline profile,
- The AppleTV set-top box supports the Baseline and Main profiles
- Adobe Flash on a desktop PC supports the Baseline, Main, and High profiles

YouTube now uses the H.264 codec to encode high-definition videos playable through Adobe Flash. YouTube also provides H.264 encoded video for mobile devices, like the iPhone and smart phones running the Android mobile operating system.

Also, H.264 is one of the video codecs mandated by the Blu-ray specification. Blu-ray discs that carry video on them generally use the H.264 High profile while encoding the original video source content.

Most nonPC devices that play H.264 video (i.e. iPhones, Blu-ray players) actually do the decoding on a dedicated chip, since their main CPUs are nowhere near powerful enough to decode the video in real time. Many desktop graphics cards also support decoding H.264 within their hardware.

Regretfully, the H.264 codec standard is bound by several patents. Licensing is required and acquired through the MPEG LA group.

Video processed using the H.264 video codec can be embedded in most popular container formats including MP4 and MKV (*used primarily by noncommercial video enthusiasts*).

Theora

The Theora codec has evolved from the VP3 codec. It has been developed by the Xiph.org Foundation.

Theora is a royalty-free codec and is does not have and patents that prevent its usage other than the original VP3 patents, which have been licensed by Theora royalty-free.

Although the Theora standard was "frozen" since 2004, the Theora project only released Version 1.0 of its codec in November 2008 and Version 1.1 in September 2009.

Theora video can be embedded in any container format, although it is most often seen in an Ogg container. All major Linux distributions support Theora, and Mozilla Firefox 3.5 includes native support for Theora video in an Ogg container.

Here native means that Theora support is available on all platforms without platform-specific plug-ins being required.

Videos compressed using the Theora codec can also be played on Windows or the Mac after the installation of Xiph.org's open source decoder software for that specific operating system.

VP8

VP8 is another video codec from On2, the same company that originally developed VP3 (*which later came to be known as Theora*).

Technically, it is similar in quality to H.264 Baseline, with lots of potential for future improvements.

In 2010, Google acquired On2 who were the owners of the VP8 video codec and published the video codec specification and a sample encoder and decoder as open source.

Google also released all the patents that On2 had filed on VP8 by licensing them royalty-free.

When patents are licensed as royalty free, and then anyone can use the technologies that the patents cover without paying anything or negotiating any patent licenses. As of May 19, 2010, VP8 is a royalty-free, modern video codec.

Audio Codecs

All videos have an audio track. Like video codecs, audio codecs are encoding programs, for audio streams. Just as with video codecs, there are lossy and lossless audio codecs. Lossless audio is really too big to use on the Web, so this material will focus on lossy audio codecs.

Actually, there are different categories of lossy audio codecs. Audio is used in many places where video is not. Hence, there is an entire category of audio codecs optimized only for encoding speech. Many of these codecs will not be used for ripping a music CD because of their poor audio quality, but they work perfectly for Telephony based audio encoding (i.e. *UHF Walky Talkies*). These audio codecs can compress human speech into an audio file a fraction of the size of the same speech compressed by general purpose audio codecs.

However, due to lack of support natively in Browsers and the lack of third-party plug-ins, speech-optimized audio codecs never really took off on the Web. Hence, in this material the focus is on general purpose, lossy, audio codecs.

When an audio file is being listened to the computer is doing several things at once:

1. Interpreting the audio content - container format
2. Decoding the audio stream
3. Sending the audio stream appropriately to speakers

The audio codec specifies how to do #3 above, i.e. decoding the audio stream, and turning it into digital waveforms that speakers then turn into sound.

There are all sorts of tricks used to minimize the amount of information stored in the audio stream when the original audio content was being encoded to produce an output file that is much smaller in size than the original audio file.

Since these are lossy audio codecs, audio information is being permanently lost during the recording encoding decoding listening lifecycle. Different audio codecs throw away different things, but they all have the same purpose, to trick human ears into not noticing the parts of the audio are missing.

Audio content has channels. Sound is being sent to speakers. Normally with computers there maybe only two speakers, one on the left and one on the right. Today modern laptops have multi speaker, surround sound systems that can have six or more speakers. Each speaker needs to be fed a particular channel of the original recording.

The theory is that a user can sit in the middle of these six speakers and literally be surrounded by six separate channels of sound.

Most general-purpose audio codecs can handle two channels of sound. During recording, the sound is split into left and right channels; during encoding, both channels are stored in the same audio stream; and during decoding, both channels are decoded and each is sent to the appropriate speaker.

Some audio codecs can handle more than two channels, and they keep track of which channel is which so your player can send the right sound to the right speaker.

There are really tons of audio codecs, but on the Web, there are really only three audio codecs one needs to be familiar with: MP3, AAC, and Vorbis.

MPEG-1 Audio Layer 3

MEPG-1 audio layer 3 is colloquially known as *MP3.*

MP3s can contain up to two channels of sound and can be encoded at different bitrates:

- 64 kbps
- 128 kbps
- 192 kbps
- And a variety of others, from 32 to 320

Higher bitrates mean larger output file sizes from the encoding process and better-quality audio. Having said that the ratio of audio quality to bitrate is not linear.

Audio content encoded at a 128 kbps bit rate will produce an output audio stream that sounds *more than* twice as good as audio content encoded at a 64 kbps bitrate, but audio content encoded at a 256 kbps bitrate does not sound twice as good as audio encoded at a 128 kbps bitrate.

The MP3 audio file format (*standardized in 1991*) also allows variable bitrate encoding. This means that some parts of the original audio content is compressed a lot more during encoding than others.

A great example is, silence between musical notes which can be encoded at a very low bitrate, then the bitrate can spike up a moment later when multiple instruments start playing to produce a complex sound. MP3s can also be encoded with a constant bitrate. This is called - constant bitrate encoding.

Strangely the MP3 audio encoding standard does not define exactly how to encode MP3s. It does define exactly how to decode them. Hence, different MP3 audio encoders use different psychoacoustic models that can and do produce wildly different results, but are all decodable by MP3 enabled players.

The open source LAME project is the best free MP3 encoder, possibly the best MP3 encoder, for all but the lowest encoding bitrates.

Unfortunately the MP3 format is bound by several patents, which is why Linux cannot play MP3 files out of the box.

Pretty much every portable music player supports standalone MP3 files, and MP3 audio streams can be embedded in any video container. Adobe Flash can play both standalone MP3 files and MP3 audio streams within an MP4 video container.

Advanced Audio Coding

Advanced Audio Coding is also known as *AAC*. AAC was standardized in 1997. AAC was chosen by Apple as the default format for the iTunes store. When the iTunes store started, all the AAC files purchased and downloaded were encrypted with Apple's proprietary DRM scheme, FairPlay.

Today many songs in the iTunes store are available as unprotected AAC files, which Apple calls *iTunes Plus*.

Unfortunately the AAC audio format is bound by a number of patents. The AAC licensing rates are available online.

AAC audio encoding was designed to provide superior sound quality than MP3 at the same bitrate. AAC can encode audio at any bitrate. MP3 is limited to a fixed number of bitrates, with an upper limit of 320 kbps. AAC can encode up to 48 channels of sound, although in practice no one does that.

The AAC encoding format also defines multiple profiles, similar to the H.264 encoding format, and for the same reasons.

The AAC *low complexity* profile is designed to be played on devices with limited CPU power. Higher profiles offer better sound quality at the same bitrate, at the expense of slower encoding and decoding.

Currently Apple products, which include iPods, AppleTV, and QuickTime, support certain profiles of AAC in standalone audio files and in audio streams placed within a MP4 video container. Adobe Flash supports all profiles of AAC in MP4, as do the open source MPlayer and VLC video players.

Vorbis

Vorbis often called Ogg Vorbis, although this is technically incorrect. Ogg is just a container format. Vorbis is an audio stream which can be embedded in the Ogg container or other containers.

The Vorbis codec is not bound by patents and is therefore supported out of the box by all major Linux distributions and by portable devices running the open source Rockbox firmware.

Mozilla Firefox 3.5 and above supports Vorbis audio files in an Ogg container, or Ogg videos with a Vorbis audio track. Android mobile phones can also play standalone Vorbis audio files.

Vorbis audio streams are usually embedded in an Ogg or WebM container, but they can also be embedded in an MP4 or MKV container, or, with some difficulty, in AVI container.

Vorbis supports an arbitrary number of sound channels. There are open source Vorbis encoders and decoders, including the OggConvert encoder, the ffmpeg decoder, the aoTuV encoder, and the libvorbis decoder. There are also QuickTime components for Mac OS X and DirectShow filters for Windows.

What Works on the Web

Here is how the complicated subject of video and its associated audio is related to HTML5.

HTML5 includes a single element for embedding video into a web page <video>. There are no restrictions on the video codec, audio codec, or container format that can be use for actual video content file.

A single HTML5 element can link to multiple video files. It's the Browser which will choose the first <video> video content file that it can actually play. It is up to the HTML5 coder to know which Browsers support which containers and which codecs.

Here is a chart of Browsers and what type of video and audio encoding they support at the time of creating this material. Use this table as a guideline because on the web things change very rapidly.

Browser	Video	Audio	Container
Mozilla Firefox 3.5 >	Theora	Orbis	Ogg
Opera 10.5 >	Theora	Orbis	Ogg

Google Chrome	Theora	Orbis	Ogg
	H.264 video	AAC audio	All containers
Safari	H.264 video	AAC audio	MP4
IE9	H.264 video	AAC audio	MP4

Table 1.

Regretfully, if video content must be displayed in HTML5 compliant Browsers that there is no single combination of video/audio codecs and containers that will work in all HTML5 browsers. While this may not likely to change in the immediate future give time there will be a change in the video/audio codecs and container space to make it compatible with the HTML5 <video> element.

Hence, currently to make video content watchable across all Browsers and platforms, the source video content will have to be encoded more than once.

For to get the maximum video content compatibility across Browsers and platforms:

1. Encode original video content using Theora video and Vorbis audio and place this in an Ogg container
2. Make a second version that uses WebM (VP8 + Vorbis)
3. Make a third version that uses H.264 Baseline video and AAC low-complexity audio in an MP4 container

Link to all three video files from a single HTML5 <video> element, and also have a fall back to a Flash <video> based video player.

HTML5 <video> Markup

There are techniques that HTML5 offers to include/display video on a web page. Both techniques use the <video> element. If there is only one video file, simply link to it in a *src* attribute. This is similar to including an image with an *<img src="...">* tag.

For example: <video src="pr6.webm"></video>

Technically, that is all that's required. To improve this codespec, i.e. add value to the displaying Browser within the codespec, always include the *height* and *width* attributes in the <video></video> tags.

The *height* and *width* attributes can be the same as the maximum height and width specified when the source video was being encoded:

For example: <video src="pr6.webm" width="320" height="240"></video>

Even if one dimension of the video file is a little smaller than specified the browser will center the video inside the box defined by the <video> tag. The video content will never be squashed or stretched out of proportion.

By default, the <video> element will not expose any sort of video player controls. Create your own controls with HTML, CSS, and JavaScript. The <video> element has methods like *play()* and *pause()* and a read/write property called *current Time*. There are also read/write and properties like *volume* and *muted*. So really everything required build an interface is available.

The Browser can also be instructed to display a built-in set of controls. To do this, just include the controls attribute in the <video> tag:

For example: <video src="pr6.webm" width="320" height="240" controls="controls"></video>

There are two other useful (*but optional*) <video> element attributes, they are *preload* and *autoplay*:

The *preload* attribute informs the browser that it should start downloading the video file as soon as the page loads. This makes sense if the entire point of the page is to view the video.

On the other hand, if the video content is just supplementary material on the web page, (*i.e. that only a few visitors will decide to watch video*), set *preload* to *none* to inform the browser that the video content does not have to be downloaded automatically when the web page loads.

And here's an example of a video that will not start downloading as soon as the page loads:

For example: <video src="pr6.webm" width="320" height="240" preload="none"></video>

Here's an example of a video that will start downloading (*but not playing*) as soon as the page loads:

For example: <video src="pr6.webm" width="320" height="240" preload="preload"></video>

> **Note:** *This can also be coded as: <video src="pr6.webm" width="320" height="240" preload></video>*

The HTML5 <video> element *autoplay* attribute tells the Browser that it should start downloading the video file as soon as the page loads, and that it should start playing the video content automatically as soon as possible. Some site visitors will love this, some site visitors will hate this.

Here's an example of video content that will start downloading and playing as soon as possible after the page loads.

For example: <video src="pr6.webm" width="320" height="240" autoplay="autoplay"></video>

> **Note:** This can also be coded as: <video src="pr6.webm" width="320" height="240" autoplay></video>

Now the issue here is that that all Browsers cannot play all video file formats. Some Browsers have native support for one video content format and some Browsers for another video content format. Please take a quick look at **Table 1**.

- The first type of video content could be in *<filename>*.ogv file format.
- The second type of video content could be in *<filename>*.mp4 file format.
- The Third type of video content could be in *<filename>*.webm file format.

HTML5 provides a way to link to all three of them: the <source> element.

Each <video> element can contain as many <source> elements as required. The Browser, in which this codespec is being executed will go down the list of video sources, in order, and play the first one that it has native support for.

That raises the question, how does a Browser know which video it can play? In the worst-case scenario, the Browser downloads each of the videos and tries to play them. That's a big waste of Internet bandwidth.

A lot of network traffic can be saved if the Browser is told up front about each video type. This is done using the *type* attribute of the *<source>* element.

For example:

```
<video width="320" height="240" controls>
   <source src="pr6.mp4" type='video/mp4; codecs="avc1.42E01E, mp4a.40.2"'>
   <source src="pr6.webm" type='video/webm; codecs="vp8, vorbis"'>
   <source src="pr6.ogv" type='video/ogg; codecs="theora, vorbis"'>
</video>
```

Code Snippet 1

Here is and explanation of code snippet 1.

The <video> element specifies the *width* and *height* of the video content display area. The <video> element does not actually link to any video file.

Nested within the <video> element are three <source> elements.

Each <source> element is linked to a single video file via its *src* attribute. The video file format, bound to the *src* is specified in the *type* attribute.

There are multiple values passed to the *type* attribute. Each value is separated from the other using a semicolon (;).

These are: type='*video/webm*; codecs="*vp8, vorbis*"'

(i) The video file container format
(ii) The video content file format
(iii) The audio content file format

The benefit of coding using the codespec specified in code snippet 1, is that the Browser will be able to check <source> element's the *type* attribute first to see if it can play a particular video file format.

If a Browser decides it cannot play a particular video file format, it will not download the file. This saves on Internet bandwidth, and your web site visitor will see the video playing in their Browser, faster.

Using Appropriate MIME Types With The <video> Element

A misconfigured web server can lead to endless frustration when videos play on your local computer but the same videos fail to play when they are downloaded from a website, i.e. delivered to a requesting Browser by the website's web server.

The root cause for this problem is that most likely the web server's probably MIME types have been misconfigured.

If you're using Apache web server, use the AddType directive in its httpd.conf file or mention the appropriate MIME types in a .htaccess file in the folder where the video files are stored. If you use any web server, please consult the web server's documentation and find out on how to set the HTTP header for specific file types.

For Apache web server the AddType directives that must be included are:

- AddType video/ogg .ogv (i.e. *This line is for videos in a Ogg container*)
- AddType video/mp4 .mp4 (i.e. *This line is for videos in a MPEG-4 container*)
- AddType video/webm .webm (i.e. *This line is for videos in a WebM container*)

These AddType values must be in the Apache httpd.conf file once. If not, your videos will fail to play in some Browsers, even if you include the MIME type in the *type* attribute in HTML markup.

Dealing With Internet Explorer

Microsoft has released a *developer preview* of Internet Explorer 9. It does not yet support the HTML5 <video> element, but Microsoft has publicly promised that the final version of IE9 will support H.264 video and AAC audio in an MPEG-4 container, just like Safari on desktop Macs and Mobile Safari.

The question remains - What about older versions of Internet Explorer, up to and including IE 8?

Most people who use Internet Explorer also have the Adobe Flash plug-in installed. Modern versions of Adobe Flash support H.264 video codec and AAC audio codec in an MPEG-4 container. Once you've encoded the original video content in these codecs and placed them in an MPEG4 container, this file will play cheerfully in any Flash enabled video player.

HTML5 is well designed to handle this kind of situation, largely because an element can be nested within a element in HTML5. Hence within the HTML5 <video> element coders can nest the <object> element.

Older Browsers that do not support the HTML5 <video> element will simply ignore this element render the nested <object> element instead. The <object> element will invoke the Flash plug-in, which will play the video file since it's in the correct format to play within a flash player. Browsers that support HTML5 <video> element will find a video source they can play and play it, and ignore the nested <object> element altogether.

HTML5 specifies that all elements (*other than <source> elements*) that are children of a <video> element must be ignored altogether. That allows you to use HTML5 video element in Browsers that support HTML5 and fall back to Flash gracefully in older Browsers, without requiring any fancy JavaScript coding.

A Complete Example

Here is an example of HTML5 codespec that uses all the above techniques. The final markup uses a <video> element for HTML5 video, with a nested <object> element for Flash fallback:

```
<video id="movie" width="320" height="240" preload controls>
  <source src="example1.mp4" type='video/mp4; codecs="avc1.42E01E, mp4a.40.2"' />
  <source src="example1.webm" type='video/webm; codecs="vp8, vorbis"' />
  <source src="example1.ogg" type='video/ogg; codecs="theora, vorbis"' />
  <object width="320" height="240" type="application/x-shockwave-flash"
      data="flowplayer-3.2.1.swf">
    <param name="movie" value="flowplayer-3.2.1.swf" />
    <param name="allowfullscreen" value="true" />
    <param name="flashvars" value='config={"clip":
    {"url": "http://wearehugh.com/dih5/good/bbb_480p.mp4",
    "autoPlay":false, "autoBuffering":true}}' />
    <p>Download video as <a href="pr6.mp4">MP4</a>,
    <a href="pr6.webm">WebM</a>, or <a href="pr6.ogv">Ogg</a>.</p>
  </object>
</video>
```

With this combination of HTML5 and Flash, this video should be viewable in almost any browser. The Output of the above Example is shown in diagram 6.1

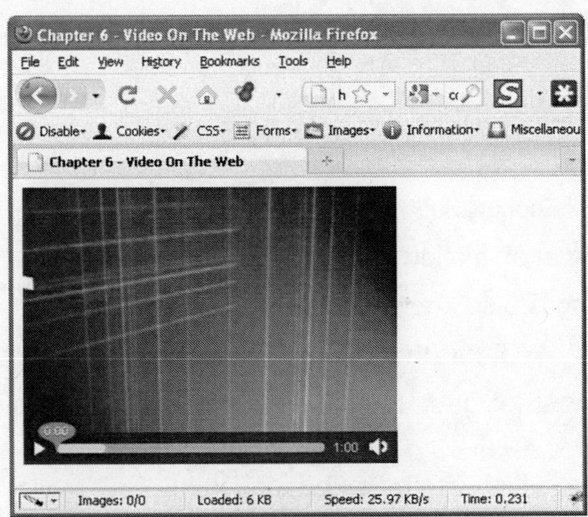

Diagram 6.1

Self Review Questions

Fill In The Blanks

1. HTML5 defines a standard way to embed any video in a web page, using the ______________ element.
2. When watching a video within a Browser, the Browser is handling a combination of one ________________file streaming content and one ______________ streaming content.
3. The Browser is really not handling two different files, its handling the *video* file which could be resident within an ___________or ____________ container.
4. Files with either the __________ or ___________ extension are MPEG-4 video content containers.
5. The ______________container is based on Apple's older QuickTime container (.mov).
6. Flash Video is, owned and used by________________.
7. ___________is an open standard that is open source friendly and is not covered by any known patents.
8. A _______________ is a program by which a video stream (i.e. video content) is encoded.
9. The word *codec* is a combination of the ________________ and ______________.
10. ______________ video codec produces output video files that are much too big to be useful on the Web.
11. The H.264 standard is split into multiple _________________.
12. _______________ is one of the video codecs mandated by the Blu-ray specification.

13. _____________ codecs are encoding programs, for audio streams.

14. Most general-purpose audio codecs can handle ___________ channels of sound.

True Or False

15. MEPG-1 audio layer 3 is colloquially known as *MP4.*
16. The MP3 audio file format also allows variable bitrate encoding.
17. Advanced Audio Coding is also known as *AAC.*
18. AAC was not chosen by Apple as the default format for the iTunes store.
19. AAC audio encoding was designed to provide superior sound quality than MP3 at the same bitrate.
20. Vorbis is a video stream which can be embedded in the Ogg container or other containers.
21. HTML5 includes multiple elements for embedding video into a web page <video>.
22. The *preload* attribute informs the browser that it should start downloading the video file as soon as the page loads.
23. The HTML5 <video> element *autoplay* attribute tells the Browser that it should start downloading the video file before the page loads.
24. Each <video> element cannot contain as many <source> elements as required.

Hands-on Exercise

1. Create a Web Page which makes use of handsonexercise.mp4 and handsonexercise.ogg file. Please use all the HTML5 elements that have been learned in this chapter. Output of this exercise is shown in diagram 6.2

Diagram 6.2

7. Geo Location In HTML5

Geolocation is the art of figuring out where a site visitor is located are in the world, and optionally sharing that information with any trusted network. There are many ways to figure out where a site visitor is located an IP address, wireless network connection, the cell tower that a mobile phone is communicating with, dedicated GPS hardware that receives latitude and longitude information from satellites in the sky and more.

Privacy is a concern when sharing your physical location with a remote web server. Fortunately the HTML5 geolocation API explicitly states: "User Agents must not send location information to websites without the express permission of the user." In other words, if a user does not want to share their location, they don't have to.

The Geolocation API

The geolocation API lets a site visitor share their location with trusted websites. The latitude and longitude of a site visitor are available to JavaScript embedded in the web page, which in turn can send that information back to a remote web server which and then do fancy location aware things like finding local businesses to the site visitor or showing their location on a map and so on.

The geolocation API is well supported in several major Browsers, on desktops and in mobile devices. Additionally, some older browsers and can use wrapper libraries to support the GEO Location API. The geolocation specification states: "The geographic coordinate reference system used by the attributes in this interface is the World Geodetic System (2d) [WGS84].

Browsers that have native support for the Gro location API

Firefox 3.5 and >	Safari 5.0 and >	Chrome 5.0 and >

Basic Geolocation Code Snippets

The geolocation API centers around a new property on the global navigator object which is: navigator.geolocation.

The simplest use of geolocation would be:

```
function get_location() {
        navigator.geolocation.getCurrentPosition(show_map);
}
```

There is no detection, no error handling, and no options. To detect Browser support for the geolocation API, *Modernizr* can be used as follows:

```
function get_location() {
    if (Modernizr.geolocation) {
    navigator.geolocation.getCurrentPosition(show_map);
}
else
{
// no native support; maybe try Gears?
}
}
```

Note: *For the GeoLocation code snippets to work, the code requires access to the latest modernizr Javascript library. Download the latest modernizr library from http://www.modernizr.com .*

Modernizr is a small and simple JavaScript library that helps programmers take advantage of emerging web technologies (i.e. *HTML5, CSS3*) while still maintaining a fine level of control over older Browsers that may not support these new technologies.

Modernizr detects support for:

@font-face	CSS Animations	Drag and Drop
Canvas	CSS Columns	hashchange
Canvas Text	CSS Gradients	X-window Messaging
HTML5 Audio	CSS Reflections	History Management
HTML5 Video	CSS 2D Transforms	applicationCache
rgba()	CSS 3D Transforms	Touch events
hsla()	CSS Transitions	Web Sockets
border-image	Geolocation API	Web Workers
border-radius	localStorage	Web SQL Database
box-shadow	sessionStorage	WebGL
text-shadow	SVG	IndexedDB
opacity	SMIL	Input Types†
Multiple backgrounds	SVG Clipping	Input Attributes‡
Flexible Box Model	Inline SVG	

Let's understand what happens during that call to getCurrentPosition() is made. Remember, geolocation support is opt-in. That means no Browser can ever force any site visitor to reveal their current physical location to a remote server. The user experience differs from browser to browser.

In Mozilla Firefox, calling the getCurrentPosition() function of the geolocation API will cause the browser to pop up an "infobar" at the top of the browser window. The infobar looks like diagram 7.1.

Diagram 7.1

For the site visitor there is lot of work happening between the Browser and the web page from where the geolocation request was triggered. The site visitor end is informed:

- That a website wants to know their location
- Which website wants to know their location
- Can click through to Mozilla's "Location-Aware Browsing" help page, which explains what is happening
- Choose to share their location
- Choose not to share their location
- Can tell their browser to remember their choice (i.e. *share or do not share*) so as site visitor one never has to see this infobar again for this specific website

Additionally, the Firefox infobar is:

- Nonmodal, so it will not prevent the site visitor from switching to another browser window or tab
- Tab-specific, so it will disappear if the site visitor switched to another browser window or tab and will reappear when the site visitor comes back to the tab where the geolocation query was raised
- Unconditional, - there is no way for any website to bypass it
- Blocking, so there is no chance that the website can determine their location while it's waiting for their answer

The JavaScript code that causes this infobar to appear in Firefox, is a single function call that takes a callback function *show_map()*.

The call to show_map() will return immediately, but that does not mean that everyone has access to the getCurrentPosition() of the user's location.

The callback function looks like this:

function show_map(position)

```
{
    var latitude = position.coords.latitude;
    var longitude = position.coords.longitude;
    // let's show a map or do something interesting!
}
```

The callback function will be called with a single parameter, an object with two properties: *coords* and *timestamp*

The timestamp is, the date and time when the location was calculated. The object has *coords* properties like latitude and longitude that represent the site visitors physical location in the world.

The position object's properties are listed in Table 1.

coords.latitude double	coords.longitude double	coords.altitude double	coords.accuracy double
coords.altitudeAccuracy double	coords.heading double	coords.speed double	timestamp DOMTimeStamp

Table 1.

Only three of the properties are guaranteed to be available they are coords.latitude, coords.longitude and coords.accuracy. The rest may come back null, depending on the capabilities of requesting device and the backend positioning server with which it communicates. The heading and speed properties are calculated based on the user's previous position, if possible.

Focus:

Before attempting to execute GeoLocation codespec, check if the Browser in use has GeoLocation support or not. The Codespec 1 below checks if the Browser being used supports GeoLocation or not.

```
function checkGeoInBrowser()
{
    var checkGeoService = navigator.geolocation;

    if (checkGeoService)
    {
        alert("Great!! Your Browser supports GeoLocation.");
    }
```

```
    else
    {
        alert("Sorry Your Browser does not support GeoLocation.
    Upgrade Your Browser or use a different Browser.");
    }
}
```

Codespec 1

The JavaScript function above i.e. *checkGeoInBrowser()* determines if a Browser has Geolocation support built in or not.

The function queries the standard navigator object first. If the Browser supports Geolocation, then an alert with the message *"Great!! Your Browser supports GeoLocation."* is displayed as shown in diagram 7.3.

The Output of the above Codespec is shown in diagram 7.2, 7.3 and 7.4

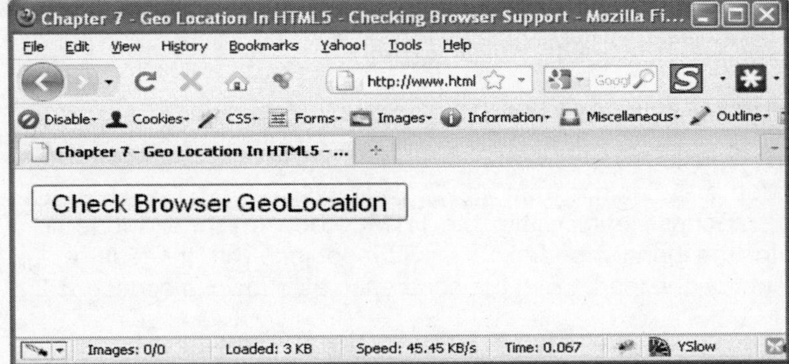

Diagram 7.2

Diagram 7.3

If your Browser does not support GeoLocation, you will be prompted with an Error Message *"Sorry Your Browser does not support GeoLocation. Upgrade Your Browser or use a different Browser"* as shown in diagram 7.4

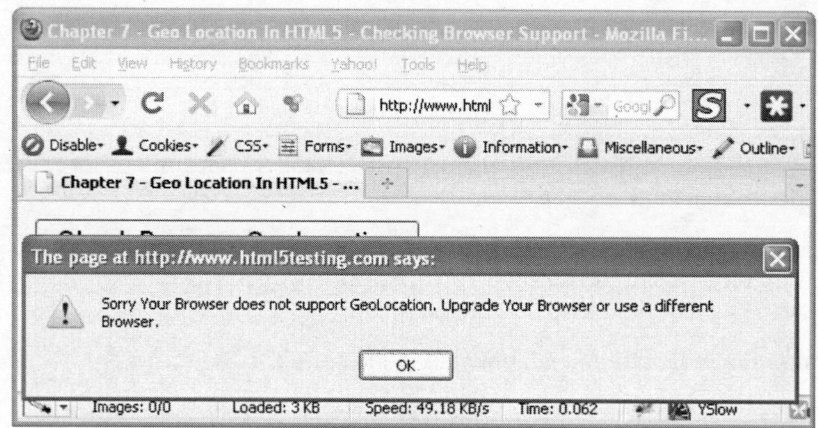

Diagram 7.4

Using Modernizr in within a code snippet

Follow these steps to include Modernizr:

1. Download modernizr-1.5.min.js from http://www.modernizr.com
2. Include the JavaScript library within the HTML code. Initialize Modernizr when the page loads. It creates the global Modernizr JavaScript object, with the feature objects created.
3. Create geotest.html and load it with the code spec as shown in codespec 2

Complete CodeSpec 2 - **Geo Location In HTML5 - Using Alerts**

```
<!DOCTYPE html>
<html>
<head>
    <meta charset="utf-8">
    <title>Chapter 6 - Geo Location In HTML5 - Using Alerts</title>
    <script type="text/javascript" src="js/modernizr-1.6.min.js"
     language="javascript"></script>
    <script type="text/javascript">
        function getGeoLocationTracking()
        {
            alert("Start GeoLocation Tracking.");
```

```
        if (Modernizr.geolocation)
        {
            alert("Great!! Your Browser supports GeoLocation.");
            navigator.geolocation.getCurrentPosition(show_map);
        }
        else
        {
            alert("Sorry Your Browser does not support GeoLocation.
            Upgrade Your Browser or use a different Browser.");
        }
    }
    function show_map(position)
    {
        var latitude = position.coords.latitude;
        var longitude = position.coords.longitude;
        alert("Latitude = " + latitude);
        alert("Longitude = " + longitude);
    }
  </script>

</head>
<body>
  <input type="button" value="Get GeoLocation" onClick="getGeoLocationTracking()"/>

</body>
</html>
```

Codespec 2

The Output of the Codespec 2 is shown in diagram 7.5 to diagram 7.10

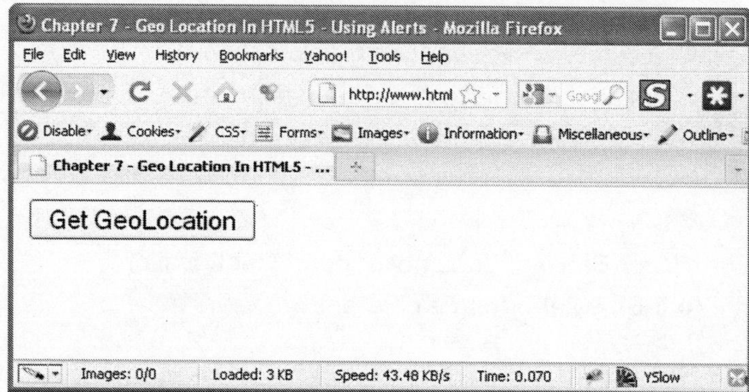

Diagram 7.5

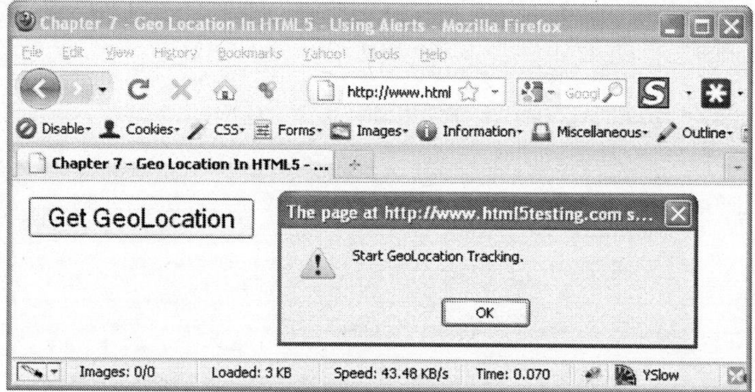

Diagram 7.6

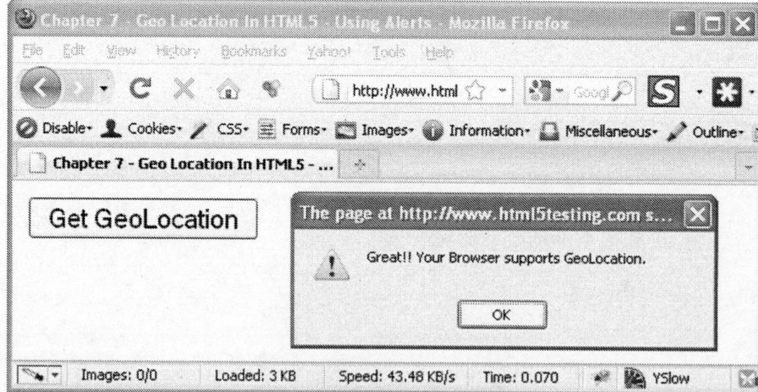

Diagram 7.7

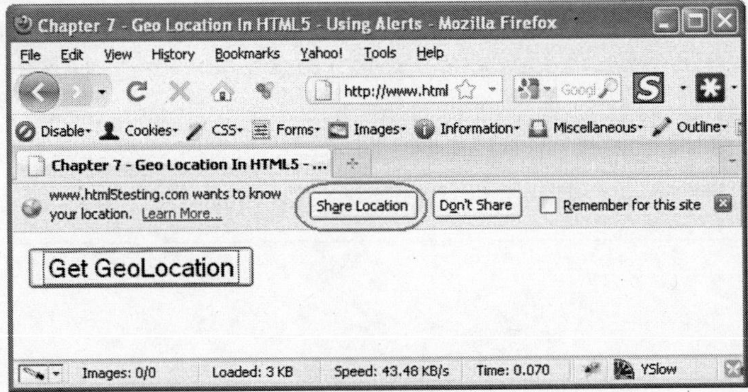

Diagram 7.8

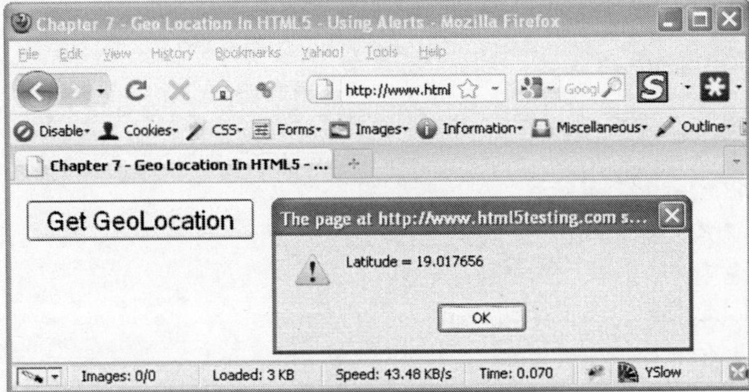

Diagram 7.9

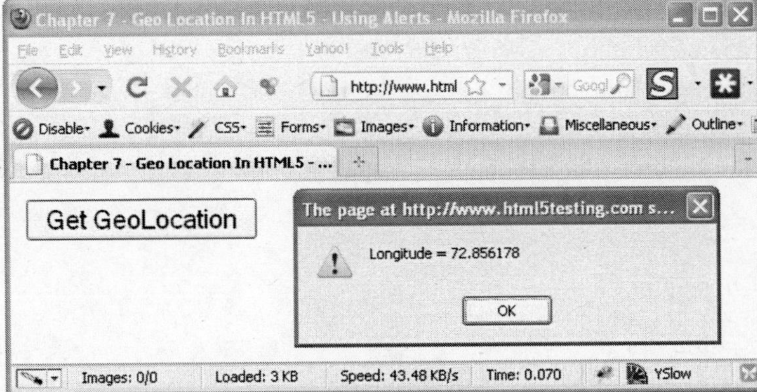

Diagram 7.10

Note: *Most programmers do not like to use Alerts. Instead of an alert they use prefer to use <div></div>. Therefore in codespec 3 output messages are displayed in DIV's.*

Example of Using GeoLocation in HTML 5:

Complete CodeSpec 3 - **Geo Location In HTML5 - Using Divs**

```
<!DOCTYPE html>
<html>
<head>
    <meta charset="utf-8">
    <title>Chapter 6 - Geo Location In HTML5 - Using Divs</title>
    <script type="text/javascript" src="js/modernizr-1.6.min.js" language="javascript"></script>
    <script type="text/javascript">
        function getGeoLocationTracking()
        {
            document.getElementById("divStartGeoLoc").innerHTML =
            "Start GeoLocation Tracking.";
            if (Modernizr.geolocation)
            {
                document.getElementById("divBrowSuppGeoLoc").innerHTML =
                "Great!! Your Browser supports GeoLocation.";
                navigator.geolocation.getCurrentPosition(show_map);
            }
            else
            {
                document.getElementById("divBrowSuppGeoLoc").innerHTML =
                "Sorry Your Browser does not support GeoLocation.
                Please Upgrade Your Browser or use a different Browser.";
            }
        }
        function show_map(position)
        {
            var latitude = position.coords.latitude;
            var longitude = position.coords.longitude;
            document.getElementById("divMyLatitude").innerHTML =
            "Latitude = " + latitude;
```

```
            document.getElementById("divMyLongitude").innerHTML =
            "Longitude = " + longitude;
        }
    </script>
</head>
<body>
    <input type="button" value="Get GeoLocation" onClick="getGeoLocationTracking()"/><br
/><br />
    <div id="divStartGeoLoc"></div><br />
    <div id="divBrowSuppGeoLoc"></div><br />
    <div id="divMyLatitude"></div><br />
    <div id="divMyLongitude"></div><br />

</body>
</html>
```

Codespec 3

The Output of the Codespec 3 is shown in diagram 7.11 and diagram 7.12

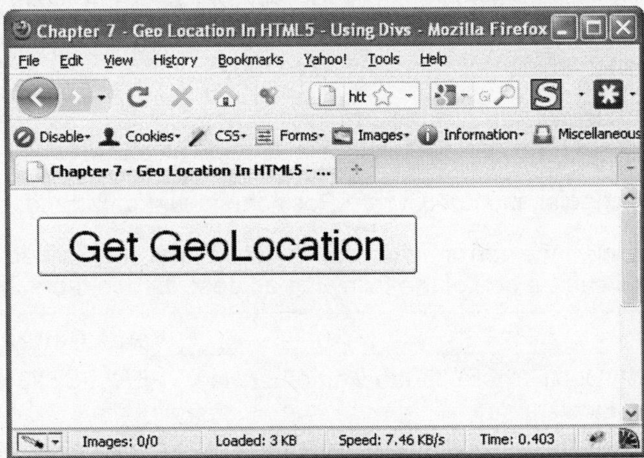

Diagram 7.11

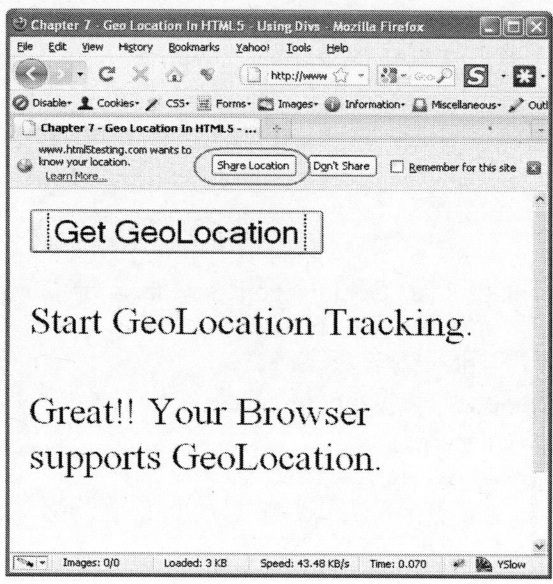

Diagram 7.12

Handling Errors

Geolocation is complicated. Many things can (*and do*) go wrong. It could be something simple like the user refusing permission or the network taking too long to calculate the user's position or the positioning satellites being uncontactable and more.

This is how these issues are handled in codespec. Use a second argument to getCurrentPosition() i.e. an error handling callback function as shown below:

For Example: navigator.geolocation.getCurrentPosition(show_map, handle_error)

If anything goes wrong, the error callback function will be called with a object. The PositionError properties can be one of the following as described in table 2.

Reason	**Value Returned**
If the user clicks the "Don't Share" button or otherwise denies access to their location	PERMISSION_DENIED **1**
If the network is down or the positioning satellites can't be contacted	POSITION_UNAVAILABLE **2**
If the network is up but its taking too long to calculate the user's position	TIMEOUT **3**
If anything else goes wrong	UNKNOWN_ERROR **0**

Table 2

For example:

function handle_error(err)

```
{
    if ( err.code == 1)
    {
    // The user said no!
    }
}
```

Geo Location In HTML5 Complete CodeSpec 4 - Using Alerts + Error Handling

```
<!DOCTYPE html>
<html>
<head>
    <meta charset="utf-8">
    <title>Chapter 6 - Geo Location In HTML5 - Using Alerts + Error Handling</title>
    <script type="text/javascript" src="js/modernizr-1.6.min.js"
    language="javascript"></script>
    <script type="text/javascript">
        var watchPositionID=0;
        function getGeoLocationTracking()
        {
            alert("Start GeoLocation Tracking.");

            if (Modernizr.geolocation)
            {
                alert("Your Browser supports GeoLocation");
                watchPositionID =
                        navigator.geolocation.watchPosition(showCurrentLocation,errHandler,
                { enableHighAccuracy: true});
            }
```

```
            else
            {
                alert("Sorry Your Browser does not support GeoLocation.
                Upgrade Your Browser or use a different Browser.");
            }
        }
        function showCurrentLocation(position)
        {
            var latitude = position.coords.latitude;
            var longitude = position.coords.longitude;
            alert("Latitude = " + latitude);
            alert("Longitude = " + longitude);
        }
        function errHandler(error)
        {
            alert("Error while retrieving current position. Error code: " + error.code);
        }
    </script>
</head>
<body>
    <input type="button" value="GetGeoLocation" onClick="getGeoLocationTracking()"/>
</body>
</html>
```

Codspec 4

The Output of the Codespec 4 is shown in diagram 7.13 to diagram 7.18

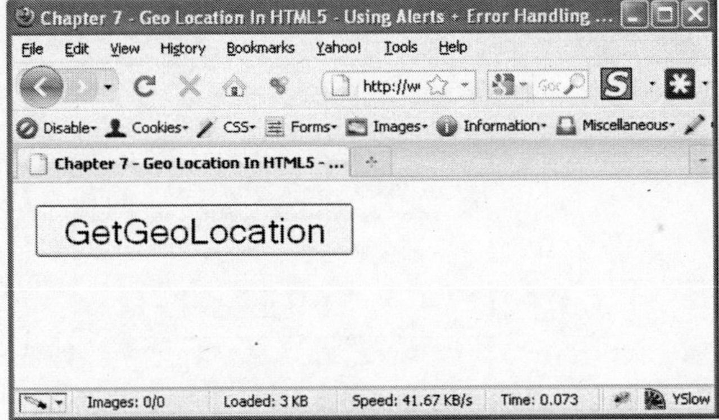

Diagram 7.13

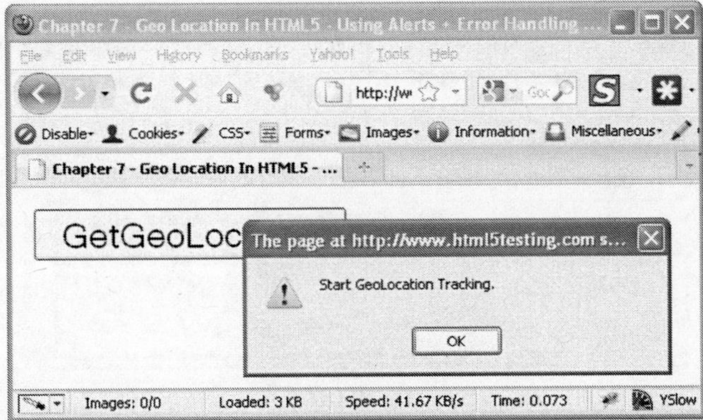

Diagram 7.14

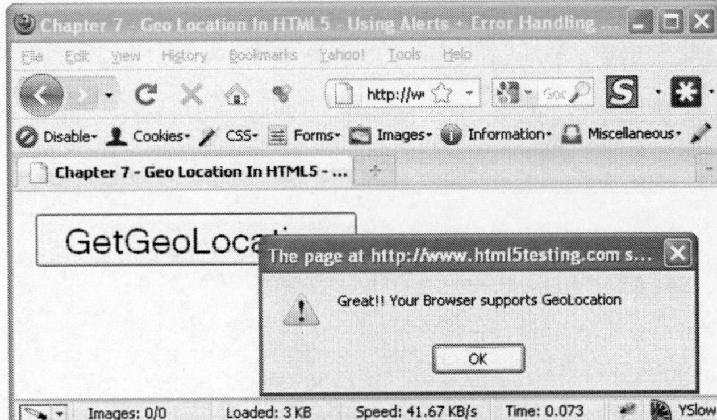

Diagram 7.15

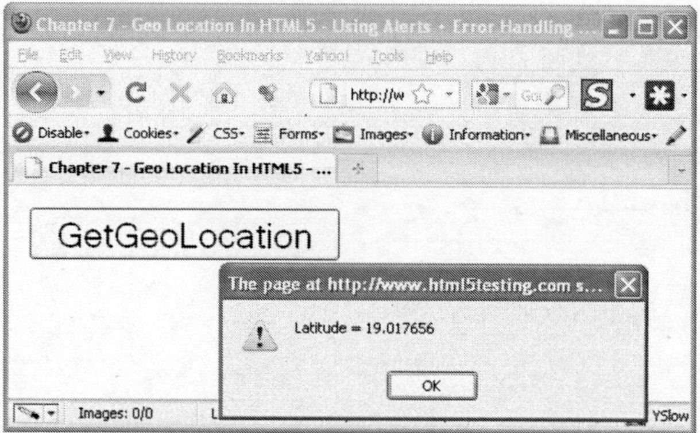

Diagram 7.16

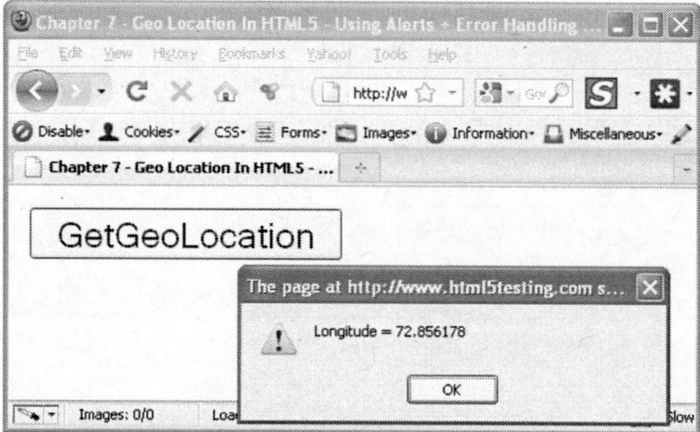

Diagram 7.17

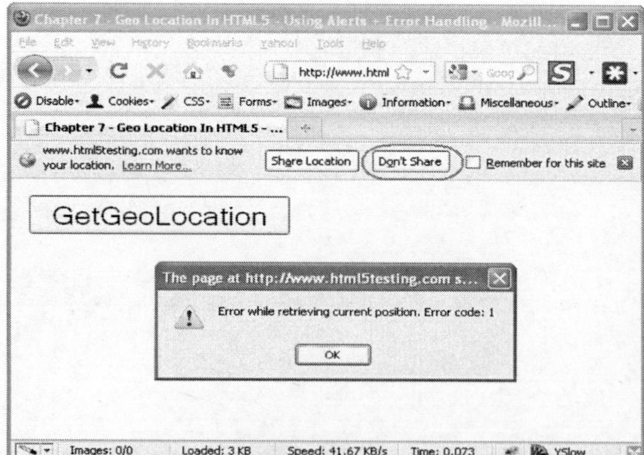

Diagram 7.18

Self Review Questions

Fill In The Blanks

1. The geolocation API lets a site visitor share their _____________ with trusted websites.
2. The geolocation API centers around a new property on the global navigator object which is: ___________________.
3. Only three of the properties are guaranteed to be available they are ___________________, __________________and ___________________.

True or False

4. Geolocation is the art of figuring out where a site visitor is located are in the world, and optionally sharing that information with any trusted network.
5. The timestamp is, the date and time when the visitor visited the site was calculated.
6. Geolocation is simple.

Hands-on Exercise

1. Create an HTML5 file which displays the *latitude*, *longitude* and *accuracy* using *<div></div>* and handle Error conditions. Use the HTML5 elements that have been learned in this chapter. The output of this exercise is shown in diagram 7.19

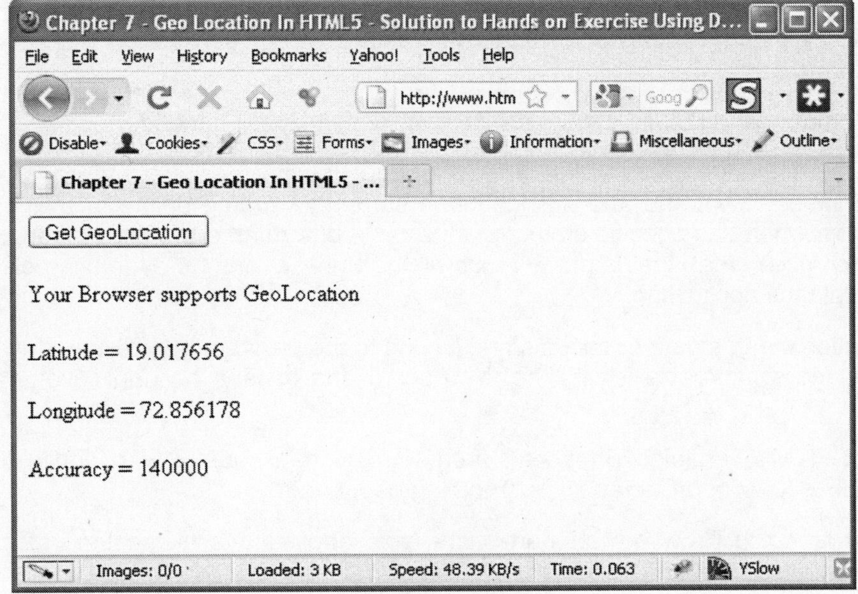

Diagram 7.19

8. Working Off-Line In HTML5

Working offline using a web application? This really sounds strange. Web pages are traditionally things that are downloaded and rendered in a Browser in real time. Downloading webpage information implies an Internet connection. Then comes the question - How can you download anything while offline? Of course, you can't, but data can be downloaded whenever online. That's how HTML5 *offline* applications work.

An offline web application is just a list of URLs which point to HTML, CSS, JavaScript files, images, and/or any other kinds of resources that may be required by the application. The home page of the offline web application points to this list. This list is called a manifest file. It is just a text file containing this information located on the Web server.

Any Browser that implements HTML5 offline applications:

- Reads the list of URLs contained in manifest file
- Download the resources
- Caches them locally

And

- Automatically keep the local copies up to date as and when they change

When an attempt is made to access the web application without an Internet connection, the Browser automatically switches over to the copies cached locally instead.

The instant this happens, most of the work is up to the web developer. There is a flag in the DOM which indicates whether the application is currently working online or offline. There are events that fire when this specific status changes (i.e. one minute the application is offline the next online, or vice versa), that is pretty much all the Browser can do everything else has to be coded for within the application.

If the application creates data or saves state, it is up to the programmer to store that data locally while offline and synchronize it with the Web server the instant the application can go back online.

Hence using HTML5 enabled Browsers, programmers can code a web application to work offline as well as to work online as though nothing happened.

Table 1 shows which Browsers support offline web applications at the time of creating this material.

IE	FireFox	Chrome	Opera	Safari
Not Available	Available	Available	Not Available	Available

Table 1.

In order to ensure that all the resources required are downloaded by an HTML5 enabled Browser and cached locally, the HTML codespec must point to the manifest file, using the *manifest attribute* within the opening <html> element. As follows:

```
<!DOCTYPE HTML>
<html manifest="/cache.manifest">
    <body>
    ...
    </body>
</html>
```

The manifest file can be located anywhere on the Web server, but it must be served with its content type specified as *text/cache-manifest*.

If Apache is the web server, add an AddType directive either in the .htaccess file available in the root folder of the website or in the httpd.conf (*which is normally not exposed in shared hosting hence the use of the .htaccess file*)

For example: AddType text/cache-manifest .manifest

Make sure that the name of the manifest file is *{filename}*.manifest. If a different Web server is used, consult the server's documentation on how to control *Content-Type* header information.

> **Note:** *If the website consists of multiple pages then every page of the website needs a manifest attribute nested within the start <HTML> element that points to the {filename}.manifest that will hold URLS for the resources consumed by the entire website.*

Every one of the HTML pages therefore points to *{filename}*.manifest. This file is delivered to the requesting Browser by the Web server with the proper Content-Type header. Now focus a little bit on the contents of *{filename}*.manifest.

The very first line contained within *{filename}*.manifest is:

CACHE MANIFEST

All *{filename}*.manifest files are divided into three sections.

- The "explicit" section
- The "fallback" section

And

- The "online whitelist" section

Each section has a *header*, on a separate line. If a manifest file does not have any section headers, all the listed resources within it are determined to be in an *explicit* section by the Browser handling the *{filename}*.manifest.

Here is the content of a valid *{filename}*.manifest file. There are individual resources listed on separate lines the resources are - a CSS file, a JavaScript file, and a JPEG image.

CACHE MANIFEST

/clock.css

/clock.js

/clock-face.jpg

This manifest file has no section headers defined. Hence, all the listed resources are in the *explicit* section by default. All resources listed in the *explicit* section of any manifest file get downloaded and cached locally. These resources will be used instead of the ones online whenever the application is disconnected from the Internet.

As soon as an HTML5 enabled Browser reads the manifest attribute within the start <HTML> element the Browser will download clock.css, clock.js, and clock-face.jpg from the root directory of the web server as save them locally. To test this simply unplug from the Internet and refresh the page, and all of these resources will be available offline.

Handling Web Applications That Consist Of Multiple Pages

There are times when a web application is contained within a single HTML page. If that is so then, make sure that the <HTML> element has the manifest attribute specified that points to all the resources required by that page to render correctly in a HTML5 enabled Browser. The Browser assumes that the page itself is part of the application hence there is no need to explicitly name the page within the entries in *{filename}*.manifest.

Often web applications consist of more than one HTML page. If that is so, then each HTML required by the application should be listed in the manifest, the browser will not know that there are other HTML pages that need to be downloaded and cached from the Web server.

Network Section

Here is a slightly more complex example. Suppose a clock application was being used to track site visitors, using a tracking script that is loaded dynamically via a <img src> attribute. If this resource was to be cached locally it would completely defeat the purpose of why it is being used in the first place. Hence, this specific resource should never be cached locally and thus never be available offline.

Here's how to do this:

```
CACHE MANIFEST
NETWORK:
/tracking.cgi

CACHE:
/clock.css
/clock.js
/clock-face.jpg
```

This manifest file includes section headers.

The line marked NETWORK: marks the beginning of a section which holds resources that are never downloaded from the Web server and available locally. Any attempt to access these resources by the application when being executed offline will result in an error.

The line marked CACHE: marks the beginning of the *explicit* section. Each of the resources listed under CACHE: will be downloaded from the Web server and cached locally.

Fallback Sections

There is one more type of section that can be added to a manifest file: a fallback section.

In a fallback section, substitutions for online resources can be defined that, cannot be cached or were not cached successfully.

The HTML5 specification offers this as an example of using a fallback section:

```
CACHE MANIFEST
FALLBACK:
/ /offline.html
NETWORK:
*
```

Consider Wikipedia a site that contains millions of pages. It just would be impossible to download the entire web site. For a huge website site like Wikipedia if a part of it must be made available offline, how should the decision on which pages to cache locally be made?

Perhaps this could be an acceptable approach:

Every page viewed on Wikipedia could be downloaded and cached locally.

This will include:

- Every encyclopedia entry visited
- Every talk page

And

- Every edit page

That is what the manifest file entry described above does.

Every HTML page on Wikipedia, *entry, talk page, edit page, history page*, visited is checked against what is available in the local cache. If the Browser recognizes that it has never downloaded this particular file, it will set up a new offline *appcache* (i.e. *an abbreviation for application cache*), download all the resources listed in the cache manifest, and then add the current page to the appcache.

If the page exists in an appcache but the file on the Web server has been updated the updated resources are downloaded and added to the appcache.

Either way, the page just visited ends up in the appcache. This means that it's possible to have an offline web application that adds pages as an when they are visited. Every single one of the website's HTML page resources is not defined within the manifest file content.

The fallback section in this manifest file contains only one line. This is not a URL, It's really a URL pattern.

The first single slash (/) matches any page on the website, not just the home page. When a request is made to visit any page on that website while offline, the Browser will first look for the page within the *appcache*. If the browser finds the page in the appcache (because it had been visited earlier while online, and the page was implicitly added to the appcache at that time), the Browser will display the cached copy of the page.

If the browser does not find the page in the appcache, instead of displaying an *error message*, it will display the page */offline.html*, as specified in the second half of the line in the fallback section.

Now to examine the NETWORK section:

The network section in this manifest also has just a single line, which contains just a single character (*). This character has special meaning in a network section. It's called the *online whitelist wildcard flag*.

This simply tells the Browser that anything not in the appcache can still be downloaded from the original web address, as long as there is an Internet connection.

This approach is important for an open-ended, offline web application.

Continuing with the example, it means that while browsing the hypothetical offline-enabled Wikipedia while online, the Browser will fetch images, videos and other embedded resources normally, even if they are in a different domain.

This is really very common in huge websites, (*even if their pages are not coded to be part of an offline web application*) their HTML pages are generated and served locally, while images and videos are served from a another Web server entirely.

Without this wildcard flag, the hypothetical offline-enabled, Wikipedia website would not load any externally hosted images or videos or other resources.

Is this example complete? Certainly not.

Huge websites like Wikipedia are more than just HTML files. They use:
- Common CSS
- Common and unique JavaScript
- Specific images

For each page.

Each of these resources would need to be listed explicitly in the CACHE: section of the manifest file in order for pages to display and behave properly offline.

But the purpose of a fallback section is that it's possible to have an open-ended, offline web application that extends beyond the resources that have been explicitly listed in a manifest file.

The Flow Of Events

So far when describing the construction of offline web applications lots of things seem to happen as if by magic when an HTML5 enabled Browser starts interpreting an HTML page that has the attribute *manifest* specified within the opening <HTML> element.

Here is a brief explanation of the flow of events within the Browser's - **D**ocument **O**bject **M**odel (DOM) when an HTML5 enabled Browser encounters an HTML page that has the attribute *manifest* specified within the opening <HTML> element.

When an HTML5 enabled Browser starts to interpret any webpage that points to a manifest files, The Browser fires a series of events that belong to the window.applicationCache object.

Here's the process:

1. As soon as the Browser notices a manifest attribute on the <html> element, the Browser fires a *checking* event. All the events described in this material belong to and are fired from the:
   window.applicationCache object.

Note: *The checking event is always fired by the Browser, regardless of whether this page has been previously visited this page or not.*

2. If the Browser has never seen encountered this manifest file before:

- A downloading event is fired. This starts the download of the resources listed in the manifest file.
- While these resources are downloading, the Browser will periodically fire *progress* events. *progress* events contain information on how many files resources been downloaded already and how many resources are still queued to be downloaded.

- After all resources listed in the manifest have been downloaded successfully, the Browser fires one final event, *cached*.
- This is the signal that the offline web application is fully cached and ready to be used offline. That's it the job is done.

3. On the other hand, if the Browser has previously visited this page the Browser already knows about this manifest file and may already have some (*or all*) resources in the *appcache*.

Now the question to be handled is, has the contents of manifest file cached locally, changed on the Web server since the last time the Browser made a request to the Web server for resources.

- If the answer is no, the Browser will immediately fire a *noupdate* event. That's it the job is done.
- If the answer is that the local cache and the content on the Web server are *not the same*, the Browser will fire a *downloading* event and start re-downloading every single resource listed in the cache manifest.
- While downloading these resources, the Browser will periodically fire *progress* events, which contain information on how many files have been downloaded and how many files are still queued to be downloaded.
- After all resources listed in the manifest have been re-downloaded successfully, the browser will fire one final event, *updateready*.
- This is the signal that the new version of the offline web application is fully cached and ready to be used offline.

The new version is not yet in use. To hot-swap to the new version, i.e. without forcing the user to reload the page, manually call the window.applicationCache.swapCache() function.

If, at any point in the whole process of creating the offline resource cache, something goes horribly wrong, the Browser will fire an *error* event and stop. Here is a very tiny list of things that could go wrong. This is provided just as an illustration.

- The manifest returned an HTTP 404 (*Page Not Found*) or 410 (*Permanently Gone*) error.
- The manifest was found and had not changed, but the HTML page that pointed to the manifest failed to download properly.
- The cache manifest was found and had changed, but the browser failed to download one of the resources listed in the cache manifest.

Debugging Such Code

If even a single resource listed in the manifest file fails to download properly, the entire process of caching the resources required by the offline web application will fail. The Browser will fire the *error* event and stop, but there will be no indication whatsoever of what the actual problem was. This can make debugging offline web applications extremely frustrating.

The issue is something that is not, technically speaking an error, but it will look like a serious Browser bug. It has to do with exactly how the Browser checks whether a manifest file has changed or not.

This is a three-phase process.

1. Using normal HTTP semantics, the Browser will check whether the manifest has expired. Just like with any other file being served via HTTP, by the Web server the file will typically include *meta* information about the file in the HTTP response headers.

The *Expires* and *Cache-Control,* HTTP headers tell the Browser how whether to cache manifest file content without the Browser explicitly having to ask the Web server whether the manifest file content had changed.

This kind of information provided by the Web server has nothing specifically to do with offline web applications alone. This kind of information is delivered to the Browser by the Web server for every HTML page, stylesheet, script, image, or other resource being requested for.

2. If the manifest has expired (according to its HTTP headers), the Browser will ask the Web server whether there is a new version and, if so, will download it.

To do this, the Browser issues an HTTP request that includes the *last-modified date* of manifest file, which the Web server had included in its HTTP response headers the last time the Browser downloaded the manifest file.

If the Web server determines that the manifest file has not changed since that date, it will simply return a 304 (*Not Modified*) status code. None of this is specific to offline Web applications. It actually happens for virtually all resources on the Web.

3. If the Web server believes that the manifest file has changed since that date, it will return an *HTTP 200* (OK) status code, followed by the contents of the new manifest file along with new Cache-Control headers and a new last-modified date. This ensures that steps 1 and 2 will work properly the next time.

> **Note:** *If the Web server must send a requesting Browser a file, it does everything it can to ensure that it does not need to send the same file it twice for no reason.*

Once the Browser has downloaded the new manifest file, the Browser will check the contents against the manifest file copy it downloaded last time. If the contents of the manifest file are the same as they were last time, the Browser will not re-download any of the resources listed in the manifest file.

> **Note:** *The Browser uses an ASCII comparison routine to check for differences between the manifest file it has in its cache and the new manifest file it has just downloaded.*

Any one of these steps can trip break the offline web application being tested. For example, a manifest file is deployed on the Web server, then 10 minutes later, another resource needs to be added to it. The manifest file will be updated locally and uploaded to the Web server as is usually the case

Here's what will happen. When the webpage is reloaded, the Browser notices the <HTML> *manifest* attribute. The Browser fires the *checking* event. Then nothing happens.

The Browser behaves as though the manifest file has not changed.

Why? Because, by default, a Web server is configured to tell Browsers to cache static files for a few hours, via HTTP semantics, using *Cache-Control* headers.

That means that the Browser will never get past Phase 1 of the three phase process. Sure, the Web server knows that the manifest file has been changed, but the Browser asks the Web server for the new manifest file.

Why? Because the last time Browser downloaded the manifest file, the Web server told the Browser to cache it for a few hours via HTTP semantics, using *Cache-Control* headers. Now, just 10 minutes later, that's exactly what the Browser is supposed to do. In any sort of clash between a Browser and Web server the Web server always wins. What this really means is that only after a few hours will the Web server deliver the Browser the updated manifest file, not before.

This is not a Web server bug, it's a Web server feature. Everything is working exactly the way it's supposed to. If Web servers did not have a way to tell Browsers and Proxy servers to cache things, the Web would either collapse or crawl. But that is not comforting after you've spent a few hours trying to figure out why your Browser will not notice that the manifest file has been updated.

Additionally, if one waits long enough (*couple of hours – timing as set in the Web server configuration file*), the Browser will mysteriously recognize that the manifest file has been updated and everything will start working again! – Reason**:** The HTTP cache has expired! - Just like it was instructed to via its configuration file entries.

Here is what has to be done**:** reconfigure the Web server so that the manifest file is not cacheable by HTTP semantics. If Apache is your web server, these two lines in the **.**htaccess file will do the trick.

ExpiresActive On

ExpiresDefault "access"

This will actually disable caching for every file from the root directory and all subdirectories. That is probably not what is required in production Web server. Hence these entries must be qualified with a <Files> directive so that these directives affect only the manifest file, or create a subdirectory that contains nothing but this **.**htaccess file and the cache manifest file.

> **Note:** *Never forget that configuration details vary from Web server to Web server, so consult your Web server's documentation for how to control HTTP caching headers.*

Just disabling HTTP caching on the manifest file itself won't solve all problems, though. There will be times when one of the resources in the appcache has changed, but it's still at the same URL on the Web server.

Here, step 2 of the three phase process will throw up problems. If your manifest file has not changed, the Browser will never notice that one of its previously cached resources has changed.

Consider this example:

```
CACHE MANIFEST
# rev 42
clock.js
clock.css
```

If clock.css was changed and redeployed, the Browser will not reflect changes, because the manifest file itself has not changed.

Every time change is made to any one of the resources used in an offline web application, a change must be made within the cache manifest file itself. This can be as simple as changing a single character.

The real easy way to accomplish this is to include a comment line with a revision number in the manifest file. Any time you change one of the resources, change the revision number in the comment.

The Web server will return the newly changed manifest file to the Browser. The Browser will notice that the contents of the file have changed, and it will kick off the process to re-download all the resources listed in the manifest and everyone lives happily ever after.

```
CACHE MANIFEST
# rev 43
clock.js
clock.css
```

Self Review Questions

Fill In The Blanks

1. The manifest file can be located anywhere on the Web server, but it must be served with its content type specified as ________________.
2. Every one of the HTML pages points to ____________________.
3. The very first line contained within *{filename}*.manifest is ____________________
4. All *{filename}*.manifest files are divided into three sections: ____________ ____________ and ______________
5. Each section has a ____________, on a separate line.

6. All resources listed in the ______________ section of any manifest file get downloaded and cached locally.
7. The line marked ______________ marks the beginning of a section which holds resources that are never downloaded from the Web server and available locally.
8. The line marked ______________ marks the beginning of the *explicit* section.
9. The ______________ section in this manifest file contains only one line.

True Or False

10. Each of the resources listed under CACHE: will not be downloaded from the Web server and cached locally.
11. In a fallback section, substitutions for online resources can be defined that, can be cached or were cached successfully.
12. If the page exists in an appcache but the file on the Web server has been updated the updated resources are downloaded and added to the appcache.
13. It's not possible to have an offline web application that adds pages as an when they are visited.
14. Every single one of the website's HTML page resources is defined within the manifest file content.
15. A single character (*) has special meaning in a network section, it's called the *online whitelist wildcard flag.*
16. If even a single resource listed in the manifest file fails to download properly, the entire process of caching the resources required by the offline web application will fail.
17. Never forget that configuration details does not vary from Web server to Web server.

9. Building Forms In HTML5

HTML5 defines more than twelve new input types that can be used when crafting HTML based forms. These new input types can be used right now without any JavaScript based hacks, or workarounds.

Not all of the new input types are actively supported in every modern Browser, but in modern Browsers where there is support for the new form input types as defined in HMTL5 the forms created using these new input types will work surprisingly well, in legacy (older non HTML5 compliant Browsers) the forms created using the new input types will still work, but without the new input type functionality.

All of the new input types defined in HTML5 degrade gracefully to the older input types and therefore work in all earlier versions of Browsers including IE6.

Placeholder Text

HTML5 permits the placement of placeholder text within an input field. Placeholder text is text displayed inside the input field as long as that field is empty and the form cursor in not on the field. As soon as the form user clicks on the input field (*or tabs to it*) the placeholder text disappears.

Here is an example:

Observe the Google search box in Mozilla Firefox 3.7 and > this includes placeholder text as shown in diagram 9.1.

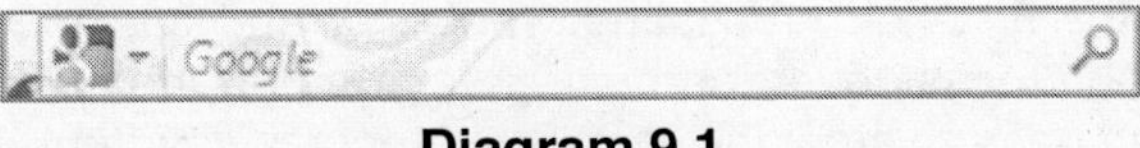

Diagram 9.1

As soon as the cursor is placed within the search box the placeholder text disappears as shown in diagram 9.2.

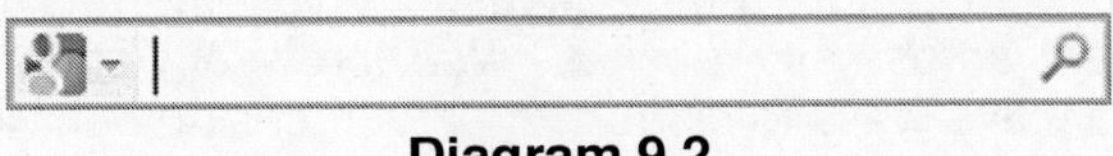

Diagram 9.2

Table 1, is a short list of Browsers that support placeholder text.

Firefox	Safari	Chrome	Opera
Version 3.7 and >	Version 4.0 and >	Version 3.0 and >	Version 10 and >

Table 1.

Here is an HTML5 code snippet to include placeholder text in an input box in when creating a form:

```
<form>
    <input name="q" placeholder="Search Bookmarks and History">
    <input type="submit" value="Search">
</form>
```

Browsers that don't support the *placeholder* attribute will simply ignore it.

Formatting Placeholder Text:

The placeholder attribute can only contain text, not HTML markup. However, there are some vendor specific CSS extensions that allow the styling to placeholder text in some Browsers.

Autofocus Fields

Many websites that use forms also use JavaScript to place the form cursor on the first input field of the form automatically.

The home page of Google.com is a great example. The home page of Google.com will autofocus the form cursor in search input box so that the user can just type in their search keywords without having to manually click on the search input box to position the form cursor there.

While this is convenient for most people, it can be pretty annoying for others. If a user clicks on a form field when the form is loading, and begins to type, when the form loads the cursor automatically jumps to the first field disrupting work flow and causing data to be typed in the wrong place. Because autofocusing is done using JavaScript, there is little that users can do if they do not want the web page to steal the form input focus away from them.

To solve this problem, HTML5 introduced the *autofocus* attribute on all web form controls. The autofocus attribute does exactly what it says, as soon as the page loads, it moves the input focus to a particular input field on the form. Because it is just markup instead of Javascript, this behavior will be consistent across all websites. Also, browser vendors (or extension authors) can offer users simple effective ways to disable the autofocusing behavior.

Table 2 shows which Browsers support autofocus.

Safari	Chrome	Opera
Version 4.0 and >	Version 3.0 and >	Version 10 and >

Table 2.

Here is an HTML5 code snippet to include autofocus on an input box in when creating a form:

```
<form>
    <input name="q" autofocus>
    <input type="submit" value="Search">
</form>
```

Browsers that don't support the *autofocus* attribute will simply ignore it.

If autofocus is to work in all Browsers, not just HTML5 compliant browsers, use Javascript as follows:

1. Add the autofocus attribute to the HTML form markup as appropriate
2. Detect whether the browser supports the autofocus attribute, if it does not, execute the Javascript autofocus code to place the form cursor on the required input field.

```
<form name="f">
    <input id="q" autofocus>
    <script>
    if (!("autofocus" in document.createElement("input"))) {
    document.getElementById("q").focus();
    }
    </script>
    <input type="submit" value="Go">
</form>
```

Codespec 1

This will do the trick nicely.

The manner in which the Javascript code is blended with HTML code in code snippet 1, may appear a little unorthodox, here's the reason why this approach has been taken.

Often web page coders use the window.onload event of the page to set a form's cursor to an appropriate input field, unfortunately the window.onload event fires only after all the images on the webpage have completed loading.

If the web page has a lot of images to load, then this event would fire perhaps after the site visitor has begun interacting with the form (i.e. *typing information into the form fields*), and abruptly re-focus the form cursor on a specific form field. This can cause the site visitor to type in information into a form field wrongly. This can also be quite irritating to a site visitor.

The approach taken in code snippet 1, places the autofocus Javascript code immediately after the form field bound to the Javascript code. If for any reason Javascript code cannot be inserted in the middle of the form's codespec then consider using a custom event defined within a Javascript library like JQuery (i.e. $(document).ready() instead of window.onload.

Email Addresses

For a long time, web forms just used a few kinds of input types the most common are listed in Table 3.

Field type	HTML code
Checkbox	<input type="checkbox">
Radio button	<input type="radio">
Password	<input type="password">
Drop-down list box	<select><option>...
File picker	<input type="file">
Submit button	<input type="submit">
Command button	<input type="button">
Text box	<input type="text">

Table 3 Some common Input types in HTML 4

All of these input types still work in HTML5. If you are upgrading HTML4 codespec to HTML5, perhaps by changing the doctype declaration, not a single line of form code needs to be changed. HTML5,in this regard has perfect backward compatibility with HTML4.

HTML5 defines several new field types. There is no reason not to start using them immediately.

Type="email" – used as follows:

```
<form>
   <input type="email">
   <input type="submit" value="Go">
</form>
```

All Browsers support type="email". Unfortunately many just do nothing special when they encounter that specific input type. Browsers that do not recognize the type="email" attribute added to *input* will simply render it as type="text" i.e. a plain text field.

The Web has millions of forms that ask for an email address to be entered, all of them use <input type="text"> (i.e. *a text box*), into which an email address is typed.

Now HTML5 has defined a new type="email" attribute. Every single browser on Earth treats an unknown type="email" attribute as type type="text" even IE 6.

Hence, web page forms can be immediately upgraded to use the <input > right now.

As of writing this material the HTML5 specification does not mandate type="email" any particular behavior for the new input types. Thus different Browser manufacturers have handled the type="email" attribute differently. Opera styles the form field with a small email icon. Other HTML5 browsers, like Safari and Chrome, simply render it as a text box exactly like type="text" so your site visitors will never know the difference unless they view the page source.

Web Addresses

Web addresses known as URLs, or URIs, are another type of specialized text. The structure of a web address is controlled by relevant Internet syntax.

Here's an example:

```
<form>
    <input type="url">
    <input type="submit" value="Go">
</form>
```

If a web address has to be entered into a form, what will be expected is something like http://www.google.com. Forward slashes and periods are common. Spaces are forbidden. A domain suffix like ".com" or ".org" expected. What's not expected is "A/5, Jay Chambers Nanda Patkar Road".

Since, (*as of writing this material*) the HTML5 specification does not mandate any particular behavior for the new input types Browsers that don't support HTML5, will treat type="url" exactly like type="text", so there's no real reason why type="url" cannot be used on web page forms.

Using Numbers

Capturing a number in a web form is trickier than asking for an email or web address. Numbers are more complicated than an Email ID or a URL/URI.

Most often an arbitrary number is not asked for, more likely a number in a particular range is required, or numbers within a range, maybe whole numbers only are required but not fractions or decimals, or something even more tricky like numbers divisible by 10. Here is how this is done in.

For example: <input type="number" min="0" max="10" step="2" value="6">

Here is an explanation:

- type="number" means that this is a number field.
- min="0" specifies the minimum acceptable value for this field.
- max="10" is the maximum acceptable value.
- step="2", combined with the value, defines the acceptable numbers in the min range: 0, 2, 4, and so on, up to the max value.
- value="6" is the default value.

This should be familiar value="6" the same attribute always used to specify values for form fields. That's the markup side of a number field.

Keep in mind that all of those attributes are optional. For example: A min attribute maybe specified but no max attribute. The default step value is 1, omit the step attribute unless a different step value is required then specify it. If no default value is required, the value attribute can be an empty string or even omitted altogether.

HTML5 does not stop there. These handy JavaScript methods are available for use with <input type="number"> as well:

input.stepUp(n) - Increases the field's value by n

input.stepDown(n) - Decreases the field's value by n

input.valueAsNumber() - Returns the current value as a floating-point number
(*Note: the property input.value is always a string*)

The exact interface of a number control is up to Browser manufacturers. Different browser manufacturers have implemented type="number" support in different ways.

In the desktop version of Opera, the type="number" field is rendered as a *spinbox* control, with little up and down arrows that can be clicked to change the value within the control as shown in diagram 9.3.

Diagram 9.3

Opera respects the *min*, *max* and *step* attributes, so an acceptable numeric value will always be loaded in the input box. If value is increased to the maximum, the up arrow in the *spinbox* is grayed out as shown in diagram 9.4.

Diagram 9.4

As with all the other new HTML5 input types, browsers that don't support type="number" will treat it as type="text". The default value will show up in the field since it's stored in the value attribute, but the other attributes, like min, max and step, will be ignored.

These attributes can be manually implemented in Javascript or reuse one of the many JavaScript frameworks that have already implemented spinbox controls. Just check for native HTML5 support and if this is not available manually handle this.

Numbers As Sliders

Spinboxes, as described above are not the only way to capture Numeric input from a site visitor, slider type controls can also be used to capture numeric type input.

To use slider type controls as shown in diagram 9.5, in web forms to capture numeric input from a site visitor use the following markup: <input type="range" min="0" max="10" step="2" value="6">

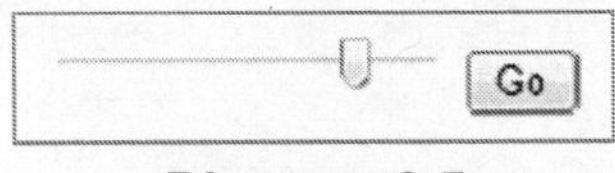

Diagram 9.5

For example:

```
<form>
    <input type="range" min="0" max="10" step="2" value="6">
    <input type="submit" value="Go">
</form>
```

The difference in capturing a numeric value from a site visitor is in the user interface. When an HTML5 enabled Browser encounters the type="range" attribute instead of a field for typing in a value, the Browser is expected to render type="range" as a *slider* control. At the time of creating this material, the latest versions of Safari, Chrome, and Opera all do this.All other Browsers simply treat the input field as type="text", so there's no reason at all why HTML coders cannot start to future proof their web page forms using the *type="range"* attribute for *input* immediately.

Date Pickers

HTML 4 did not include a date picker control. Various JavaScript frameworks offer date picker controls such as, Dojo, jQuery UI, YUI, and MooTools but to use a date picker control means one of these Javascript framework needs to be adopted by the HTML coder.

Regretfully, the use of multiple Javascript libraries with a single web page form tends to cause clashes when specific methods are invoked. HTML5 finally defines a way to include a native date picker control without having the following six attributes: date, month, week, time, date + time, and date + time – timezone.

Regretfully, Browser support is sparse. Opera 9.0 and > is the only Browser that has supported these HTML5 attributes at the time of creating this material. Diagram 9.6 shows how Opera renders an <input type="date"> field in a web form.

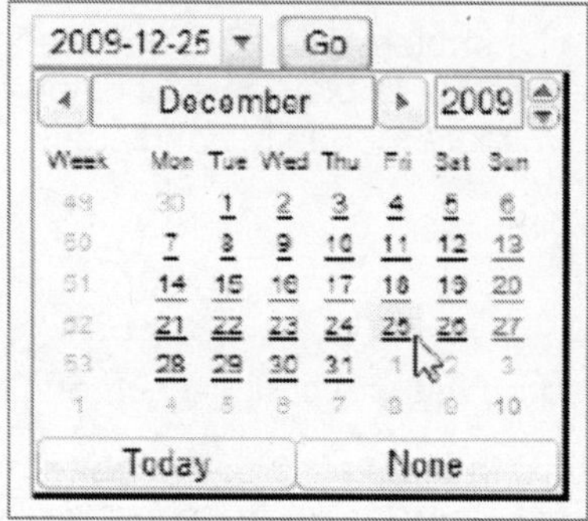

Diagram 9.6

If time is required along with date, Opera also supports <input type="date time"> as shown in diagram 9.7.

Diagram 9.7

If only need a month and year is required in the date picker, used perhaps with a credit card expiration date input field, Opera can render the date picker as shown in diagram 9.8.

Diagram 9.8

Less commonly used in web forms but available, is the facility of coders in HTML5 to provide website visitors with the ability to pick a specific week of a year with <input type="week"> as shown in diagram 9.9.

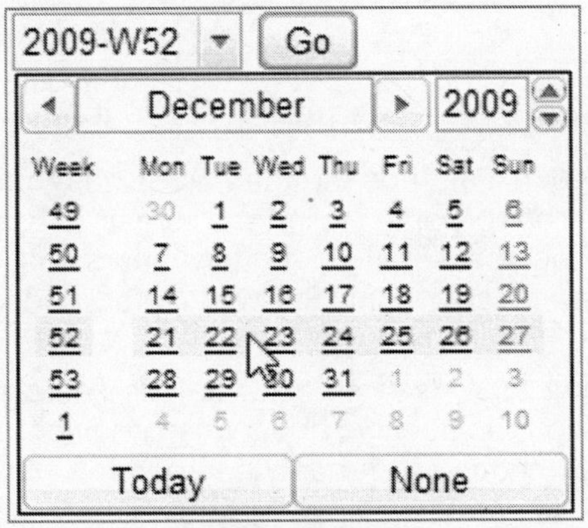

Diagram 9.9

Last but not least, a time picker will be rendered in Opera when it encounters <input type="time"> as shown in diagram 9.10.

Diagram 9.10

It just makes good programming sense to use <input type="date"> Opera users will be happy when they visit the website page, and wait for other Browsers to catch up. Hopefully they soon will. Alternatively, as explained earlier, detect whether the site visitor's Browser has native support for <input type="date">, if not then use one of the Javascript libraries to deliver a Date picker for the web form. All this goes a long way to future proofing the web form.

Search Boxes

Search. Not just Google Search or Yahoo! Search. Any search box, on any page, on any site. Amazon has a search box. Newegg has a search box. Most blogs have a search box. They are normally marked up using <input type="text"> just like every other text box used on a web page form.

With HTML5, this changes as shown below:

```
<form>
    <input name="q" type="search">
    <input type="submit" value="Find">
</form>
```

In most browsers, this codespec will make no difference at all. What will be noticed is a regular HTML4 text box. you But if Safari on the Mac OS X is being used by the site visitor, the type="search" input box it will look like diagram 9.11.

Diagram 9.11

The search input box displayed in Safari on the Mac OS X has rounded corners. When the user starts typing in this search box, Safari inserts a small "x" button on the right side of type="search" the box. Clicking the small "x" button clears the contents of the search box. Google Chrome, which shares much technology with Safari under the hood, also exhibits this behavior.

The Apple website uses <input type="search"> for its site-search box. It helps give the site a "Mac-like" feel. There is nothing Mac-specific about this behavior. It's just markup. Hence, each Browser on each platform can choose to render the search box according to platform specific conventions.

As with all the other *new input types*, Browsers that do not recognize *type="search"* attribute will treat it like type="text", so there is absolutely no reason not to start using type="search" for all web page, search boxes today.

Note: *There is one good reason why coders may not want to use <input type="search">. Safari will not apply any coder defined CSS styles to use the <input type="search"> field. User defined CSS styling will not be applied but the search field will have rounded corners.*

Color Pickers

HTML5 has also defined the type="color" input attribute. This attribute will spawn a color picker which lets the site visitor pick a color and returns that color's hexadecimal value. Regretfully, no Browser supports this input attribute yet.

Automatic Input Validation

Something really exciting that HTML5 brings to the table is automatic input validation. Consider validating site visitor input when entering an email address into a web form. This is probably done using some client-side validation in JavaScript, followed by server-side validation in PHP or Python or some other server-side scripting language.

- There are two big problems with validating email addresses in JavaScript:
  A surprising number of your visitors (probably around 10 percent) won't have JavaScript enabled
- You'll get it wrong

Determining whether a random string of characters entered in to an input field is a valid email address is unbelievably complicated. The harder you look, the more complicated it gets. It would be wonderfully easy to offload the entire email ID validation headache to the Browser.

The functionality of validating an Email ID has been present since Opera 9. The only markup required is setting the input *type attribute* to *email* i.e. (*<input type="email">*). If this code is executed in any version of Opera 9 and higher, Opera automatically offers RFC-compliant email validation, even if Javascript is disabled as shown in diagram 9.12.

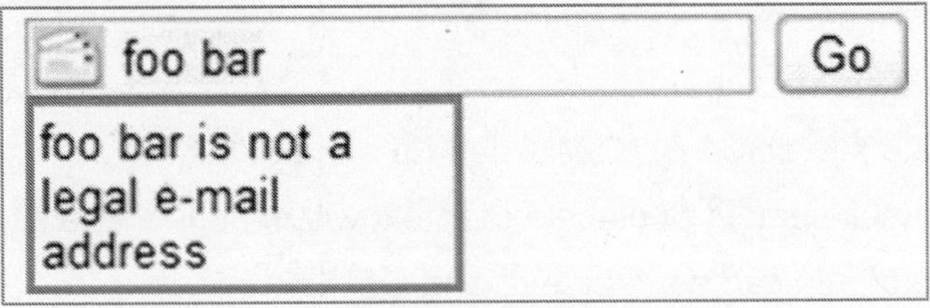

Diagram 9.12

Opera also offers validation of web addresses entered into text fields whose type has been specified as url i.e. <input type="url"> and the validation of numbers entered in into text fields whose type has been specified as number i.e. <input type="number">.

During validation of numbers Opera even takes into account the min and max attributes. Hence, Opera will not let users submit the form if they enter a number that is larger than the max value specified in the max attribute as shown in diagram 9.13. Unfortunately, no other browser supports automatic HTML5 form validation yet.

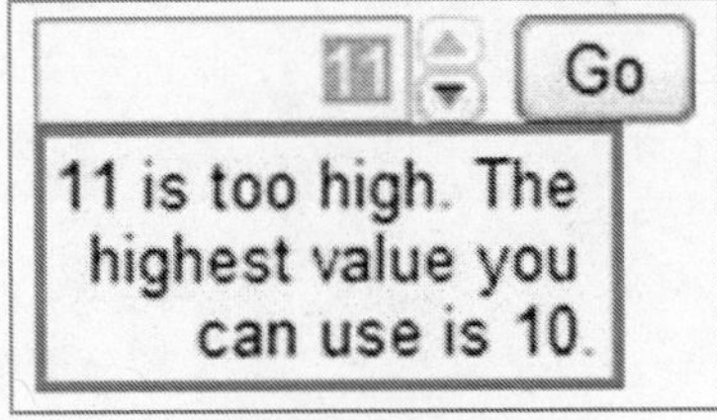

Diagram 9.13

Self Review Questions

Fill In The Blanks

1. HTML5 defines more than __________ new input types that can be used when crafting HTML based forms.
2. type="number" means that this is a ____________ field.
3. min=_________ specifies the minimum acceptable value for this field.
4. value=__________ is the default value.
5. In the desktop version of Opera, the type="number" field is rendered as a ___________ control
6. type=__________ input attribute will spawn a color picker which lets the site visitor pick a color and returns that color's hexadecimal value.

True Or False

7. Placeholder text is text displayed inside the input field as long as that field is not empty and the form cursor is on the field.
8. Web addresses known as URLs
9. The placeholder attribute can only HTML markup and not text.
10. HTML5 permits the placement of placeholder text within an input field.
11. The placeholder attribute can contain text, and HTML markup.
12. Many websites that use forms also use JavaScript to place the form cursor on the first input field of the form automatically.
13. Browsers that do not recognize the type="email" attribute added to *input* will simply render it as type="text"

Hands-on Exercise

1. Create a Registration Form which makes use of the following information. Please use all the HTML5 elements that have been learned in this chapter. Output of this exercise is shown in diagram 9.14

First Name
Last Name
Contact Number
Email Id
Website URL
Date of Birth
Abilities to Learn New Technology
Time of Registration

Registration Form

First Name:	
Last Name:	Please Enter Last Name
Contact Number:	Please Enter Contact Nun
Email Id:	Please Enter Email Addre
Website URL:	Please Enter Website UR
Date of Birth:	2000-10-10
Abilities to learn new technology:	
Time of Registration:	00:00
Submit	

Diagram 9.14

Answers To Self Review Questions

1. An Introduction To HTML5

Fill In The Blanks

1	<canvas>
2	XHTML version 1
3	HTML
4	**W**eb **A**ccessibility **I**nitiative - **A**ccessible **R**ich **I**nternet **A**pplications
5	advanced graphics, typography, animation, transitions
6	Apple, Google
7	<aside>
8	XMLHttpRequest DOM
9	Web Forms
10	Geolocation
11	HTML4
12	blog article
13	JavaScript, JavaScript DOM
14	<figure>
15	XHTML version 2.
16	web page links
17	HTML 5
18	<video>
19	HTML5
20	**W**eb **H**ypertext **A**pplication **T**echnology **W**orking **G**roup
21	<header>
22	JavaScript
23	<audio>, <video>

True Or False

1	False
2	True
3	False
4	True
5	True
6	False
7	True
8	False
9	True
10	True
11	False
12	True
13	False
14	False
15	True
16	False
17	True

2. The HTML4 Doctype Declaration

Fill In The Blanks

1 HTML5 doctype
2 *siblings*
3 rel="archives"
4 *pingback*
5 XHTML
6 *type*
7 author
8 <html>
9 *standards mode*
10 HTML4, XHTML1
11 syntactical
12 HTML5
13 `<!DOCTYPE html>`
14 characters, symbols
15 HTML
16 *<head>*
17 metadata
18 rel="external"
19 height, width
20 rel="nofollow"
21 Google

True Or False

22 True
23 True
24 True
25 False
26 True
27 False
28 True
29 False
30 True
31 True
32 True
33 False
34 False
35 True
36 False

3. HTML5 Is Open To Interpretation

Fill In The Blanks

1 Syntactical, Semantic
2 language
3 Semantic
4 HTML
5 HTML5
6 *section, article*
7 outline
8 *Article*
9 *section*
10 *aside*
11 Blog posts
12 *article*
13 *explicit*
14 *implicit*
15 Headings
16 *div*

True Or False

17 True
18 False
19 False
20 True
21 False
22 True
23 False
24 True
25 True
26 False

4. WAI-ARIA And HTML5

Fill In The Blanks

1 ARIA
2 XHTML 1.1
3 role
4 *banner* role
5 *banner*
6 *contentinfo*
7 *main*
8 *navigation*
9 *note*
10 *search*

True Or False

11 False
12 False
13 True
14 False
15 True
16 True
17 False
18 False
19 True

5. Drawing With The Canvas Element

Fill In The Blanks

1 Canvas
2 quadraticCurveTo();
3 JavaScript
4 strokeRect
5 line art
6 *beginPath()*
7 lines, arcs, text
8 bezierCurveTo();
9 filled-in rectangles

True Or False

1 False
2 True
3 True
4 False
5 True
6 False
7 False
8 True
9 True

6. Video On The Web

Fill In The Blanks

1 <video>
2 video, audio
3 AVI, MP4
4 .mp4, .m4v
5 MPEG-4
6 Adobe
7 Ogg
8 video codec
9 words *coder, decoder*
10 Lossless
11 *profiles*
12 H.264
13 Audio
14 two

True Or False

15 False
16 True
17 True
18 False
19 True
20 False
21 False
22 True
23 False
24 False

7. Geo Location In HTML5

Fill In The Blanks

1 location
2 navigator.geolocation
3 coords.latitude, coords.longitude, coords.accuracy

True Or False

4 True
5 False
6 False

8. Working Off-Line In HTML5

Fill In The Blanks

1 *text/cache-manifest*
2 *{filename}*.manifest
3 CACHE MANIFEST
4 explicit, fallback, online whitelist
5 *header*
6 *explicit*
7 NETWORK:
8 CACHE:
9 fallback

True Or False

10 False
11 False
12 True
13 False
14 False
15 True
16 True
17 False

9. Building Forms In HTML5

Fill In The Blanks

1 twelve
2 number
3 "0"
4 "6"
5 *spinbox*
6 "color"

True Or False

7 False
8 True
9 False
10 True
11 False
12 True
13 True

Solutions To Hands On Exercises

Chapter 2 - The HTML4 Doctype Declaration

1)

```
<!DOCTYPE html>
<html>

   <head>
      <meta charset="utf-8">
   </head>

<body>

   <header>
      <hgroup>
         <h1>Lorem Ipsum</h1>
         <h2>Come learn how to use lorem ipsum</h2>
      </hgroup>

      <p>1st January 2011</p>

       <nav>
          <ul>
             <li>Home  | </li>
             <li>About  | </li>
             <li>Demo  | </li>
             <li>Affiliates  | </li>
             <li>Contact Us</li>
          </ul>
        <nav>
</header>
```

```
Lorem Ipsum
Presenter: John
    Lorem Ipsum is simply dummy text of the printing and typesetting industry. Lorem Ipsum has been the industry's standard dummy text ever since the 1500s, when an unknown printer took a galley of type and scrambled it to make a type specimen book. It has survived not only five centuries, but also the leap into electronic typesetting, remaining essentially unchanged. It was popularized in the 1960s with the release of Letraset sheets containing Lorem Ipsum passages, and more recently with desktop publishing software like Aldus PageMaker including versions of Lorem Ipsum.
<footer>
        <p>&copy;2011. All Right Reserved. <br />
        Terms and Conditions | Privacy Policy</p>
</footer>
</body>
</html>
```

Chapter 3 - HTML5 Is Open To Interpretation

1)

```
<!DOCTYPE html>
<html>
<head>
    <meta charset="utf-8">
    <title>Lorem Ipsum</title>
</head>
<body>
    <header>
        <hgroup>
            <h1>Lorem Ipsum</h1>
            <h2>Come learn how to use lorem ipsum</h2>
        </hgroup><!-- hgroup  ENDS -->
        <p>1st January 2011</p>
         <nav>
           <ul>
               <li>Home  | </li>
               <li>About  | </li>
               <li>Demo  | </li>
               <li>Affiliates  | </li>
               <li>Contact Us</li>
           </ul>
       <nav><!-- nav  ENDS -->
    </header><!-- header  ENDS -->
    <div id="divMainContent">
        <section class="track">
            <article>
                <header>
                    <hgroup>
                        <h3>Lorem Ipsum</h3>
                    </hgroup>
```

```
        <figure>
            <img src="" alt="" >
            <figcaption>Presenter: John</figcaption>
        </figure>
    </header>

    <p>Lorem Ipsum is simply dummy text of the printing
    and typesetting industry. Lorem Ipsum has been the industry's
    standard dummy text ever since the 1500s, when an unknown
    printer took a galley of type and scrambled it to make a type
    specimen book. It has survived not only five centuries, but also
    the leap into electronic   typesetting, remaining essentially
    unchanged. </p>

    <p>It was popularized in the 1960s with the release of Letraset
    sheets containing Lorem Ipsum passages, and more recently
    with desktop publishing software like Aldus
    PageMaker including versions of Lorem Ipsum. There are many
    variations of passages of Lorem Ipsum available, but the
    majority have suffered alteration in some form, by
    injected humour, or randomized words which don't look even
    slightly believable. </p>
</article>

<article>
    <header>
        <hgroup>
            <h3>Google vs Microsoft:
            The game becomes filthier</h3>
        </hgroup>

        <figure>
            <img src="" alt="">
            <figcaption>Presenter: Vidya</figcaption>
        </figure>
    </header>
```

```
    <p>Google is enjoying its dominance in the search arena,
    which is challenged by Microsoft Corp, the software giant, which
    had updated its search engine with a
    new Decision Engine, called Bing in June last year. While,
    Microsoft leads in operating system, enterprise applications and
    web browsers market, Google holds the lead
    in search arena.</p>
    <p>Meanwhile, the search giant is gearing up in various fields
    like operating system, web based apps and web browser, to
    compete with the software giant.
    But, besides healthy competition, the two biggies are also trying
    other ways out to beat each other in various fields. </p>
</article>
<article>
    <header>
        <hgroup>
            <h3>Essential add-ons for Twitter and
            FaceBook</h3>
        </hgroup>

        <figure>
            <img src="" alt="">
            <figcaption>Presenter: Sneha</figcaption>
        </figure>
    </header>
    <p>FaceBook is the world's number one social networking
    website with over 400 million active users worldwide. Similarly,
    Twitter is a leading micro-blogging social website, where users
    can send and read messages called as tweets, consists of upto
    140 characters. Recently, Twitter has achieved yet another
    milestone by reaching 10 billion "tweets."</p>
```

```
            <p>Today, people are actively using these mediums to connect
            socially with their friends, reaching new markets and also for
            promoting their business profiles.
            Users love to play games on the FaceBook like FarmVille, Mafia
            Wars, and also create their company's social profile to promote
            or make the followers on its home page.</p>
        </article>
    </section> <!-- track-->
    <aside id="aideSidebar">
        <form>SEARCH</form>
        <section id="subBrought2uBy">
            <h3>BROUGHT TO YOU BY</h3>
            <section id="subSponsors">
                <h4>OUR SPONSORS</h4>
            </section> <!-- subSponsors ENDS -->
            <section id="subPartners">
                <h4>OUR PARTNERS</h4>
            </section> <!-- subPartners ENDS -->
        </section> <!-- subBrought2uBy ENDS -->
    </aside> <!-- aideSidebar ENDS -->
</div> <!-- divMainContent  ENDS -->
<footer>
    <section id="secSubscribe">
        <h3>REGISTER WITH OUR SITE</h3>
        <p>Subscribe to our monthly newsletter to stay up-to date with the new
        technologies</p>
        <form>
            <label>User Name:</label><br />
            <label>Password:</label><br />
            <label>Confirm Password:</label><br />
            <label>Email Id:</label><br />
```

```
                <input type="button" value="Register" />
            </form>
        </section><!-- secSubscribe Ends -->

        <p>&copy; All Rights Reserved.</p>

        <section id="secFooterMenu">
            Terms and Conditions | Privacy Policy
        </section><!-- secFooterMenu Ends -->

    </footer><!-- footer  ENDS -->

</body>
</html>
```

Chapter 4 - WAI-ARIA And HTML5

1)

```
<!DOCTYPE html>
<html>
<head>
    <meta charset="utf-8">
    <title>Personal Profile Professional Profile</title>
</head>
<body>
    <header role="banner">
        <hgroup role="heading">
            <h1>Lorem Ipsum</h1>
            <h2>Come learn how to use lorem ipsum</h2>
        </hgroup><!-- hgroup  ENDS -->
        <p>1st January 2011</p>
        <nav role="navigation">
            <ul>
              <li>Home | </li>
              <li>About | </li>
              <li>Demo | </li>
              <li>Affiliates | </li>
              <li>Contact Us</li>
            </ul>
        <nav><!-- nav  ENDS -->
    </header><!-- header  ENDS -->
    <div id="divMainContent">
        <section class="track">
            <article>
                <header>
                    <hgroup>
                        <h3>Lorem Ipsum</h3>
                    </hgroup>
```

```
        <figure>
            <img src="" alt="" >
            <figcaption>Presenter: John</figcaption>
        </figure>
    </header>

    <p>Lorem Ipsum is simply dummy text of the printing and
    typesetting industry. Lorem Ipsum has been the industry's
    standard dummy text ever since the 1500s,
    when an unknown printer took a galley of type and scrambled it
    to make a type specimen book. It has survived not only five
    centuries, but also the leap into electronic
    typesetting, remaining essentially unchanged. </p>

    <p>It was popularized in the 1960s with the release of Letraset
    sheets containing Lorem Ipsum passages, and more recently
    with desktop publishing software like Aldus
    PageMaker including versions of Lorem Ipsum. There are many
    variations of passages of Lorem Ipsum available, but the
    majority have suffered alteration in some form, by
    injected humour, or randomized words which don't look even
    slightly believable. </p>
</article>

<article>

    <header>
        <hgroup>
            <h3>Google vs Microsoft: The game becomes
            filthier</h3>
        </hgroup>

        <figure>
            <img src="" alt="">
            <figcaption>Presenter: Sneha</figcaption>
        </figure>
    </header>
```

```
        <p>Google is enjoying its dominance in the search arena, which
        is challenged by Microsoft Corp, the software giant, which had
        updated its search engine with a
        new Decision Engine, called Bing in June last year. While,
        Microsoft leads in operating system, enterprise applications and
        web browsers market, Google holds the lead
        in search arena.</p>
        <p>Meanwhile, the search giant is gearing up in various fields
        like operating system, web based apps and web browser, to
        compete with the software giant.
        But, besides healthy competition, the two biggies are also trying
        other ways out to beat each other in various fields. </p>
      </article>
    </section> <!-- track-->
    <aside id="aideSidebar" role="complementary">
      <form>SEARCH</form>
      <section id="subBrought2uBy">
        <h3>BROUGHT TO YOU BY</h3>
        <section id="subSponsors">
          <h4>OUR SPONSORS</h4>
        </section> <!-- subSponsors ENDS -->
        <section id="subPartners">
          <h4>OUR PARTNERS</h4>
        </section> <!-- subPartners ENDS -->
      </section> <!-- subBrought2uBy ENDS -->
    </aside> <!-- aideSidebar ENDS -->
  </div> <!-- divMainContent  ENDS -->
```

```
    <footer>
        <section id="secSubscribe">
            <h3>REGISTER WITH OUR SITE</h3>
            <p>Subscribe to our monthly newsletter to stay up-to date with the
            new technologies</p>
            <form>
                <label>User Name:</label><br />
                <label>Password:</label><br />
                <label>Confirm Password:</label><br />
                <label>Email Id:</label><br />
                <input type="button" value="Register" />
            </form>
        </section><!-- secSubscribe Ends -->

        <p role="contentinfo">&copy; All Rights Reserved.</p>

        <section id="secFooterMenu">
            Terms and Conditions | Privacy Policy
        </section><!-- secFooterMenu Ends -->

    </footer><!-- footer  ENDS -->

</body>
</html>
```

Chapter 5 - Drawing With The Canvas Element

1) Create a “No Parking” sign using the HTML5 elements that have been learned in this chapter.

```
<html>
<head>
    <title>Chapter 5 - Drawing with the Canvas element –
        Solution for Hands-On-Exercise 1 </title>
    <style type="text/css">
        canvas { border: 2px solid red; }
    </style>
    <script type="text/javascript">
    function loaderCanvas()
    {
        var canvas=document.getElementById('canvas');
        var context=canvas.getContext('2d');
        context.beginPath();
        context.fillStyle="#000";
        context.font="40pt sans-serif";
        context.fillText("NO",120,50);
        context.closePath();
        context.beginPath();
        context.fillStyle="#fff";
        context.strokeStyle="red";
        context.lineWidth=4;
        context.arc(150, 150, 75, 0,Math.PI*2, true);
        context.shadowOffsetX=2;
        context.shadowOffsetY=2;
        context.shadowBlur=3;
        context.stroke();
```

```
        context.shadowOffsetX=0;
        context.shadowOffsetY=0;
        context.shadowBlur=0;

        context.fill();
        context.closePath();

        context.beginPath();

        context.fillStyle="#000";
        context.font="100pt sans-serif";
        context.fillText("P",114,205);

        context.moveTo(100,95);
        context.lineTo(210,210);

        context.lineWidth=4;

        context.stroke();

        context.closePath();

        context.beginPath();

        context.fillStyle="#000";
        context.font="40pt sans-serif";
        context.fillText("PARKING",50,300);

        context.closePath();

    }

    </script>

</head>

<body onLoad=" loaderCanvas();">

    <canvas id="canvas" width="350" height="350"></canvas>

</body>
</html>
```

2) Create a "Warning Sign" using the HTML5 elements that have been learned in this chapter.

```
<html>
<head>
   <title>Chapter 5 - Drawing with the Canvas element –
   Solution for Hands-On-Exercise 2 </title>
   <style type="text/css">
      canvas { border: 2px solid red; }
   </style>
   <script type="text/javascript">
   function loaderCanvas()
   {
      var canvas=document.getElementById('canvas');
      var context=canvas.getContext('2d');
      context.beginPath();
      context.StrokeStyle="red";
      context.lineWidth=5;
      context.strokeStyle="red";
      context.moveTo(75,50);
      context.lineTo(125,125);
      context.lineTo(25,125);
      context.closePath();
      context.shadowColor="#fff";
      context.shadowOffsetX=2;
      context.shadowOffsetY=2;
      context.shadowBlur=3;
      context.stroke();
      context.shadowOffsetX=0;
      context.shadowOffsetY=0;
      context.shadowBlur=0;
      context.fillStyle="black";
      context.font="60px sans-serif";
```

```
        context.fillText("!",63,120);
        context.closePath();
    }
    </script>

</head>
<body onLoad="loaderCanvas();">
    <canvas id="canvas" width="150" height="150"></canvas>
</body>
</html>
```

Chapter 6 - Video On The Web

1)

```
<!DOCTYPE html>
<html>

<head>
    <title>Chapter 6 - Video On The Web - Solution to Hands-On-Exercise</title>
</head>

<body>
    <h1>HTML 5 Video</h1>
    <video height="100" width="400"  src="handsonexercise.ogg" autoplay
    type='video/ogg; codecs="theora, vorbis"' preload controls >

    <object width="320" height="240" type="application/x-shockwave-flash"
    data="flowplayer-3.2.1.swf">
        <param name="movie" value="flowplayer-3.2.1.swf" />
        <param name="allowfullscreen" value="true" />
        <param name="flashvars" value='config={"clip": {"url":
        "http://wearehugh.com/dih5/good/bbb_480p.mp4", "autoPlay":false,
        "autoBuffering":true}}' />
        <p>Download video as <a href="handsonexercise.ogv">Ogg</a>.</p>
    </object>

    </video>

</body>

</html>
```

Chapter 7 Geo Location In HTML5

1)

```
<!DOCTYPE html>
<html>
<head>
    <meta charset="utf-8">

    <title>Chapter 7 - Geo Location In HTML5 - Solution to Hands on Exercise Using
    Divs</title>

    <script type="text/javascript" src="js/modernizr-1.6.min.js"
    language="javascript"></script>
    <script type="text/javascript">
        function getGeoLocation()
        {
            if (Modernizr.geolocation)
            {
                document.getElementById("divBrowSuppGeoLoc").innerHTML =
                "Your Browser supports GeoLocation";
    navigator.geolocation.watchPosition(show_map,errHandler,{enableHighAccuracy: true});
            }
            else
            {
                document.getElementById("divBrowSuppGeoLoc").innerHTML =
                "Sorry Your Browser does not support GeoLocation. Upgrade
                your Browser or use a different Browser.";
            }
        }
        function show_map(position)
        {
            var latitude = position.coords.latitude;
            var longitude = position.coords.longitude;
            var accuracy  = position.coords.accuracy;
```

```
            document.getElementById("divMyLatitude").innerHTML =
            "Latitude = " + latitude;

            document.getElementById("divMyLongitude").innerHTML =
            "Longitude = " + longitude;

            document.getElementById("divAccuracy").innerHTML =
            "Accuracy = " + accuracy;
        }
        function errHandler(error)
        {
            document.getElementById("divAccuracy").innerHTML = "Error while retrieving
current position. Error code: " + error.code;
        }
    </script>

</head>
<body>

    <input type="button" value="Get GeoLocation" onClick="getGeoLocation()"/>
    <br /><br />

    <div id="divBrowSuppGeoLoc"></div><br />

    <div id="divMyLatitude"></div><br />

    <div id="divMyLongitude"></div><br />

    <div id="divAccuracy"></div><br />

    <div id="divError"></div><br />

</body>
</html>
```

Chapter 9 – Building Forms In HTML5

1) Create a Registration Form

```
<!DOCTYPE HTML>
<html>
<head>
   <title>Registration Form</title>
   <meta charset="utf-8">
   <style type="text/css">
      #fsRegiForm { width:400px; }
   </style>
</head>
<body>
<form method="get">
   <fieldset id="fsRegiForm">
      <legend>Registration Form</legend>
      <table cellspacing="0" cellpadding="4" border="1" width="100%">
         <tr>
            <td><label for="name">First Name</label>:</td>
            <td><input
            arprops=",,149px,14px,none,none,static,auto,visible,,,"
            name="fname" id="fname"
            placeholder="Please Enter First Name" autofocus=""
            type="text"></td>
         </tr>
         <tr>
            <td><label for="name">Last Name</label>:</td>
            <td><input
            arprops=",,149px,14px,none,none,static,auto,visible,,,"
            name="lname" id="lname"
            placeholder="Please Enter Last Name" type="text"></td>
         </tr>
```

```
<tr>
    <td><label for="telephone">Contact Number</label>:</td>
    <td><input
    arprops=",,149px,14px,none,none,static,auto,visible,,,"
    name="telephone" id="telephone"
    placeholder="Please Enter Contact Number" type="tel"></td>
</tr>
<tr>
    <td><label for="email">Email Id</label>: </td>
    <td><input
    arprops=",,149px,14px,none,none,static,auto,visible,,,"
    name="email" id="email"
    placeholder="Please Enter Email Address" type="email"></td>
</tr>
<tr>
    <td><label for="website">Website URL</label>:</td>
    <td><input
    arprops=",,149px,14px,none,none,static,auto,visible,,,"
    name="website" id="website"
    placeholder="Please Enter Website URL" type="url"></td>
</tr>
<tr>
    <td><label for="DOB">Date of Birth</label>:</td>
    <td><input
    arprops=",,149px,14px,none,none,static,auto,visible,,,"
    name="DOB" id="DOB" value="2000-10-10" type="date"></td>
</tr>
<tr>
    <td><label for="AbilTech">Abilities to learn new
    technology</label>:</td>
    <td><input
    arprops=",,149px,14px,none,none,static,auto,visible,,," min="1"
    max="5" step="1" name="AbilTech" id="AbilTech"
    type="range"></td>
```

```
            </tr>
            <tr>
                <td><label for="AbilTech">Time of Registration</label>:</td>
                <td><input type="time" value="00:00"></td>
            </tr>
            <tr>
                <td colspan="2"><input value="Submit" type="button"></td>
            </tr>
        </table>
    </fieldset>
</form>
</body>
</html>
```

Section 2

CSS3

10. Using CSS Today

For several years now web page designers and programmers have been using CSS to create flexible, accessible websites that are visually pleasing and are easy to maintain and expand when necessary.

Because different Browsers handled HTML code differently, generally causing web pages to render differently in different Browsers, great looking in some and horribly broken in others, in 2001, Jeffrey Zeldman wrote a great article *To Hell With Bad Browsers*, signaling the dawn of the CSS Age. If you would like to read that slice of CSS history here is the link http://www.alistapart.com/articles/tohell/.

It was the content of this article that woke a lot of web designers to the power and use of CSS. CSS rules began to be used for a lot more than just setting fonts and font color and styling web page links to blend well with webpage content. Several years have gone by. A ton of articles have been shared describing various techniques for doing something close to magic on web pages. This helps keep clients very happy with jaw dropping visuals supporting well crafted web page content.

2001 to about 2006 was an exciting time of experimentation, pushing of boundaries, and figuring out complex ways of handling web pages to render exactly the same across multiple Browsers and multiple versions of the same Browser. All the while keeping a very sharp eye on flexibility, improved accessibility, and reducing code spec to the minimum possible.

Somewhere around 2006 or so, all the buzz around CSS on various forums and Blogs went quiet. Most of the web page content formatting issues were solved and documented. Common Browser bugs had multiple workarounds available.

Subsequent to 2006 was the time when Browser changes were relatively few and far between and largely cosmetic. This was a period when re-useable codespec came into being, best practices were established and perhaps things got a bit complacent for CSS coders in general.

Then things changed rapidly, Browsers began to change rapidly, the changes were more to conform to standards suggested by W3C and other bodies. Browser updations started coming out regularly FireFox and Safari, began to gain market share slowly but substantially. These Browser manufacturers thrived on a quick development cycle compared to IE, they brought solid adherence to standards along with quite a few experimental properties as well.

It was Browser vendors that pushed CSS codespec significantly forward periodically.

CSS3, the next big leap forward in CSS coding, has morphed into series of modules that are designed to be implemented separately and independently from each other.

The modular approach to CSS3 growth is a good thing. This modular approach has enabled sections of CSS3 code spec to move faster than other sections. This in turn has encouraged Browser manufacturers to implement those sections of CSS3 specification into their Browser core code that are completed (*or so close to completion that their logical end is insight*) before the entire CSS3 specification is considered finished.

W3C explains that they have adopted this modular approach because rather than attempting to shove dozens of updates into a single monolithic CSS3 specification, it is much easier (*and more efficient to be able to update individual pieces of the CSS3 specification*) when agreement has been reached.

Modules enable CSS3 specification to be updated quicker and faster, thus allowing the CSS3 specification to evolve more flexibly and quickly.

The obvious benefit here is that Browser manufacturers adopt such updated modules into their Browser core code giving rise to faster update cycles for Browsers that expand their support for CSS3 with every update. This empowers web designers the ability to use many CSS3 properties before waiting until they become full-fledged CSS3 recommendations, perhaps a few years from now.

Hence it's far more practical to focus on the sections of CSS3 specifications that are currently implemented and usable in Browsers today. It is these CSS3 sections that this material handles. A great deal of CSS3 skill can be acquired by simply dissecting and learning from real world CSS3 examples in use in a multitude of web pages today.

CSS3 can be sued by anyone, instead of waiting until the entire CSS3 specification comes into being, there are several CSS3 modules already implemented in most modern Browsers FireFox, Opera, Safari, Chrome and the truth is web designers can begin to use CSS3 right now.

Note: *As is expected IE is not a Browser that is attempting to change its core code to empower web designers to use CSS3, although in their defense, Microsoft has promised that IE 9.0 will be CSS3 compliant. Only time will reveal exactly how many CSS3 modules have be adopted within IE 9.0.*

Fortunately web designers do not have to think differently or make dramatic changes in the way they craft websites in order to use CSS3 today. Today all web designers can use CSS3 with any project. In this material how CSS3 code spec is blended into web page code spec is carefully chosen based on real world experience.

Web designers have been doing a ton of things correctly over the past several years, they have been building websites based upon a foundation of web standards, such as semantic HTML and CSS, leaving must of the web page's interaction and effects to technologies such as Flash and JavaScript.

Today with CSS3 properties being slowly, but steadily introduced in modern Browsers, some web page's interaction and effects (*normally left to other technologies*) can be shifted to style sheets.

Most website designers lean heavily on the design side rather than the programming side when creating a user interface, hence the more that they can do for a user interface to make it eye catching and useful at the same time using familiar tools such as HTML and CSS the better.

CSS3 is for web designers. They can start using portions of CSS3 today. All they need to know is what can be used in CSS3 and exactly how use this in web design bound to real world examples.

When applying CSS3 to a website's visual experience, it's necessary to group things into two categories that which is critical and that which is non critical as shown in (Table 1).

Web page areas like branding, usability, and layout are crucial to any website's success, and as such utilizing technology that's not fully supported by all browsers would be a risky there. For example, in the evolving CSS3 specifications there are multiple drafts for controlling web page layout something drastically needed.

CRITICAL	**NON-CRITICAL**
Branding	Interaction
Usability	Visual Rewards
Accessibility	Feedback
Layout	Movement

Table 1

The *float* of a *div* is normally used to handle the visual layout of web pages for years now. A real layout engine is an absolute necessity. Having said that, the three new CSS3 layout modules have not yet been implemented by any Browser manufacturer yet.

The CSS3 layout engine specifications are currently confusing and difficult to grasp and probably not the final solution. Hence, this specification is going to change after a while, hence currently, CSS3 is really not the correct tool for defining page layouts as of the time of creating this material.

To understand the non critical issues of a web page, these could be hover, focus, form elements, animation and so on that have been implemented to an extent in all modern Browsers, hence this is a great time to begin to implement CSS3 in these areas of a web page right now.

This material is focused on applying CSS3 to these areas of a web page while keeping the important characteristics of any web page intact for all Browsers irrespective of how much (*or how little*) the Browser supports CSS3.

Since the focus is strictly on non-critical areas of a website's visuals, CSS3 can be used freely to enrich a user's interaction with the website without worrying that the core message of the website, its layout and accessibility will not be damaged in any way.

CSS3 Properties That Are Usable Today

Since the web page areas in which CSS3 can be safely and intelligently applied have been identified its now time to identify the core CSS3 properties that can be used today, simply because most modern Browsers have already implemented these in their core code. Hence, it is practical to use these CSS3 properties today.

Large chunks of CSS3 specifications have not yet been implemented in any Browser. Hence, it makes a great deal of sense focusing on what actually works in CSS3 across Browsers, and luckily there is a fair amount now that does.

Here is a quick look at a relatively small set of core CSS3 properties that will be used in this material. They are merely being introduced here. They will be examined in greater depth later in this material when advanced syntax and real world usage are being examined later.

border-radius

This CSS3 property rounds the corners of an element with the specified radius value.

This CSS3 property is supported in Safari 3+, Chrome 3+, Firefox 1+, Opera 10.5+, and IE9 Beta.

For example:

```
.divLoginReg {
border-radius: 10px;
}
```

text-shadow

This CSS3 property adds a shadow to hypertext, with options for the *direction* of the shadow, *amount* of blur, and *color* of the shadow.

Supported in Safari 1.1+, Chrome 2+, Firefox 3.1+, and Opera 9.5+.

For example:

```
H1 H2 H3 {
text-shadow: 1px 1px 2px #999;
}
```

box-shadow

This CSS3 property adds a shadow to an element. *Identical syntax to textshadow*

Supported in Safari 3+, Chrome 3+, Firefox 3.5+, Opera 10.5+, and IE9 Beta.

For example:

```
divAdvert1
{
    box-shadow: 1px 1px 2px #999;
}
```

This CSS3 property adds multiple background images to an element (*separated with commas*), as opposed to just one background image as in the past.

Supported in Safari 1.3+, Chrome 2+, Firefox 3.6+, Opera 10.5+, and IE9 Beta.

For example:

```
body {
background: url(image1.png) no-repeat top left,
url(image2.png) repeat-x bottom left,
url(image3.png) repeat-y top right;
}
```

opacity

This CSS3 property defines how opaque an element is. A value of 1 means completely opaque, while a value of 0 means fully transparent.

Supported in Safari 1.2+, Chrome 1+, Firefox 1.5+, Opera 9+, and IE9 Beta.

For example:

```
.divFooterIcons {
/* .divFooterIcons will be 50% transparent */
opacity: 0.5;
}
```

RGBA

This is not a CSS3 property, but rather a new color model introduced in CSS3. This adds the ability to specify a level of opacity to an element to which the CSS rule is bound along with an RGB color value.

Supported in Safari 3.2+, Chrome 3+, Firefox 3+, Opera 10+, and IE9 Beta.

For example:

```
.divCopyright {
/* .divCopyright black with an opacity of 75%  */
color: rgba(0, 0, 0, 0.75);
}
```

The above examples of CSS3 properties are far from exhaustive. CSS3 contains many more properties and tools, many of which are still being developed and are not yet implemented in any browser.

Every CSS3 property mentioned above has a reached a certain threshold of Browser support, they work in at least two of the major browsers, in some cases, support is promised in future versions of Internet Explorer and Opera.

Hence, now there is a nice concise list of CSS3 properties to play with, based on their relatively decent support in Safari, Chrome, Firefox, and Opera. These CSS3 properties do not work across the board yet. This material will help you on how to plan for such non-uniform, Browser support, later in the book.

Vendor Specific Prefixes

The CSS3 specification is a series of modules that are being slowly rolled out by Browser manufacturers. In some cases the roll out involves experimental support. What this means is that while the CSS3 specification is being debated at W3C, a Browser manufacturer might choose to add support for certain CSS3 properties anyway, thus permitting these CSS3 properties to be tested in the real world.

This is a healthy part of the CSS3 evolutionary process, the feedback obtained from such experimental usage is often used to make specific, useful and at times significant changes in the CSS3 specification.

Alternatively, a Browser manufacturer may want to introduce an experimental property that is not yet part of any module in the CSS3 specification being created at W3C, but may become one at a later date. Such experimental properties are handled by Browser manufacturers by the use of a Browser vendor specific prefix such as: *-webkit-border-radius*

The hyphenated prefixed, keyword attached to the beginning of a CSS3 property flags this property as *work in progress* specific to that Browser's implementation and interpretation of this evolving specification. If and when this experimentation becomes part of a finished CSS3 module, Browsers will support the non-prefixed property name from then on.

Each Browser manufacturer has their own prefix, essentially *namespacing* their experimental properties. Other Browsers will simply ignore the CSS3 rules containing prefixes that they do not recognize. Hence the CSS codespec will throw up no errors.

Table 2 shows the most widely-used Browser manufacturers and their associated prefixes. The WebKit, Mozilla, and Opera prefixes will be used, as they pertain to CSS3, in the examples in the material ahead.

Browser icon	Name	Hyphenated prefix used
	WebKit	–webkit–
	Mozilla	–moz–
	Opera	–o–
	Konqueror	–khtml–
	Microsoft	–ms–
	Chrome	–chrome–

Table 2

How Vendor Based CSS3 Prefixes Work

Assume that an element with rounded corners whose radius was 5 pixels was required.

Here is the CSS codespec that would do it.

```
.divPgHeader {
-webkit-border-radius: 5px;
-moz-border-radius: 5px;
border-radius: 5px;
}
```

WebKit, the Browser engine used in Safari, mobile Safari, and Chrome and *Gecko* the browser engine used in Firefox each support the *border-radius* property using their own vendor prefixed names. Opera supports this property without a vendor prefix. IE9 will also support *border-radius* without a vendor prefix.

Optimal Ordering

When using Browser vendor specific prefixes, it's important to keep in mind the order in which such formatting rules are listed in the CSS file. Vendor-prefixed properties are listed first, *followed by the non prefixed CSS3 property*.

Why put the actual CSS3 property last? Because such CSS type styling will likely work in more Browsers in the future, progressively enhancing the webpage designs as Browsers evolve and support such properties.

Hence, when a Browser manufacturer finally implements support for the specific CSS3 property as defined in the CSS3 specification, that real property will be used and experimental names ones will be simply be ignored. Hence non prefixed CSS property name comes last in the list. Should the implementation for the vendor-specific CSS3 property differ from the implementation of the real CSS3 property, being placed last helps ensure that the final standard CSS3 property reigns supreme.

This approach is really a great way forward. It's certainly not the messy approach that non-CSS3 solutions might bring to the table and an important part of the evolution of the CSS3 specification as well.

Additionally, by using these vendor specific CSS3 properties, the behavior of these properties can be tested giving valuable feedback to Browser makers before the CSS3 specification becomes final.

Such vendor specific prefixes are always tied to proposed CSS3 standards. Hence, this is the big difference from other hack type of CSS workarounds used periodically to solve cross-browser issues.

Some programmers may compare Browser vendor specific prefixes to syntax exploits used to target specific Browser versions (for example, *using w\idth: 200px or _width: 200px to target specific versions of IE*). This is not true, using Browser vendor specific prefixes are really an important part of the CSS3 standards implementation process, which allows the evolution of a CSS3 property in the real-world.

Hence, do not be overly concerned over Browser vendor specific prefixes. Use them knowing that you are a part of a process that allows CSS3 work to get done today, while paving the way toward a future when all such Browser vendor specific CSS3 prefixes can be dropped completely.

Repeating Such Properties In The CSS Rule Sheet

Currently it may be a bit of a pain to repeat what seems like the same CSS3 property three or four times so that the web page will work correctly in different Browsers, and I might agree with you on that. The reality is that non-CSS3 solutions would likely require inflexible and more complex code, that maybe a just little less repetitive.

Such CSS3 properties will not have to be repeated forever, for now it's just a temporary step to permit different Browsers to understand same CSS3 property due to varying CSS3 implementations between Browsers.

To go forward and start doing magical things with the handful of usable CSS3 properties (*and their respective vendor prefixes*), let's get a grasp of CSS transitions.

Understanding CSS transitions and how they operate will help web designers combine them with other CSS3 properties to create wonderful user experiences on a website.

Self Review Questions

Fill In The Blanks

1. Experimental properties are handled by Browser manufacturers by the use of a Browser vendor specific prefix such as ___________
2. ___________ CSS3 property adds a shadow to an element.
3. The ___________ approach to CSS3 growth is a good thing.
4. The ___________ of a *div* is normally used to handle the visual layout of web pages.
5. ___________ CSS3 property rounds the corners of an element with the specified radius value.
6. ___________ CSS3 property adds a shadow to hypertext, with options for the *direction* of the shadow, *amount* of blur, and *color* of the shadow.
7. A value of ___________ means completely opaque, while a value of ___________ means fully transparent.
8. ___________ *is identical syntax to textshadow.*
9. Opacity CSS3 property defines how ___________ an element is.
10. RGBA is not a ___________, but rather a new color model introduced in CSS3.

True Or False

11. Each Browser manufacturer does not have their own prefix, essentially *namespacing* their experimental properties.
12. When using Browser vendor specific prefixes, it's important to keep in mind the order in which such formatting rules are listed in the CSS file.
13. Vendor specific prefixes are somteimes tied to proposed CSS3 standards.
14. Vendor-prefixed properties are listed first, *followed by the non prefixed CSS3 property.*
15. The reality is that non-CSS3 solutions would likely require inflexible and more complex code, that maybe a just little less repetitive.
16. Some programmers may compare Browser vendor specific prefixes to syntax exploits used to target specific Browser versions.
17. border-radius CSS3 property is not supported in Safari 3+, Chrome 3+, Firefox 1+, Opera 10.5+, and IE9 Beta.
18. *box-shadow is not identical syntax to textshadow.*
19. RGBA is a CSS3 property.
20. The CSS3 specification is a series of modules that are being slowly rolled out by Browser manufacturers.

11. Understanding CSS Transitions

Transitions in webpages were normally driven by JavaScript. The best remembered example being a menu item that magically changed when the mouse cursor hovered over it or when it was clicked on. The image used to represent the menu item magically seemed to transition to something else entirely.

This transition was driven by several lines of JavaScript, which used many different built-in JavaScript methods, which in turn accessed multiple images stored in the /images folder (*hopefully*) and swapped these images faster than the eye could see, so that the user did not really notice the actually image transition process but just noticed that the menu image had changed.

As mentioned in Chapter 10, web designers can start using some CSS3 properties right away as long as where they are used in a web page is carefully chosen.

This is true for CSS transitions as well. CSS transitions will not replace existing technologies like Flash, JavaScript, or **S**calable **V**ector **G**raphics (i.e. *SVG*) without broader Browser support, but as of today when CSS transitions are used in conjunction with core CSS3 properties by web designers the result can increase user delight a great deal.

CSS transitions are relatively easy to implement, only taking a few lines of code. Hence any web designer already familiar with CSS will have no trouble using this technique.

CSS transitions were initially developed solely by the WebKit team for Safari. CSS Transitions have now gone on to become a working draft specification at W3C. CSS Transforms and CSS Animations share that same lineage.

This is a real example of a Browser manufacturer's experiment being accepted as having great potential and thus being included within the working draft specification for CSS3 at W3C. Opera has recently added CSS transitions support in version 10.5 and Firefox has pledged support for version 4.0. Although it is a W3C draft specification and evolving, it's stable enough for Opera and Firefox to be taking it seriously enough and adding support for it within their Browser's core. More than that, CSS transitions are no longer proprietary to Safari only.

What Are CSS Transitions?

CSS Transitions are what allow changes to attribute:*values* of an element specified in the CSS rules to occur smoothly when triggered by user interactions like hovering, clicking, and focusing the mouse cursor on an element of a web page.

This type of smoothing animates the changing of a elements attribute:*value* specified with CSS rules and when triggered by a mouse click, focus or active state, or any changes to the element (*including even a change on the element's class attribute*).

A Simple Example

Our Focus: Is to add a CSS transition to the background color of a link. When the mouse cursor is hovered over it the link's background will change. A CSS transition will be used to smooth out the change in the background color of the link. This was previously possible only using Flash or JavaScript, but is now possible with a few simple lines of CSS.

Here is the HTML markup used:

```
<div id="divTopMenu">
  <ul>
    <li><a href="#" class="cssTransitions">Home</a></li>
    <li><a href="#" class="cssTransitions">About</a></li>
    <li><a href="#" class="cssTransitions">Contact</a></li>
  </ul>
</div>
```

Next, a declaration that styles the link state with a little padding and a light green background, followed by the background swap to a darker green on hover is added. (diagram 11.1)

```
a.cssTransitions{
  padding: 0px 40px;
  text-decoration:none;
  background: #68841D;
  color: #fff;
    text-decoration:none;
    background: #68841D;
    color: #fff;
}
a.cssTransitions:hover{
  padding: 4px 40px;
  color: #fff;
  background: #9c3;
}
```

Now let's add a transition to that background color change. This will smooth out and animate the difference over a specified period of time. For now, only the vendor-prefixed properties which currently work in WebKit-based browsers i.e. *Safari* and *Chrome* will be used to keep things simple. Later, vendor prefixes for Mozilla and Opera can be added.

Diagram 11.1

Here is the CSS3 transition code snippet.

```
a.cssTransitions {
  padding: 5px 10px;
  background: #9c3;
  -webkit-transition-property: background;
  -webkit-transition-duration: 0.3s;
  -webkit-transition-timing-function: ease;
}
a.cssTransitions: hover {
  padding: 4px 40px;
  color: #fff;
  background: #9c3;
}
```

There are three parts of to a transition declaration:

transition-property: The property to be transitioned (in this case, the background property)

transition-duration: How long the transition should last (0.3 seconds)

transition-timing-function: How fast the transition happens over time (ease)

The output is as shown in diagram 11.2.

Diagram 11.2

The transition timing function value allows the speed of the transition to be controlled by defining one of six possibilities: *ease*, *linear*, *ease-in*, *ease-out*, *ease-in-out*, and *cubic-bezier* (*which allows the web designer to define their own timing curve*).

For our simple example, the duration of the transition is pretty fast (i.e. *just 0.3 seconds*) hence it could be difficult to tell the difference visually between the six options available.

For longer animations, the timing function chosen becomes important as there is now time enough to notice the speed of change over the length of the animation. When in doubt, use *ease,* which is the default value or *linear,* either should work just fine for short timed transitions.

Delaying The Transition

The transitions in our example can be delayed from the moment the triggering event occurs on the screen. For example: Assume that the background transition should happen half a second after the triggering event occurs on the screen, this is done using the *transition-delay* property.

```
a.cssTransitions{
  padding: 0px 40px;
  text-decoration:none;
  background: #68841D;
  color: #fff;
  -webkit-transition-property: background;
  -webkit-transition-duration: 0.3s;
  -webkit-transition-timing-function: ease;
  -webkit-transition-delay: 0.5s;
}
a.cssTransitions: hover {
  padding: 4px 40px;
  color: #fff;
  background: #9c3;
}
```

Shorthand Used In CSS3 Transitions

The CSS3 transition (i.e. *the non delayed code spec*) can be simplified significantly by using the transition shorthand as follows:

```
a.cssTransitions{
  padding: 0px 40px;
  text-decoration:none;
  background: #68841D;
  color: #fff;
  -webkit-transition: background 0.3s ease;
}
```

```
a.cssTransitions: hover {
  padding: 4px 40px;
  color: #fff;
  background: #9c3;
}
```

This transition CSS3 rule is much more compact and accomplishes exactly the same thing.

Using Transition Shorthand With A Delay

Here is the shorthand code spec for a CSS3 transition with a delay.

```
a.cssTransitions{
  padding: 0px 40px;
  text-decoration:none;
  background: #68841D;
  color: #fff;
  -webkit-transition: background 0.3s ease 0.5s;
}
a.cssTransitions:hover {
  padding: 4px 40px;
  color: #fff;
  background: #9c3;
}
```

Now all these CSS3 transitioning rules work just fine in Browsers built using the WebKit engine, i.e. *Safari* and *Chrome*, but what about other (*non compliant*) Browsers.

Browser Support

CSS3 transitions were initially developed by WebKit, and have been recognized by Safari and Chrome since version 3.2. Opera supports them as well in version 10.5. Firefox has promised support in version 4.0.

Note: *All these Browsers will support CSS3 transitions when appropriate vendor prefixes are used.*

Coding The Full CSS3 Transition Stack

The revised CSS3 transition declaration, adding the –moz- and –o- prefixes as well as the actual CSS3 transition property is given below. Again, the non-prefixed CSS3 property is placed last in the stack to ensure that the final CSS3 implementation will work perfectly as the CSS3 transition property moves from *draft* to *finished* status.

```
a.cssTransitions{
  padding: 0px 40px;
  text-decoration:none;
  background: #68841D;
  color: #fff;
  -webkit-transition: background 0.3s ease;
  -moz-transition: background 0.3s ease;
  -o-transition: background 0.3s ease;
  transition: background 0.3s ease;
}
a.cssTransitions:hover {
  padding: 4px 40px;
  color: #fff;
  background: #9c3;
}
```

With this codespec, the background color transition will be smoothened out in current versions of Safari, Chrome, and Opera, as well as future versions of any browser (i.e. *FireFox 4.0*) that choose to support it.

Transitioning States

It would seem to make more sense if the transition properties were placed in *:hover* since that's the trigger for this transition. What happens is that there are other states of an element besides *:hover*, and web designers would likely want such a transition to happen on each of those stated without duplication.

For instance, web designers may want this transition to happen with the *:focus* or *:active* pseudo-classes of a link as well. Hence, instead of adding the CSS3 transition code to each of the pseudo-classes the CSS3 transition instructions are attached to the *normal state* and therefore declared only once.

The following code spec example adds the same background transition to *:focus*. This ensures that the transition will be triggered from either hovering over or focusing on the link.

```
a.cssTransitions{
  padding: 0px 40px;
  text-decoration:none;
  background: #68841D;
  color: #fff;
  -webkit-transition: background 0.3s ease;
  -moz-transition: background 0.3s ease;
  -o-transition: background 0.3s ease;
  transition: background 0.3s ease;
}
a.cssTransitions:hover,
a.cssTransitions:focus {
  padding: 4px 40px;
  color: #fff;
  background: #9c3;
}
```

Transitioning Multiple Properties

Let's assume that a web designer wants the background color of the link as well as the link Text color to transition as well. This can be done very simply by stringing multiple CSS3 transitions together, each separated by a comma. Each CSS3 transition can its own varying duration and timing functions if required, as shown in diagram 11.3.

```
a.cssTransitions{
  padding: 0px 40px;
  text-decoration:none;
  background: #68841D;
  color: #fff;
  -webkit-transition: background .3s ease, »color 0.2s linear;
  -moz-transition: background .3s ease, »color 0.2s linear;
  -o-transition: background .3s ease, color 0.2s linear;
  transition: background .3s ease, color 0.2s linear;
}
```

```
a.cssTransitions:hover,
a.cssTransitions:focus {
  padding: 4px 40px;
  color: #fff;
  background: #9c3;
}
```

Home About Contact

Diagram 11.3

Transitioning All Possible Properties

An alternative to listing multiple CSS3 transitioning properties is using *all*. This will transition all available CSS3 properties. Here is how this is added to the CSS3 transitioning codespec being used in all the earlier examples. All the CSS transitioning properties will now share the same duration and timing.

```
a.cssTransitions {
  padding: 0px 40px;
  text-decoration:none;
  background: #68841D;
  color: #fff;
  -webkit-transition: all 0.3s ease;
  -moz-transition: all 0.3s ease;
  -o-transition: all 0.3s ease;
  transition: all 0.3s ease;
}
a.cssTransitions:hover,
a.cssTransitions:focus {
  padding: 4px 40px;
  color: #fff;
  background: #9c3;
}
```

This is a convenient way of applying CSS3 transitioning code spec to all the events associated with a link *:hover*, *:focus*, or *:active* without having to list each property to transition.

Which CSS Properties Can Be Transitioned?

Now that the background and Text color of a hyperlink were successfully transitioned, there are many other CSS properties that can be transitioned, including width, opacity, position, and font-size. It is easy to see from this that a whole lot of wonderfully fluid transitional user experiences can be built into a web page.

Why Not Use JavaScript Instead?

With all Browsers not supporting CSS3 Transitions natively, why not use a JavaScript solution to handle such animation? Popular frameworks such as jQuery, Prototype, and script.aculo.us have enabled animations via JavaScript that work cross-browser for some time now.

Well it all depends on how crucial such transitions are to user experience for that specific web page.

Web designers can embrace the simplicity and flexibility of CSS3 if you choose the appropriate parts of the user interface to apply it to enriching user interactions that happen on that page. Hence, a few simple lines of CSS rules to trigger a simple animation within supporting Browsers, rather than using a JavaScript framework seems like a smart choice, and one most web designers are glad they have at their disposal.

Be Smart Be Subtle

Like the many new innovations that are happening with web Browsers it's important to use CSS3 transitions appropriately. Do not go overboard using CSS3 transitions just because it is available. Web designers should carefully look at the web page being designed and consider where CSS3 transitions will delight the user and where CSS3 transitions will annoy the user and cause them to navigate away from the web page.

CSS3 transitions should be used with care and solid design sensibility.

Now that a solid base of CSS transitions has been built at a technical level, this technique can be used to smooth out the user experience in the examples that follow, beginning with the very next chapter.

Self Review Questions

Fill In The Blanks

1. Transitions in webpages were normally driven by____________.
2. CSS transitions were initially developed solely by the ___________ team for Safari.
3. CSS Transitions have now gone on to become a working draft specification at __________.
4. ___________ has recently added CSS transitions support in version 10.5 and ___________ has pledged support for version 4.0.
5. The transitions can be delayed from the moment the ________ event occurs on the screen.
6. It would seem to make more sense if the transition properties were placed in ___________ since that's the trigger for this transition.
7. There are other states of an element besides :hover, and web designers would likely want such a transition to happen on each of those stated without ____________.
8. Instead of adding the CSS3 transition code to each of the ___________ the CSS3 transition instructions are attached to the normal state and therefore declared only once.
9. An alternative to listing multiple CSS3 transitioning properties is using ___________.
10. Popular frameworks such as ___________, ___________, and ___________ have enabled animations via JavaScript that work cross-browser for some time now.
11. CSS3 transitions should be used with care and solid design ____________.

True Or False

12. CSS transitions will replace existing technologies like Flash, JavaScript, or Scalable Vector Graphics without broader Browser support.
13. When CSS transitions are used in conjunction with core CSS3 properties by web designers the result can decrease user delight.
14. CSS transitions are relatively easy to implement, only taking a few lines of code.
15. CSS transitions are no longer proprietary to Safari only.
16. Web designers cannot embrace the simplicity and flexibility of CSS3.
17. Like many new innovations that are happening with web Browsers it's important to use CSS3 transitions appropriately.
18. The transition timing function value allows the speed of the transition to be controlled by defining one of six possibilities: ease, linear, ease-in, ease-out, ease-in-out, and cubic-bezier.

19. The non-prefixed CSS3 property is placed first in the stack to ensure that the final CSS3 implementation will work perfectly as the CSS3 transition property moves from draft to finished status.

Hands-on Exercise

2. Style the Left Menu of a Web page using CSS Transitions.

   Left Menu will contain the following links:
   a. Home
   b. About Us
   c. Product
   d. Forum
   e. Contact Us
   On hover of the any of the Left Menus change the background color, text color and the transition properties for menus.

   Output of this exercise is shown in diagram 11.4

   Please use all the CSS3 elements that have been learned in this chapter.

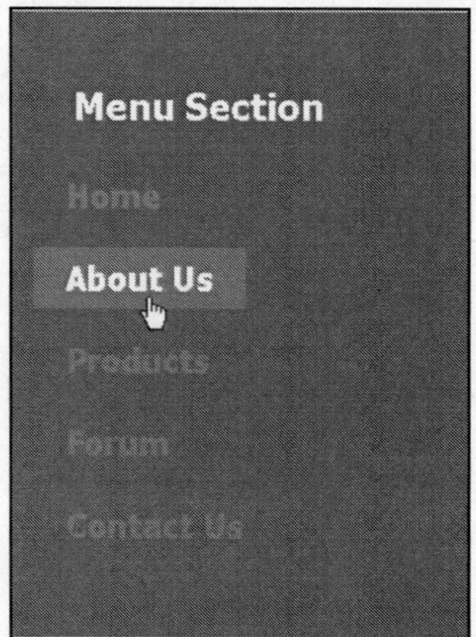

Diagram 11.4

12. Hover Crafting With CSS

Some time has been spent in understanding what is currently available for use in CSS3 today. It's in giving users delight with the website's user interface that most of the current CSS3 rules are being applied.

Here is a very brief recap of what has been covered so far:

1. There are various core CSS3 properties that are useable today
2. These CSS3 core properties can be used happily for creating user delight in the website's user interface
3. Currently Browser vendor specific prefixes permit the use of several new CSS3 properties in the real world
4. CSS3 based transitions are not Browser manufacturer, proprietary experiments but have become W3C / CSS3 draft specifications that most modern Browsers are embracing

Having got these concepts and CSS3 code spec understood, it time to have fun with the new CSS3 properties and apply them to correctly and contextually in the design of a webpage.

Hover Crafting With CSS3

Web designers are constantly communicating with site visitors when they create anything delivered by the web. Web designers often make assumptions about site visitors, such as who reads the material created on the website, what content would be appealing to the website visitors, what content would they be capable of understanding, and so on, but are never 100% sure simply because website visitor demographics is a very tricky science and apparently not fully matured except in very special circumstances.

The fact the website visitor demographics is a grayish area should not prevent web designers from using the very best technology available to deliver web page content to the website visitor.

Web designers should be especially careful when applying the very best technology to website design by ensuring that such technology degrades gracefully when being accessed and used using older Browsers that do not recognize such technology.

Fortunately CSS3 is one such technology that can be cheerfully used in website design that will bring an enhanced user experience to users that access the website content using Browsers that are CSS3 enabled and CSS3 degrades gracefully, in most cases without damaging site visitor experience, when a site visitor is accessing the website using an older Browser which is not CSS3 compliant.

The following chapters in this material tackle a sets of examples related to CSS3. This material does not attempt to tell everything there is know about CSS3, but approaches the learning of CSS3 properties by doing something specific with them that fit in with real world examples. Hence, after the examples have been worked through and understood, perhaps as web designer you will be able to apply them immediately to your latest web design job and take off from there.

Ensuring Visitor Delight

When working in web design (*as opposed to graphic design for magazines and newspapers*) the most interesting thing for the designer is that - the web as medium is alive - the web empowers web designer to build stuff that can react to a site visitor, move or morph depending on what the site visitor does. The website and the visitor can truly interact.

It is this interaction between the website and the visitor that can be made different, interesting and is easily enhanced by using CSS3 rules and a CSS3 enabled Browser to access the website. While at the same time if a visitor accesses the website using an older (*non CSS3 compliant*) Browser the website does not break, just the degree of visitor interactivity and delight just reduces to accommodate the non CSS3 compliant Browser.

A great example of such work using CSS3 can be found on Dutch designer and developer Faruk Ateş's personal site (http://farukat.es).

Its sidebar contains a list of links to various social networks that, on hover, expand and come alive due to the clever use of several CSS3 rules as shown in diagram 12.1.

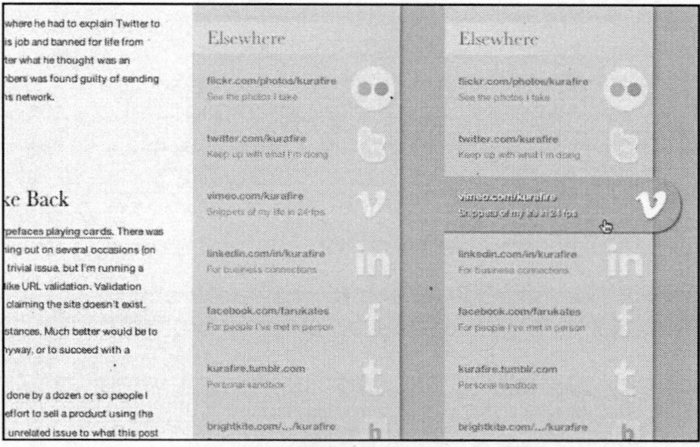

Diagram 12.1

What looks like a normal list of text with images on the right hand side suddenly morphs into something visually interesting when a site visitor places their mouse cursor on a link and is using a CSS3 enabled Browser. This is really a great example of aesthetic web design, which comes to life because of using CSS3 properties, and when viewed in Browsers that are CSS3 enabled.

Diagram 12.2 shows the same default and hover state as viewed in Internet Explorer 7, which does not support CSS3 at all. While what happens when the mouser cursor hovers over the same link is not as visually polished, it is still a usable, readable, and functional experience. Additionally, when the mouse cursor moves off the link the visual is nearly identical.

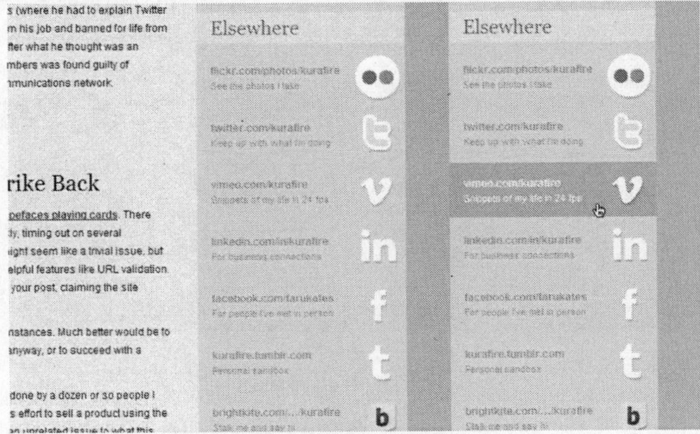

Diagram 12.2

Hovering the mouse cursor over (*or focusing on*) an element in a webpage is a great place to enhance using CSS3 properties.

Site visitors, using Internet Explorer will be served a different visual experience, until IE eventually begins to support CSS3 properties, but what's seen in IE is perfectly fine, not unexpected, and is functionally perfect.

IE users really do not know what they are missing, until they view the very same page in a copy of Safari, Chrome, Firefox, or Opera (*and then feel a tinge of jealousy*).

Do Websites Need To Look Exactly The Same In Every Browser?

To web designers, this has been a troublesome question for quite a while. My answer to this question is as shown in diagram 12.3. Do take a quick look at:
http://dowebsitesneedtobeexperiencedexactlythesameineverybrowser.com it will be a pleasant surprise.

Diagram 12.3

Its only when a site visitor begins to interact with the website that things get interesting. On the surface the site looks identical across all Browsers, CSS3 enabled or not, but the moment the mouse cursor is moved across the screen a series of CSS3 properties, transitions, and transforms are applied to the screen to make the visitor experience delightful as shown in diagram 12.4.

Diagram 12.4

Note: *If the changes in the two diagrams cannot be noticed in print, please do visit the website and see for yourself the changes that visitor interactivity with the website brings.*

The core content of this website remains the same, the visual message remains the same, usability remains the same in Browsers that at CSS3 enabled or Not, but the site design experience of a visitor is enriched if they use a CSS3 enabled Browser to visit the website.

Adding CSS3 Effects To Menu Items

Let's add a visual effect to the menu items on a website by combining *border-radius*, *text-shadow*, *RGBA*, and *CSS transitions* to delight the site visitor who visits the website using a CSS3 enabled Browser and notice the there is no difference in the functionality of the menu items whatsoever if the site visitor is using an older Browser that does not recognize CSS3 properties and rules. Take a look at diagram 12.5.

Diagram 12.5

Here is the HTML code spec that is used to markup the top navigation menu items.

```
<div id="divTopMenu">

  <ul id="nav">
    <li><a href="#">Home</a></li>
    <li><a href="#">About</a></li>
    <li><a href="#">Contact</a></li>
  </ul>

</div>
```

Now appropriate CSS3 styling can be applied to this menu item markup.

Floating The Menu Items

The entire menu item list is floated and some padding is added to position it on the *right hand side* of the the web page. Then each list item is in turn floated.

```
#nav
{
  float: left;
}
```

```
#nav li
{
  float: left;
  margin: 0px 0px 0px 5px;
  list-style: none;
}
```

Styling Menu Item Link Color With RGBA

Now add some padding to each menu item link and change its Text color to a semi-transparent white. RGBA is used to achieve this. Making the Menu Text a semi transparent white, allows some of the background color of the web page to show through the Menu Text as shown in diagram 12.6.

Note: *Setting the white Menu Item Text to 70% opacity via RGBA lets the web page background shown through, very slightly.*

```
#nav li a
{
  padding: 5px 15px;
  font-weight: bold;
  text-decoration: none;
  font-size: 11pt;
  color: rgba(255, 255, 255, 0.7);
}
```

Home About Contact

Diagram 12.6

Providing A Backup For RGBA

While RGBA is a really flexible way of specifying color along with a level of opacity, it's not supported in all browsers. Current flavors of *Safari*, *Chrome*, *Firefox*, and *Opera* all support it, it's supposed to be available in Internet Explorer 9 but what about IE6 IE7 and IE8?

Here's where specifying a backup color scheme becomes valuable. When using RGBA to assign color values, it's good practice to specify a solid color first, as a fallback CSS rule for those Browsers that do not support RGBA. As follows:

```
#nav li a
{
  padding: 5px 15px;
  font-weight: bold;
  text-decoration: none;
  font-size:11pt;
  color: #ccc;
  color: rgba(255, 255, 255, 0.7);
}
```

Browsers that support RGBA will override the solid color (*a shade of gray in this case*), while browsers that do not support RGBA yet will ignore the RGBA rule and use the solid color.

> **Note:** *Specify solid color backups for RGBA in a separate rule that appears before the RGBA rule.*

Adding *text-shadow*

Next a subtle text-shadow can be added, using RGBA to define the *text-shadow* color letting the semi-transparent black at 50% opacity blend into the web page background.

```
#nav li a
{
  padding: 5px 15px;
  font-weight: bold;
  color: #ccc;
  color: rgba(255, 255, 255, 0.7);
  text-shadow: 0 1px 1px rgba(0, 0, 0, 0.5);
}
```

Diagram 12.7 shows a comparison of the Menu Item, text links without text-shadow applied (left hand side) and the Menu Item, text links with text-shadow applied (right hand side), as viewed in Safari. The tiny shadow specified gives the Menu Item, text an almost imperceptible *lift* detail from the background.

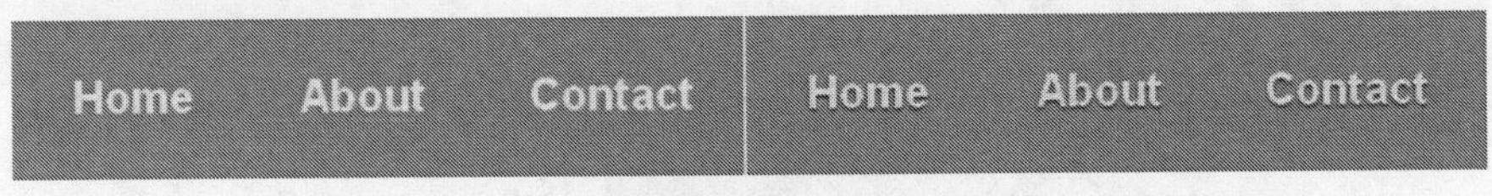

Diagram 12.7

The CSS3 property *text-shadow* works in current versions of *Safari*, *Chrome*, *Firefox*, and *Opera*. Browsers that do not support the CSS3 property *text-shadow* (*IE*) will just harmlessly ignore this CSS3 styling rule i.e. No shadow, no problem.

Now the :hover CSS3 styling rules can be added to complete the Menu Items, visual effects.

Hover And Focus Styling

A Text color change and a background color change will be added to the Menu Item links when a user hovers their mouse cursor on the menu item link. The **:hover** state of each link will be styled using CSS3 properties. Once again RGBA will be used to set a semi-transparent, white background behind the text on **:hover**.

```
#nav li a
 {
  padding: 5px 15px;
  font-weight: bold;
  text-decoration: none;
  font-size:11pt;
  color: #ccc;
  color: rgba(255, 255, 255, 0.7);
  text-shadow: 0 1px 1px rgba(0, 0, 0, 0.5);
}
#nav li a:hover,
#nav li a:focus
 {
  color: #fff;
  background: rgba(255, 255, 255, 0.15);
}
```

When the site visitor hovers their mouse cursor on the Menu Item Text, its color changes to a solid white and a background color of white with an opacity of 15% is added as well. When the Menu Items are focused on by the site visitor the very same styling is applied to the Menu items.

Diagram 12.8 shows the new **:hover** and **:focus** state of the Menu Item links. Browsers that support RGBA will set a semi-transparent white background behind bright white text.

Diagram 12.8

Rounding The Hover Background Corners With *border-radius*

Going forward, the corners of the background applied to the Menu Items when the visitor hovers their mouse cursor on a Menu Item the background corners can be rounded, which will be visible in all Browsers that are CSS3 compliant as shown in diagram 12.9.

Note: *When using the border-radius CSS3 property specific vendor prefixes must be used, as shown below:*

```
#nav li a
 {
   padding: 5px 15px;
   font-weight: bold;
   text-decoration: none;
   font-size: 11pt;
   color: #ccc;
   color: rgba(255, 255, 255, 0.7);
   text-shadow: 0 1px 1px rgba(0, 0, 0, 0.5);
   -webkit-border-radius: 14px;
   -moz-border-radius: 14px;
   border-radius: 14px;
 }
 #nav li a:hover,
 #nav li a:focus
 {
   color: #fff;
   background: rgba(255, 255, 255, 0.15);
 }
```

Diagram 12.9

Diagram 12.9 shows how the **:hover** codespec styles the Menu Items - Text and Background. This CSS3 styling rule will be obeyed in the latest versions of *Safari*, *Chrome*, *Firefox*, and *Opera*, as well as *IE9*.

> **Note:** *The non-prefixed, border-radius property is placed last in the list of CSS3 rules, this ensures when Browser manufactures ultimately implement the CSS3 property the vendor-prefixed CSS3 properties will be overridden by the common border-radius property.*

One may wonder why the CSS3 border-radius rules are being placed within the *#nav li* HTML codespec, this is because a CSS3 transition is going to be applied to add a final bit of polish to the Menu Item, Text styling.

Adding CSS3 Transition To The Menu Item Background

Last add a CSS3 Transition to the **:hover** and **:focus** for the Menu Item navigational links. This will help smooth out the appearance of the oval shaped background, subtly bringing it into focus behind the Menu Item Text. The transition will also smoothly change the text color from semi-transparent white to a full bright white as shown in diagram 12.10.

The Browser specific, pre-fixed, CSS3 Transition rules that currently work in Safari, Chrome, Firefox (4.0), and Opera are placed first, with the non-prefixed CSS Transition rule last in this declaration of CSS rules for the usual reasons.

Here is the complete block of CSS3 styling rules that does this.

```
#nav li a
 {
   padding: 5px 15px;
   font-weight: bold;
   text-decoration: none;
   font-size: 11pt;

   color: #ccc;
   color: rgba(255, 255, 255, 0.7);
   text-shadow: 0 1px 1px rgba(0, 0, 0, 0.5);

   -webkit-border-radius: 14px;
   -moz-border-radius: 14px;
   border-radius: 14px;
```

```
    -webkit-transition: all 0.3s ease-in-out;
    -moz-transition: all 0.3s ease-in-out;
    -o-transition: all 0.3s ease-in-out;
    transition: all 0.3s ease-in-out;
}
#nav li a:hover,
#nav li a:focus
{
    color: #fff;
    background: rgba(255, 255, 255, 0.15);
}
```

Note: *The CSS3 Transition properties are added to the normal state of the HTMLT element to which CSS3 transitioning must be applied. CSS3 Transitions are coded in this fashion so that the transition is applied to* the **:**hover, **:**focus and **:**active states as well. Take a look at diagram 12.10.

Additionally the *all* value is being used in the CSS Transition rule to catch all properties that can change i.e. **:**hover, **:**focus, :active, color and background in this specific case.

Alternatively, the same kind of CSS3 Transition, Menu Item behavior can be achieved by listing each of those properties explicitly in a comma-delimited list as follows**:**

```
-webkit-transition: color 0.3s ease-in-out, background 0.3s ease-in-out;
-moz-transition: color 0.3s ease-in-out, background 0.3s ease-in-out;
-o-transition: color 0.3s ease-in-out, background 0.3s ease-in-out;
transition: color .3s ease-in-out, background .3s ease-in-out;
```

The entire block of CSS3 rules specified above can be reduce by the use of the *all* CSS3 property making the CSS3 rules a lot more compact and efficient when applying CSS3 transitions to multiple property values of any HTML element.

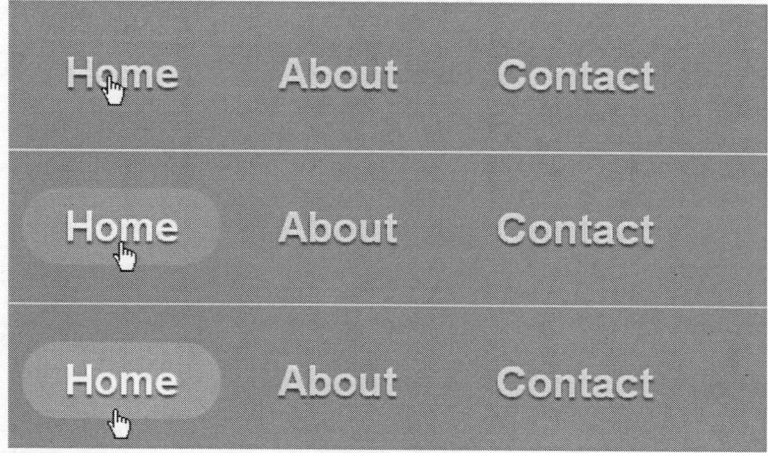

Diagram 12.10

Future Proofing CSS3 Rules

The above example of applying CSS3 styling rules the Menu Items of a webpage is a simple example of adding visuals value to the menu system of a website. CSS3 enabled Browsers will display a smooth transition from a semi-transparent, rounded background color behind text-shadowed text links to bright white Menu Item Text, very prettily.

Browsers that are not CSS3 compliant will not deliver this visual experience to the site visitor but what the site visitor will get is a semantically correct, horizontal list of Menu Item, i.e. website navigational links.

This demonstrates how efficient it is to achieve something that previously would have required Flash and/or JavaScript to achieve. The CSS3 styling rules are simple and straightforward, best they are harmless to Browsers that do not yet support them.

The CSS3 Style rules have been future proofed, by ensuring that the CSS3 property from its W3C specification is included *last* in all the CSS3 rule blocks.

Duplicating the CSS3 styling rules using appropriate vendor-specific prefixes is a necessary effort, but this effort has the golden payoff of getting to use CSS3 styling properties right now to enhance the website visitor's experience.

Simple And Flexible Icon Styling Using *opacity*

Web designers are always looking for CSS rule based solutions that offer flexibility in delivering great website visuals while saving coding time. This is exactly what CSS3 offers web designers in a very big way, the ability to achieve in a few lines of styling rule code, what used to take a lot more lines of code using multiple programming environments such as JavaScript and Flash.

Here is a creative way of using the CSS3 *opacity* property. Using the CSS3 *opacity* property a web designer can determine just exactly how visible a specific web page element is to a site visitor.

When the CSS3 *opacity* property is coupled with the CSS3 *RGBA* property this offers another method to add transparency to icons and other design elements used in a web page. Using CSS3 styling rules which combine the *opacity* and *RGBA* properties web designers can create simple and flexible hover states for hyperlinked graphics in a web page. To do this, simply variety the *opacity* of a single image and thus create multiple visual states for that image.

Finally add a custom CSS3 Transition to these changing states and the website visitor will be delighted with the visuals.

Let's take a look at how this can be achieved.

Changing The *opacity* Of Clickable Images

Diagram 12.11 shows the footer of a website underneath there is some legal copy and a disclaimer; there are three clickable logos which are used as navigable links.

Diagram 12.11

The CSS3 *opacity* property will be used to control different levels of transparency for these logo images, and a CSS transition will be used to smoothen out the transitions in the levels of transparency in the logo images.

The CSS3 styling rules that markup these footer logo images is simple and semantic and is just an unordered list of hyperlinked images, as follows:

```
<div id="divFooterLogos">
  <ul id="logos">
      <li><a href="#"><img src="images/twitter.png" alt="Twitter" width="50" height="50"
/></a></li>
      <li><a href="#"><img src="images/rss.png" alt="RSS Feed" width="50" height="50"
/></a></li>
      <li><a href="#"><img src="images/up.png" alt="Page Up" width="50" height="50"
/></a></li>
  </ul>
</div>
```

Opacity And Image Efficiency

The logo images are fully white, PNG images. Their opacity can be controlled using CSS3 styling rules. Hence multiple images are really not required. Because of the CSS3 *opacity* property web designers can begin to think differently when using images in web pages.

Here, instead of creating and saving multiple semi-transparent images in let's say, Photoshop, a single fully opaque set of images have been created whose opacity can be controlled via the CSS3 *opacity* property and adjusted by any Brower that is CSS3 compliant.

This saves quite a bit of time. It also allows the opacity level to be changed for :hover, :focus, and :active states without needing to create multiple sets of images. Take a look at diagram 12.12.

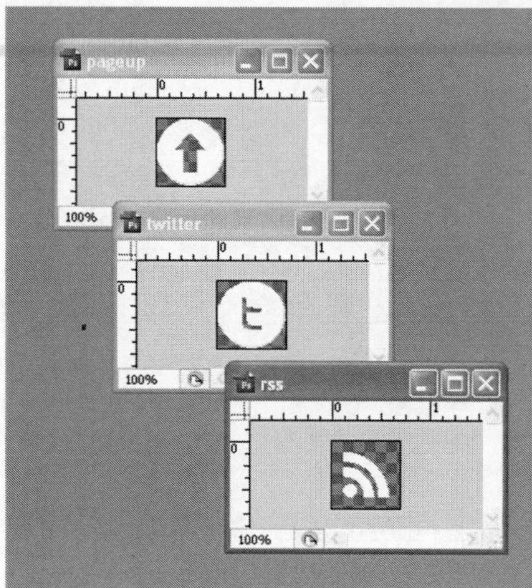

Diagram 12.12

Styling The List Of Images

The CSS styling rules will center these images in the footer. Then ensure they are displayed horizontally instead of vertically as shown in diagram 12.13.

```
#logos
{
    text-align: center;
}
#logos li {
```

```
    display: inline;
}
#logos a img
{
    border: none;
}
```

Diagram 12.13

Next, opacity rules will be added that will dim these icons images in their default state, and brightening them up bit when a visitor hovers or focuses their mouse cursor on the icon images.

Here is the CSS3 rules that achieve this.

```
#logos a img
{
    border: none;
    opacity: 0.25;
}
#logos a:hover img,
#logos a:focus img
{
    opacity: 0.6;
}
```

These CSS3 rules ensure that the images are displayed at 25% opacity initially, and then they brighten up to 60% opacity when the visitor hovers or focuses the web page cursor on the icon images. Quite simple really and requires only one set of images. Take a look at diagram 12.14.

Diagram 12.14

Note: *The CSS3 opacity property does not require Browser vendor specific prefixes, and will work in Safari, Chrome, Firefox, and Opera. IE8 and below do not support opacity. There is a IE hack solution available for anyone wants to use it.*

The IE *opacity* Hack

Opacity can be mimicked for older versions of IE by using the proprietary Microsoft filter property. Unlike vendor prefixed CSS3 properties the Microsoft filter property is not part of any proposed CSS standard being crafted at W3C. The Microsoft filter property does bring an increased performance overhead depending on where or how often it's used. It's a hack that provides a means to an end.

As long as this hack is confined to its own stylesheet, applied only when necessary, or very carefully commented in the common style sheet it becomes a viable alternative to get the same styling in older versions of Internet Explorer. Here's the IE hack codespec:

```
#logos a img
{
    border: none;
    opacity: 0.25;
    /* IE 8 hack */
    -ms-filter: "progid:DXImageTransform.Microsoft.Alpha(Opacity=25)";
    /* IE 5-7 hack */
    filter: alpha(opacity = 25);
}
#logos a:hover img,
#logos a:focus img
{
    opacity: 0.6;
    /* IE 8 hack */
    -ms-filter:"progid:DXImageTransform.Microsoft.Alpha(Opacity=60)";
    /* IE 5-7 hack */
    filter: alpha(opacity = 60);
}
```

With these IE hacks in place the same styling effects will be seen in Internet Explorer as well. Use this hack sparingly, however, if you have a website which has sizable IE traffic statistics and most website do you will have to use this hack code snippet. Please take a look at diagram 12.15.

Diagram 12.15

Adding A CSS3 *transition*

Lastly, adding a CSS3 *transition* to the *opacity* change over will make the opacity change smooth, and provide a bit of animated richness to the icon images and will tie this whole technique together nicely. Here is the CSS3 transition codespec that will do the job.

```
#logos a img
{
    border: none;
    opacity: 0.25;
     /* IE 8 hack */
    -ms-filter: "progid:DXImageTransform.Microsoft.Alpha(Opacity=25)";
     /* IE 5-7 hack */
    filter: alpha(opacity = 25);
    -webkit-transition: opacity 0.2s ease-in-out;
    -moz-transition: opacity 0.2s ease-in-out;
    -o-transition: opacity 0.2s ease-in-out;
    transition: opacity 0.2s ease-in-out;
}
#logos a:hover img,
#logos a:focus img
{
    opacity: 0.6;
    /* IE 8 hack */
```

```
    -ms-filter:"progid:DXImageTransform.Microsoft.Alpha(Opacity=60)";

    /* IE 5-7 hack */
    filter: alpha(opacity = 60);
}
```

Hover-crafting with CSS3 is about quickly and efficiently adding simple styles that enrich the site visitor's experience. Surprising and delighting site visitors how use Browsers that support these properties now. If the visitor's Browser does not support these CSS3 properties, it's perfectly OK; they really won't know what they're missing.

Self Review Questions

Fill In The Blanks

1. ____________ the mouse cursor over an element in a webpage is a great place to enhance using CSS3 properties.
2. ____________ is a really flexible way of specifying color along with a level of opacity, it's not supported in all browsers.
3. The ____________ value is being used in the CSS Transition rule to catch all properties that can change i.e. :hover, :focus, :active, color and background in this specific case.
4. The CSS3 Style rules have been future proofed, by ensuring that the CSS3 property from its W3C specification is included ____________ in all the CSS3 rule blocks.
5. Web designers are always looking for CSS rule based solutions that offer ____________ in delivering great website visuals while saving coding time.
6. Using the CSS3 ____________ property a web designer can determine just exactly how visible a specific web page element is to a site visitor.
7. Opacity can be mimicked for older versions of IE by using the proprietary ____________ property.

True Or False

8. The Microsoft filter property does bring an increased performance overhead depending on where or how often it's used.
9. Unlike vendor prefixed CSS3 properties the Microsoft filter property is part of any proposed CSS standard being crafted at W3C.
10. When the CSS3 *opacity* property is coupled with the CSS3 *RGBA* property this offers another method to add transparency to icons and other design elements used in a web page.
11. Using CSS3 styling rules with *RGBA* properties web designers can create simple and flexible hover states for hyperlinked graphics in a web page.

Hands-on Exercise

3. Style the Left Menu of a Web page using CSS Transitions.

   Left Menu will contain the following links:
   f. Home
   g. About Us
   h. Product
   i. Forum
   j. Contact Us

   On hover of the any of the Left Menus change the background color, text color and add curved corners.

   Output of this exercise is shown in diagram 12.16
   Please use all the CSS3 elements that have been learned in this chapter.

Diagram 12.16

4. Create a row with the Popular Products, using images given in the CD. Each image should have its own shadow effect. On mouse over of each image reduce the opacity of the image.

   Output of this exercise is shown in diagram 12.17
   Please use all the CSS3 elements that have been learned in this chapter.

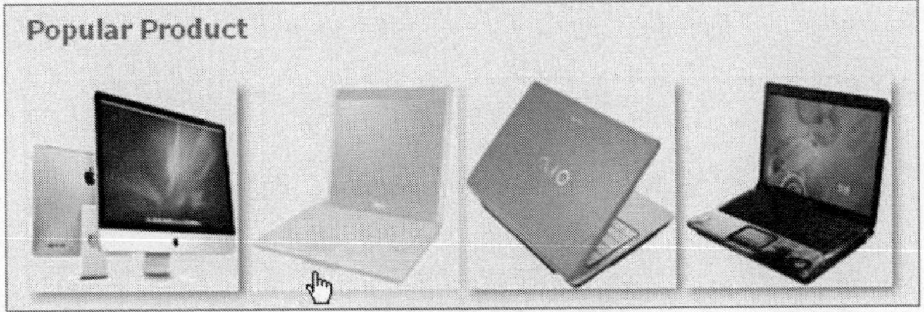

Diagram 12.17

13. Enriching Forms Using CSS3 Properties

Web forms are another aspect of a website that involves visitor interaction. Hence, forms can be groomed using CSS3 to offer greater site visitor delight. Form data capture elements like text boxes, radio buttons, check boxes and so on can differ drastically in appearance depending upon which Browser they are rendered in and on which operating system they are being viewed.

Because of this difference, the application of CSS3 properties may be applied to help contain or eliminate these visual differences and thus heighten site visitor experience. What is very important is to strike the perfect balance between the subtle modifications of the look and feel of form elements while maintaining their usability.

There is a lot that can be done styling forms using CSS3 styling rules to enrich the site visitors experience in Browsers that support CSS3 styling rules, while degrading that experience gracefully in Browsers that do not.

This chapter deals with the following three sections of CSS3 properties.

1. Powerful new selectors
2. CSS Gradients
3. CSS Animations

To understand just how web forms and CSS3 can work together let's begin work with a simple login form as shown in diagram 13.1.

Diagram 13.1

Marking Up A Simple Login Form

In terms of HTML code, this login form is as simple as it can get. A few *input* boxes. Bound to a few *labels* and a *submit* button.

Here is the HTML codespec that delivers the sign up form:

```
<div id="divLogin">
    <h3 class="alerts">Login</h3>
    <form action="/" id="loginAlerts">
        <fieldset>
            <label for="alerts-username">Username:</label>
            <input type="text" id="alerts-username" />
        </fieldset>
        <fieldset>
            <label for="alerts-password">Password:</label>
            <input type="text" id="alerts-password" />
        </fieldset>
        <fieldset>
            <input type="submit" value="Login" />
        </fieldset>
    </form>
</div> <!-- divLogin ENDS -->
```

Diagram 13.2 shows the form rendered with the default browser styles as viewed in Safari without any styling.

Diagram 13.2

Adding Styles For Fieldset and Label

To give this web form a nice shape let's start by styling its fieldset and label elements using CSS and adding some spacing between each row.

```
#loginAlerts fieldset
{
    margin: 0 0 10px 0;
    border:none;
}
#loginAlerts label
{
    display: block;
    font-weight: bold;
    line-height: 1.4;
    color: #666;
    color: rgba(0, 0, 0, 0.6);
    text-shadow: 0 1px 1px #fff;
}
```

Take a look at diagram 13.3. A *10px margin* has been added below each fieldset row. Labels have been set to display as *block* and have been placed on their own line. The color black has been assigned to the text with a 60% transparency. Additionally a backup color of gray has been defined for Browsers that cannot handle the CSS3 property of *transparency*.

Finally, a subtle white highlight has been applied to the label text with the CSS3 property *text-shadow* which makes it appear as though the Text has sunk into the background of the form.

Diagram 13.3

While it's nice to have a 10px spacing between fieldset rows, because of the padding inside the gray box, the 10px margin under the last fieldset row is unnecessary. This is the fieldset row containing the Submit button. This is a common styling issue, i.e. there are a list of elements, each requiring the same styles to be applied but the last element in the list needs to be styled a little differently.

Instead of binding either a new CSS ID class to the final element in this form, why not take advantage of the *:last-child* pseudo-class in CSS3 to remove the bottom margin as shown in the codespec below:

```
#loginAlerts fieldset
{
    margin: 0px 0px 10px 0px;
    border: none;
}

#loginAlerts label {
    display: block;
    font-weight: bold;
    line-height: 1.4;
    color: #666;
    color: rgba(0, 0, 0, 0.6);
    text-shadow: 0 1px #fff;
}
#loginAlerts fieldset:last-child
{
   margin: 0;
}
```

Note: *The :last-child pseudo-class in CSS3 is not supported in IE8 and lower. Apart from this problem this is a great way of adding a class in the markup. Diagram 13.4 shows that the bottom margin of the last fieldset element has been removed by using the :last-child pseudo-class.*

More CSS3 selectors

Since the pseudo-class, *:last-child* is being made good use of, perhaps now is a good time to point out that there are many more wonderfully convenient new selectors in CSS3.

Diagram 13.4

Styling The Text Input Boxes

Next, start customizing the text input boxes by adding styling rules to them. This time the CSS2.1 attribute selector input type="text" will be used to target the styling rules defined only to the input text boxes. Hence, this styling rule will not be applied to input type="submit" i.e. the Submit button used in this form.

If the styling rule simply stated: *#thing-alerts input*

Then all the inputs in the form (text and buttons) would have the styling rules applied to them, but if this was changed to: *#thing-alerts input[type="text"]* this will target only the text boxes and apply the styling rules declared to them alone.

> **Note:** *This helps overcome the need to add CSS - ID's or classes - to the stylesheet to style various form elements separately.*

> **Note:** *While attribute selectors are supported in IE7 and above, they are not supported in IE6.*

For this material this is just fine. Since only non-critical appearance of these form elements are being modified, IE6 can ignore these styling rules, and that's perfectly acceptable in this case.

Here is the complete CSS3 styling rules that applies a specific *width*, *padding*, and *font-size*, *turns off default borders*, adds a *backgroundcolor*, and rounds the corners of the inputs using a *border-radius* stack.

```
#loginAlerts fieldset input[type="text"]
{
    width: 215px;
    padding: 5px 8px;
    font-size: 1.2em;
```

```
    color: #666;
    border: none;
    background-color: #fff;

    -webkit-border-radius: 4px;
    -moz-border-radius: 4px;
    -o-border-radius: 4px;
    border-radius: 4px;
}
```

Diagram 13.5

Diagram 13.5 shows the application of these CSS3 styling rules to the form viewed in Safari, with similar results in Firefox and Opera. Now there are flat, rounded text input boxes which look quite nice. Next let's add some depth to make them look more like a typical, editable text input box.

Using CSS3 Gradients

A simple way to add some depth to a text input box is by using CSS gradients, which are new in CSS3. CSS3 can create a gradient from one color to another without the use of any images.

CSS gradients are currently supported in *Safari 4+*, *Chrome 2+*, and *Firefox 3.6+* **only**, but again, for non critical uses, CSS# gradients are a flexible solution that degrades well.

CSS gradients can be assigned anywhere that an image can be declared within a stylesheet:

i.e. *background-image*, *list-style-image*, *border-image*, and so on.

The syntax for declaring CSS gradients differs slightly between Safari's implementation and Firefox. Here is a excellent example of why Browser vendor prefixing is an important part of the CSS3 styling process.

Here is the syntax for creating a simple linear gradient for both WebKit and Mozilla-based browsers which can be used as part of the CSS2.1 *background* styling rule.

```
#myGradient
{
background-image: -webkit-gradient(linear, 0% 0%, 0% 100%, from(#fff), to(#999));
background-image: -moz-linear-gradient(0% 100% 90deg, #fff, #999);
}
```

Regretfully, the code spec is cumbersome and difficult to remember, with difference for both WebKit and Mozilla based Browsers.

Fortunately there is a really simple solution to this problem - go to:

http://www.westciv.com/tools/gradients/index.html

Use this tool to create whatever gradient you wish, once you've got a gradient you are happy with simply copy and paste the individual code snippets for WebKit and Mozilla into the CSS3 rules file as shown in diagram 13.6.

URL: http://www.westciv.com/tools/gradients/index.html

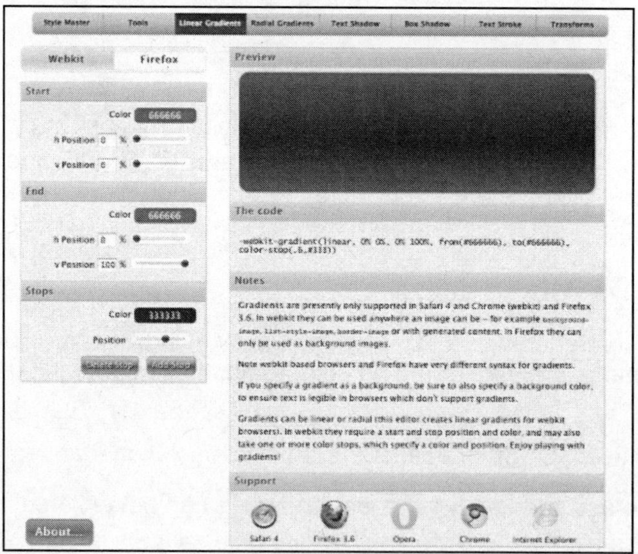

Diagram 13.6 The CSS3 gradient producing codespec tool.

The gradient required for the text input boxes in this example was very subtle, just a little lip, to make it look inset. After fiddling and entering some values into the above tool, here is the two short lines of CSS that was used which produced the gradient.

```
#loginAlerts fieldset input[type="text"]
s{
width: 215px;
padding: 5px 8px;
font-size: 1.2em;
color: #666;
border: none;
background-image: -webkit-gradient(linear, 0% 0%, 0% 12%, from(#999), to(#fff));
background-image: -moz-linear-gradient(0% 12% 90deg, #fff, #999);
background-color: #fff;
-webkit-border-radius: 4px;
-moz-border-radius: 4px;
-o-border-radius: 4px;
border-radius: 4px;
}
```

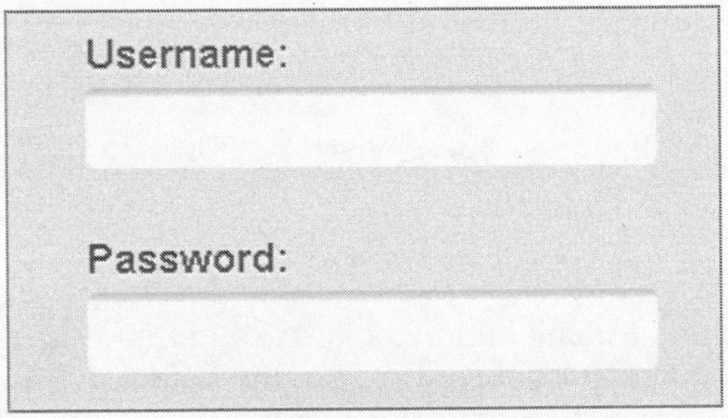

Username:

Password:

Diagram 13.7

A linear gradient was applied in this case, but radial gradients are also possible with CSS3.

The syntax differs between –webkit and –moz implementations. Essentially a small linear gradient was added that goes from light gray (#999) to white (#fff) for just 12% of the vertical height of the input text box. Browser vendor specific, prefixed, *background-image* rules are used to make that happen in Safari and Firefox.

Diagram 13.7 shows the results, the rounded input text boxes show a little inner shadow at the top without using any images. Browsers that do not yet support CSS3 gradients will ignore these *background-image* styling rules and the input text boxes will just be flat white.

That's perfectly Okay because while the look and feel of the input text boxes will appear modified in CSS3 compliant Browsers the actual functionality (*how they work*) of the input text boxes is untouched in any Browser type.

A Pure CSS Button

<Input type="button"> is one User Interface element that can demonstrate exactly how transformative CSS3 can really be. By combining many of the CSS3 styling techniques looked at earlier and ordinary form Submit button can be transformed into something far more good looking entirely using CSS3 styling rules as shown in diagram 13.8.

Diagram 13.8

The nice thing of applying CSS3 styling to a form button is that the look and feel of the button is very flexible. If the Browser does not support CSS3 properties that were used to make a great looking form Submit button, not to worry, this will degrade nicely to the default form button that the Bowser is capable of handling.

Here is the technique to produce the pretty Submit button as shown in diagram 4.8. First, add some *padding*, change the *font to Helvetica* to match the rest of the design, turn off *borders*, and set the *background color* to *white* as follows:

```
#loginAlerts input[type="submit"]
{
    padding: 8px 15px;
    font-family: Helvetica, Arial, sans-serif;
}
```

Diagram 13.9 shows what the Submit button looked like in Safari with those simple base styles applied. Already the Submit button looks nothing like the default HTML Submit button.

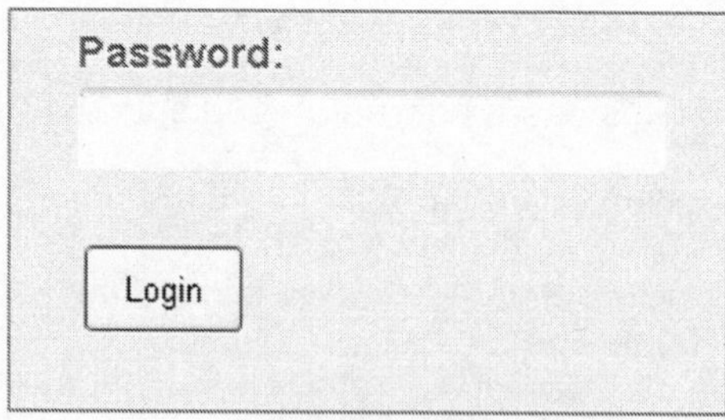

Diagram 13.9

Now let's morph this button into a pill shape by adding a *border-radius* stack to get the button rounded in shape.

```
#loginAlerts fieldset input[type="submit"]
{
    padding: 8px 15px;
    font-family: Helvetica, Arial, sans-serif;
    font-weight: bold;
    line-height: 1;
    color: #444;
    border: none;
    background-color: #fff;
    -webkit-border-radius: 23px;
    -moz-border-radius: 23px;
    -o-border-radius: 23px;
    border-radius: 23px;
}
```

After a bit of experimenting to get the right value, 23px was settled upon to get the desired pill shape as shown in diagram 13.10.

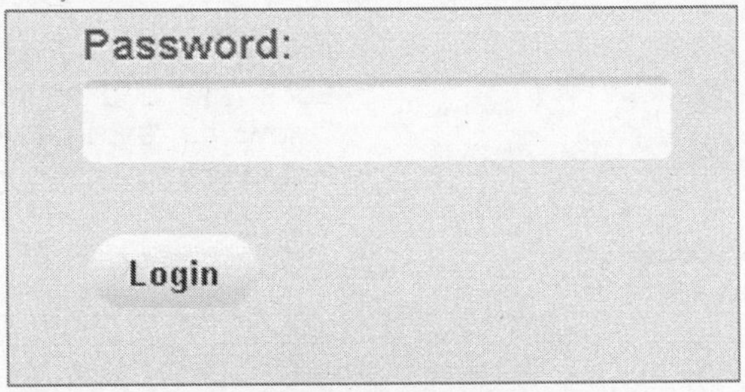

Password:

Login

Diagram 13.10

Applying A Linear Gradient

To apply a linear gradient of of light gray (#bbb) from bottom up to white (#fff) at the top of the button the gradient tool was used to get the correct gradient rule code. This code was copy / pasted into the CSS3 styling rule being created.

The code spec is what is given below:

```
#loginAlerts input[type="submit"]
{
     padding: 8px 15px;
     font-family: Helvetica, Arial, sans-serif;
     font-weight: bold;
     line-height: 1;
     color: #444;
     border: none;
     background-image: -webkit-gradient(linear, 0% 0%, 0% 100%, from(#fff), to(#bbb));
     background-image: -moz-linear-gradient(0 100% 90deg, #fff, #bbb);
    background-color: #fff;
    -webkit-border-radius: 23px;
    -moz-border-radius: 23px;
    -o-border-radius: 23px;
    border-radius: 23px;
}
```

Diagram 13.11 shows just how this the Submit button's look and feel has been transformed. Now the Submit button is a rounded button with a CSS gradient applied without any images being used only by adding a few lines of styling rules in the stylesheet.

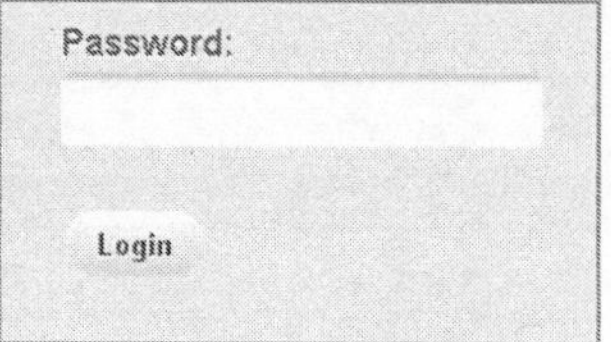

Diagram 13.11

Adding text-shadow to let the type sink in Let's now add an almost-white text-shadow below the text that will make it look as if the text is stamped into the button.

```
#loginAlerts input[type="submit"]
{
    padding: 8px 15px;
    font-family: Helvetica, Arial, sans-serif;
    font-weight: bold;
    line-height: 1;
    color: #444;
    border: none;
```

```
    text-shadow: 0 1px 1px rgba(255, 255, 255, 0.85);

    background-image: -webkit-gradient(linear, 0% 0%, 0% 100%, from(#fff), to(#bbb));
    background-image: -moz-linear-gradient(0 100% 90deg, #fff, #bbb);

    background-color: #fff;
    -webkit-border-radius: 23px;
    -moz-border-radius: 23px;
    -o-border-radius: 23px;
    border-radius: 23px;
}
```

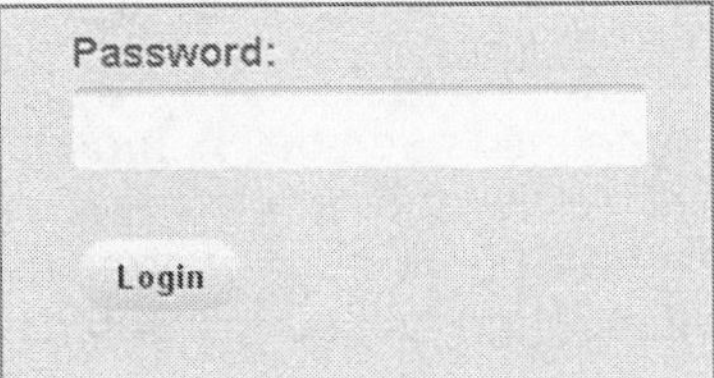

Diagram 13.12.

Next RGBA is used to tone down pure white to 85%, letting the letting the gray gradient show through just a tiny bit. Text shadow sits directly under the text by one pixel, and the shadow is blurred one pixel as well.

Diagram 13.12 adjacent shows the effect this has on the text which appears on the Submit button.

Adding A box-shadow To The Submit Button

The last CSS3 styling rule to be added to this stylish Submit button is a very slight *box-shadow* to add just another hint of dimension. This will help the Submit button sit better on the gray background behind it. Here's the CSS3 styling codespec that adds a *box-shadow* in CSS3 compliant Browsers that currently support CSS3, as well as all future CSS3 compliant Browsers.

```
#loginAlerts input[type="submit"]
{
    padding: 8px 15px;
    font-family: Helvetica, Arial, sans-serif;
    font-weight: bold;
    line-height: 1;
    color: #444;
    border: none;
    text-shadow: 0 1px 1px rgba(255, 255, 255, 0.85);
```

```
    background-image: -webkit-gradient(linear, 0% 0%, 0% 100%, from(#fff), to(#bbb));
    background-image: -moz-linear-gradient(0% 100% 90deg, #bbb, #fff);

    background-color: #fff;
    -webkit-border-radius: 23px;
    -moz-border-radius: 23px;
    -o-border-radius: 23px;
    border-radius: 23px;
    -webkit-box-shadow: 0 1px 2px rgba(0, 0, 0, 0.5);
    -moz-box-shadow: 0 1px 2px rgba(0, 0, 0, 0.5);
    box-shadow: 0 1px 2px rgba(0, 0, 0, 0.5);
}
```

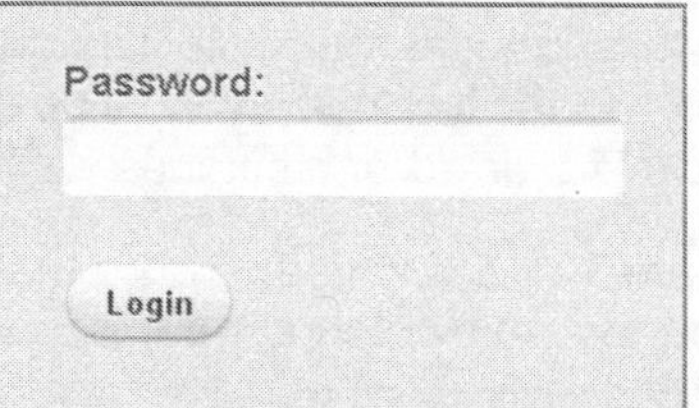

Diagram 13.13.

What happens is as shown in diagram 13.13 adjacent. Notice the gray *box-shadow* border around the Submit button, prominently seen below the button as seen in Safari.

This completes the transformation of the entire web form. Using a few extra lines of CSS3 rules a default looking web form has been transformed into something quite stylish and modern. When this web form in run in Browsers that are not CSS3 compliant it degrades very gracefully. The web form's functionality in all type of Browsers remains exactly the same.

If the web form is viewed in Internet Explorer 7, a browser that has zero support for CSS3 a perfectly acceptable, functional form is visible. All the CSS3 enhancements added via a handful of CSS3 rules in the stylesheet have been safely ignored, leaving a bare-bones form that functionally acts exactly as it should. Please take a look at diagram 13.14.

Diagram 13.14.

The web form as seen in Internet Explorer 7, a browser that has zero support for CSS3.

Using box-shadow To Create Focus States

CSS3 styling can be used to draw the site visitors attention to a text input box during web form filling time. This is achieved using the CSS3 *box-shadow* property bound to the input text box :focus pseudo class. It's quick, easy, degrades beautifully in non CSS3 compliant Browsers and site visitors will be delighted. All it requires creating a new CSS3 styling rule and binding this to :focus pseudo-class of a text input box. Here is the CSS3 styling rule codespec:

```
#loginAlerts input[type="text"]:focus
{
    -webkit-box-shadow: 0 0 12px rgba(51, 204, 255, 0.5);
    -moz-box-shadow: 0 0 12px rgba(51, 204, 255, 0.5);
    box-shadow: 0 0 12px rgba(51, 204, 255, 0.5);
}
```

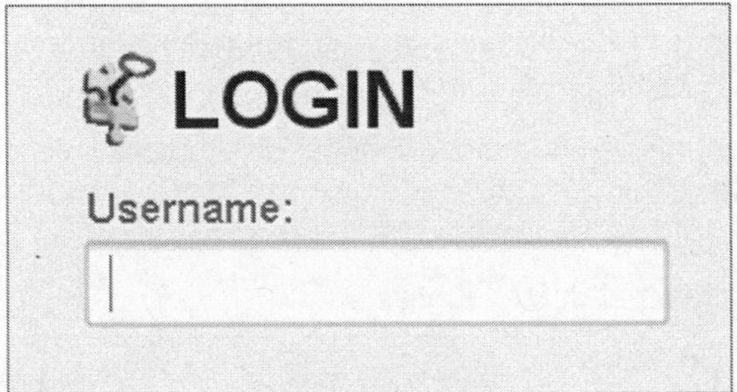

Diagram 13.15

This CSS3 style rule defines a box-shadow stack which applies a bright blue shadow at 50% opacity around a text input box when the form cursor lands on the box (*i.e. the text input box is in focus*) as shown in diagram 13.15 adjacent.

The default operating system behavior is being mimicked by the CSS3 styling, but because the code has been created by the web designer there is complete control on appearance.

Adding CSS Animation To Enrich Web Form / Visitor Interactions

To push the CSS3 *box-shadow* / focus behavior one step further, what if the box-shadow could be animated as well? Perhaps gently pulsating? The pulsations acting as a reminder to the site visitor that they have to type something into the text input box. This is completely achievable using CSS animations and Webkit powered Browsers (i.e. *Safari* and *Chrome*).

CSS3 Animations (*like CSS3 Transforms and Transitions*), were initially developed by the team that created the WebKit Browser engine, subsequently this was added as a proposed CSS3 standard at W3C.

However, unlike Transforms and Transitions, - Animations - have yet to be implemented by other Browser manufacturers. Animations currently work in *Safari* and *Chrome*. Animations do not work in *Firefox* or *Opera*, nor is there planned support in *IE9*.

For these reasons, Animations do not have a lot of attention (*at least as of now*), while they are powerful and exciting, it remains to be seen whether their adoption will be as comprehensive and swift as Transforms and Transitions have been.

Nonetheless, the concept and syntax for creating CSS Animations is rather straightforward, and for non critical enhancements of a web form that only WebKit browsers (i.e. Safari and Chrome) will enjoy for now, it could be fun to inject them into appropriate places.

Let's add a simple animation to the :focus pseudo class of a web forms input text box just to get a sense of how it all works.

Working With Keyframes

The first part of building a CSS animation is to create a *keyframes* declaration. Web designers that familiar with programming might conceptualize this as building a function that can be called and referenced from elsewhere in a stylesheet.

A *keyframe* is a specialized CSS rule. It is similar to a normal CSS declaration, but can be named with an identifier within which one can specify CSS rules and changes over the duration of time with a list of *percentage* values (or the keywords *to* and *from*).

It will be simpler to understand when a keyframe in seen in action. Hence, let's create a simple animation that will fade in and fade out the *box-shadow* that was previously added to :focus pseudo class of the web form's input text boxes.

We'll name this *keyframe* **pulse** and set three rules that differ slightly:

One rule that executes at the starting point (0%)

One rule that executes at the halfway point (50%)

And

One rule that executes at the end (100%).

Each percentage rule just adjusts the level of opacity of the blue box-shadow, from 20% up to 90% and back down to 20%. This change in opacity, when transitioned over time and looped, creates the appearance of the input text box having a pulsating border when focused upon in any WebKit-powered Browser (i.e. *Safari* and *Chrome*).

The *pulse* keyframe code spec:

```
@-webkit-keyframes pulse
{
    0%
    {
        -webkit-box-shadow: 0 0 12px rgba(51, 204, 255, 0.2);
    }
```

```
    50%
    {
      webkit-box-shadow: 0 0 12px rgba(51, 204, 255, 0.9);
    }
    100%
    {
      -webkit-box-shadow: 0 0 12px rgba(51, 204, 255, 0.2);
    }
}
```

The *keyframe* rules are being specified for WebKit engine based Browsers only, hence the use of using the –webkitvendor prefix. CSS Animations are still unsupported in any Browser but Safari and Chrome, and the –webkitvendor prefix alone is being used.

Referencing The *keyframe*

The second part of a CSS animation is referencing the *keyframe* by *name* (i.e. *pulse*) when using the CSS animation property.

In this case, a pulsing *box-shadow* should run when a website visitor focuses on a text input box in the form.

At this moment in time the keyframe will be called by name, a duration for the animation to run will be set, it will loop infinitely, and finally transition timing function will be set for easing this transition in and easing this transition out. Here is the syntax for a CSS *animation* it is similar to that of a CSS *transition*.

```
#loginAlerts input[type="text"]:focus {
    -webkit-animation: pulse 1.5s infinite ease-in-out;
}
```

With that, we're ensuring that the pulse animation runs only when a website visitor focuses on a text input box on the form (*in Safari and Chrome only*).

The result is quite stunning. Diagram 13.16 shows what happens – i.e. a slow, animated fade in/out of the box-shadow - as if the input text box is waiting to be interacted with.

Diagram 13.16

The *animation* property to used set the values for calling the animation all in one rule this is acceptable shorthand. Alternatively, each value can be specified with its own property as given below:

```
#loginAlerts input[type="text"]:focus
{
    -webkit-animation-name: pulse;
    -webkit-animation-duration: 1.5s;
    -webkit-animation-iteration-count: infinite;
    -webkit-animation-timing-function: ease-in-out;
}
```

Reusing *animation*

A nice thing about *keyframes* is that they can be reused throughout the style sheet within multiple declarations. For example, same *pulse* animation can be applied to the web forms *Submit* button whenever the site visitor hovers their mouse cursor on the Submit button or if they Focus on the Submit button. This codespec adds a blue-pulsing glow around the Submit button in any WebKit based Browser.

It's as simple as adding that same animation rule to a new :hover / :focus pseudo classes for the Submit button, just as was done with the text input boxes.

```
#loginAlerts input[type="submit"]:hover,
#loginAlerts input[type="submit"]:focus
{
    -webkit-animation: pulse 1.5s infinite ease-in-out;
}
```

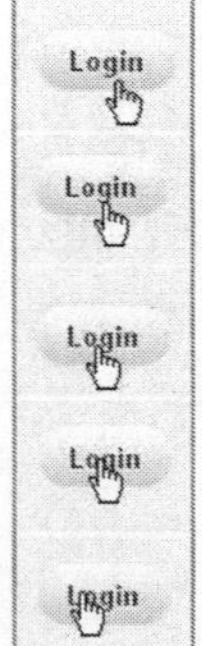

Diagram 13.17

The pulse animation we previously created for text inputs fades blue box-shadow in and out. This can be sued with the web forms Submit button as well. The special effect also works nicely), glowing softly as seen in diagram 13.17 adjacent when the Submit button is hovered or focused upon by the site visitor.

It is as if the Submit button is just waiting for the site visitor to Submit their information.

What About Other Browsers?

Adding CSS Animation is where only one Browser engine manufacturer - WebKit has been targeted. One of the primary reasons CSS3 is being used more and more is because of its adoption by Firefox, Opera, and even IE9.

The question worth asking is if it is worth considering CSS Animation and its syntax at this point in time. This is certainly something to consider.

Well either CSS Animation will remain a WebKit only technology, or it will go the way of Transitions and Transforms and be adopted by the other Browsers and move on sometime into the CSS3 recommendations at W3C.

Either way, CSS Animation is simple, requires very little overhead, and are safely ignored by Browsers that do not support them. Then CSS based animation demonstrated here is rather rudimentary, barely scratching the surface of what is possible on screen with just markup and stylesheets. It's exciting stuff, and for that reason alone it's worth experimenting with.

Focus On Interaction

It's rare when web form elements are also crucial brand elements. That is precisely why web forms are a fantastic opportunity use CSS3 to enhance their look and feel.

Form elements differ greatly in appearance depending on the site visitor's environment, but its these very difference that can embraced by choosing to enrich them with CSS3 style rules, knowing the web form will degrade to gracefully to fully-functional, familiar web form, with default form controls in Browsers that do not yet support CSS3.

Self Review Questions

Fill In The Blanks

1. ____________ are another aspect of a website that involves visitor interaction.
2. Forms can be groomed using ____________ to offer greater site visitor delight.
3. The ____________ pseudo-class in CSS3 is not supported in IE8 and lower.
4. A simple way to add some depth to a text input box is by using CSS____________, which are new in CSS3.
5. CSS3 can create a gradient from one color to another without the use of any____________.
6. CSS gradients are currently supported in ____________, ____________and __________only.
7. For non critical uses, CSS3 gradients are a ____________ solution that degrades well.

8. CSS gradients can be assigned anywhere that an image can be declared within a____________.
9. The syntax for declaring CSS gradients differs slightly between ____________ implementation and____________.
10. The syntax differs between ____________ and ____________ implementations.
11. Browser vendor specific, prefixed, ____________ rules are used to make that happen in Safari and Firefox.
12. ____________ is one User Interface element that can demonstrate exactly how transformative CSS3 can really be.

True Or False

13. Browsers that do not yet support CSS3 gradients will include *background-image* styling rules and the input text boxes will just be flat white.
14. The nice thing of applying CSS3 styling to a form button is that the look and feel of the button is very flexible.
15. If the web form is viewed in Internet Explorer 7, a browser that has zero support for CSS3 a perfectly acceptable, functional form is visible.
16. CSS3 styling cannot be used to draw the site visitors attention to a text input box during web form filling time.
17. CSS3 Animations were initially developed by the team that created the WebKit Browser engine.
18. Animations work in *Firefox* or *Opera*, and there is planned support in *IE9*.
19. The first part of building a CSS animation is to create a *keyframes* declaration.
20. A *keyframe* is not specialized CSS rule.
21. A nice thing about *keyframes* is that they can be reused throughout the stylesheet within multiple declarations.
22. Adding CSS Animation is where only one Browser engine manufacturer - WebKit has been targeted.

Hands-On-Exercise

1) Create an Register Form with the following fields:

First Name	Text Box
Last Name	Text Box
Email ID	Text Box
Password	Text Box
Confirm Password	Text Box
Register Now!!!	Submit Button

The Title **REGISTER** should be bold and should have an effect of red.

There should be an icon next to the Title **REGISTER** (register icon given in the CD).

An effect of red should be visible when focus is on each text-box.

An effect of red should be visible when focus and on mouse of of the Register Now!!

Output of this exercise is shown in diagram 13.18

Please use all the CSS3 elements that have been learned in this chapter.

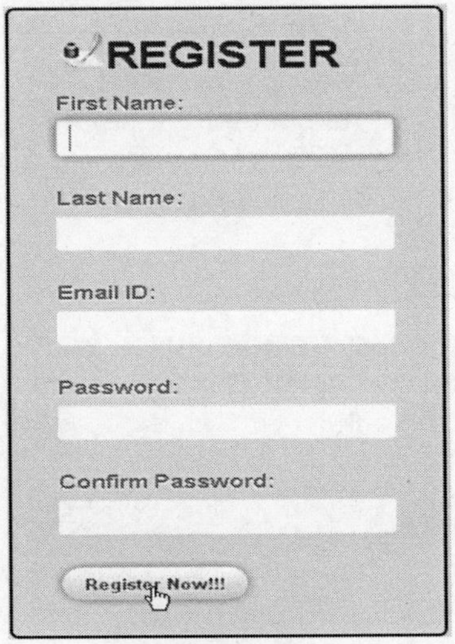

Diagram 13.18

14. Transforming The Message

CSS based transforms were also initially developed by the WebKit Browser engine team. This was then adopted and used in two separate CSS3 Working Drafts at the W3C:

1. CSS 2D Transforms (http://www.w3.org/TR/CSS3-2d-transforms/)
2. CSS 3D Transforms (http://www.w3.org/TR/CSS3-3d-transforms/)

This material focuses solely on 2D transforms they are the most practical to use right now. 2D transforms have the most Browser support, including *Safari 3.2*, *Chrome 3.2*, *Firefox 4.0*, and *Opera 10.5*.

What are CSS Transforms? W3C describes them as:

CSS 2D Transforms allow elements rendered by CSS to be transformed in two-dimensional space.

Most likely this definition was most *unhelpful*.

The very best way to understand CSS rule based transforms is to see them in action. Here is a simple example which applying various 2D transforms on a small photo gallery. Once these techniques have been understood we can put them to practice elsewhere.

The Scale Transform

Consider a horizontal list of three, subtly framed photos from a recent trip to Martha's Vineyard, a small island off the coast of Massachusetts. This is a rather typical design pattern i.e. a grid of linked images as shown in diagram 14.1.

Diagram 14.1

An HTML unordered list is going to be used to mark these three images up as shown below:

```
<ul class="gallery">
    <li><a href="#"><img src="images/photo1.jpg" /></a></li>
    <li><a href="#"><img src="images/photo2.jpg" /></a></li>
    <li><a href="#"><img src="images/photo3.jpg" /></a></li>
</ul>
```

With no CSS style rules applied to the unordered list, diagram 14.2 shows how this image list would appear by default. Notice how the images are quite a bit larger required in the final design. This is intentional, as CSS rules will be used to scale them down.

Diagram 14.2

Adding style

Now add some CSS rules to make this vertical list of photos into a horizontal grid, with a one pixel border around each image also do note the page background is a light gray #eee.

```
ul.gallery li {
float: left;
margin: 0 10px;
padding: 10px;
border: 1px solid #ddd;
list-style: none;
}
ul.gallery li a img {
float: left;
width: 200px;
}
```

Here the list items have been floated *left*, the list-style property has been used to turn bullets off, and each li has been wrapped in a one pixel gray border. The images themselves have been resized down to 200px wide.

Those two CSS rule declarations will get us where we want to go in terms of a default design as shown in diagram 14.1.

Applying The Scale Transform To The :hover Pseudo Class

Now it's time for transforms. A scale transform is being added to make a photo larger when a site visitor hovers their mouse cursor on the picture.

Note: *The original images are much larger than the 200px width specified in the CSS styles rule. This means that the image size can be safely scale up while maintaining its quality.*

Scale transforms are supported in *Safari*, *Chrome*, *Firefox*, and *Opera* each requiring a specific vendor prefix to be used when crafting the CSS3 style rule. Let's add a CSS3 rules stack that satisfies those Browsers as well as any future ones as follows:

```
ul.gallery li a:hover img {
-webkit-transform: scale(1.5);
-moz-transform: scale(1.5);
-o-transform: scale(1.5);
transform: scale(1.5);
}
```

When the image hyperlinks are hovered on, the CSS3 styling says, scale the images to 1.5 times their initial size, which was originally 200px wide. Setting scale(2) would make the image twice as large, setting scale(0.5) would the image half as large, and so on. Refer to diagram 14.3.

Diagram 14.3

Diagram 14.3 shows the result, viewed here in Safari. Notice how transform does not disturb the other two images in the HTML document, and zooms the photo out from the center, without affecting the layout around it.

Alternatively one can also optionally set a *transform-origin* that dictates where the transform scaling will expand from: *top*, *bottom*, *center*, or a *percentage*.

For example, to have the image scale out from the *bottom left* of its container instead of the *center*, this is the changed codespec:

```
ul.gallery li a:hover img
{
-webkit-transform-origin: bottom left;
-moz-transform-origin: bottom left;
-o-transform-origin: bottom left;
transform-origin: bottom left;
-webkit-transform: scale(1.5);
-moz-transform: scale(1.5);
-o-transform: scale(1.5);
transform: scale(1.5);
}
```

Adding An Appropriate Drop Shadow

To go a step further with this example, add a drop shadow to the image when it is hovered upon. This would be an appropriate use of the CSS3 *box-shadow* property, as the enlarged photo appears as if it's pulling up off the page.

Now, the drop shadow effect is often overused by web designers. It's easy to get carried away and overdo it, but in this case, an attempt is being made to add a dimension to the image when it enlarges, so it should work out quite well.

The syntax for box-shadow requires Browser vendor prefixes in order to work in *Safari*, *Chrome*, and *Firefox*. Opera 10+ and IE9 Beta support the non-prefixed box-shadow.

Let's add these CSS3 styling rules.

```
ul.gallery li a:hover img {
-webkit-transform: scale(1.5);
-moz-transform: scale(1.5);
-o-transform: scale(1.5);
transform: scale(1.5);
-webkit-box-shadow: 4px 4px 10px rgba(0, 0, 0, 0.5);
-moz-box-shadow: 4px 4px 10px rgba(0, 0, 0, 0.5);
box-shadow: 4px 4px 10px rgba(0, 0, 0, 0.5);
}
```

A CSS3 stack of rules ahs be added for the *box-shadow* property for WebKit and Mozilla browsers that support it, ending with the non-prefixed version as done with other CSS3 styling examples.

To briefly explain the syntax, a shadow is being applied to the hovered image that is 4px from the top, 4px from the left, has a 10px blur, and is black at 50% opacity, thus ensuring it will blend into whatever background or element sits behind it.

Diagram 14.4

As shown in diagram 14.4 the shadow now appears in conjunction with the scale transform when an image photo is hovered over. This combination gives the effect of having the enlarged image pop out from the page.

Smoothing Out The Zoom With A CSS3 Transition

Lastly, adding a CSS3 transition to the linked images will smooth out the scaling, giving the :hover an animated zoom-in-and-zoom-out an effect previously only possible with Flash or JavaScript, but now possible in many Browsers which are CSS3 compliant using just the few lines of CSS3 styling rules. Here is the transition block of CSS3 codespec that has been added to the complete CSS3 rules for this image gallery.

```
ul.gallery li {
float: left;
margin: 0 10px;
padding: 10px;
border: 1px solid #ddd;
list-style: none;
}
ul.gallery li a img
{
float: left;
width: 200px;
-webkit-transition: -webkit-transform 0.2s ease-in-out;
-moz-transition: -moz-transform 0.2s ease-in-out;
transition: transform 0.2s ease-in-out;
}
ul.gallery li a:hover img
{
-webkit-transform: scale(1.5);
-moz-transform: scale(1.5);
-o-transform: scale(1.5);
transform: scale(1.5);
-webkit-box-shadow: 4px 4px 10px rgba(0, 0, 0, 0.5);
-moz-box-shadow: 4px 4px 10px rgba(0, 0, 0, 0.5);
box-shadow: 4px 4px 10px rgba(0, 0, 0, 0.5);
}
```

Notice this time, the property being transitioned is the transform:scale, hence appropriate Browser vendor prefixes are in place for both *transition* and *transform* CSS3 properties.

Transforming The Experience

With all the CSS3 properties in place, the result is quite impressive for the minimal amount of CSS3 rules specified to make this happen. Most of the work done to make this effect happen is loaded on the Browsers that support it, rather than injecting Flash or JavaScript to do this.

Again, the CSS3 properties in this particular example are firmly positioned within the site visitors UI experience. When an image is hovered over, an enhanced view is offered. This effect is not critical for Browsers that do not support these CSS3 properties.

Users of Internet Explorer, for example, will just see a gallery of clickable image thumbnails, and that's perfectly OK. If the hover treatment for such images was critical, then it would be necessary to rethink the use of CSS3 to achieve this visual experience.

Rotate Skew And Translate

In addition to *scale*, there are three other transforms available for *rotating*, *skewing*, and *translating* elements. Translate moves elements via x/y coordinates. Let's add each of these to the image gallery example to quickly see how these operate.

Diagram 14.5

Adding Rotation

To rotate an image when its hovered upon, while still scaling it up, add the following rotate transform to the :hover pseudo class CSS3 styling rule.

```
ul.gallery li a:hover img {
-webkit-transform: scale(1.5) rotate(-10deg);
-moz-transform: scale(1.5) rotate(-10deg);
-o-transform: scale(1.5) rotate(-10deg);
```

```
transform: scale(1.5) rotate(-10deg);
-webkit-box-shadow: 4px 4px 10px rgba(0, 0, 0, 0.5);
-moz-box-shadow: 4px 4px 10px rgba(0, 0, 0, 0.5);
box-shadow: 4px 4px 10px rgba(0, 0, 0, 0.5);
}
```

In the above CSS3 styling rules then image is still scaling up on **:**hover, but it's also being rotated 10 degrees to the left using the *rotate* property. This will work in *Safari*, *Chrome*, *Firefox*, and *Opera*. A negative value from -1deg to -360deg will rotate any element (*in this case an image*) counterclockwise, while a positive value from 1deg to 360deg will rotate any element (*in this case an image*) clockwise. Refer to diagram 14.6.

Diagram 14.6

Alternatively, varying rotate transforms can be added to the unordered list items, so that the image (*and frame*) appear to be tossed on the table, randomly. Then the image can be rotated and scaled on **:**hover as well as shown in diagram 14.6.

This is an appropriate place to add CSS3 styling rules because this is related to the site visitor's experience domain. This does not mean that these techniques cannot be used on the default view of any web page design, provided such design elements are not critical to web page functionality and that they degrade well.

For example, should the Browser not support rotate transforms, and the photos appear perfectly straight, that would be fine. Nothing would appear broken on the web page.

The skew transform

Skew transform takes x and y coordinates and skews an element (in this case the images). To skew the images in our gallery on **:**hover, use the following CSS3 rule, skewing negative five degrees on the x coordinate, and 30 degrees on the y coordinate as shown in diagram 14.7.

```
ul.gallery li a:hover img {
-webkit-transform: scale(1.5) skew(-5deg, 30deg);
-moz-transform: scale(1.5) skew(-5deg, 30deg);
-o-transform: scale(1.5) skew(-5deg, 30deg);
transform: scale(1.5) skew(-5deg, 30deg);
}
```

Diagram 14.7

Like rotate, skew accepts positive and negative degree values. One value can be used for both x and y and the output will be as shown in diagram 14.8. Here is the CSS3 styling rule codespec.

```
ul.gallery li a:hover img {
-webkit-transform: scale(1.5) skew(30deg);
-moz-transform: scale(1.5) skew(30deg);
-o-transform: scale(1.5) skew(30deg);
transform: scale(1.5) skew(30deg);
}
```

Diagram 14.8

What was just done using the images is far from visually compelling, and admittedly, I do not use skew all that often; however, I'm convinced there are interesting uses for it. For example, skew could be used on blocks of text to create three-dimensional visuals all with semantic markup and CSS3 style rules as shown in diagram 14.9.

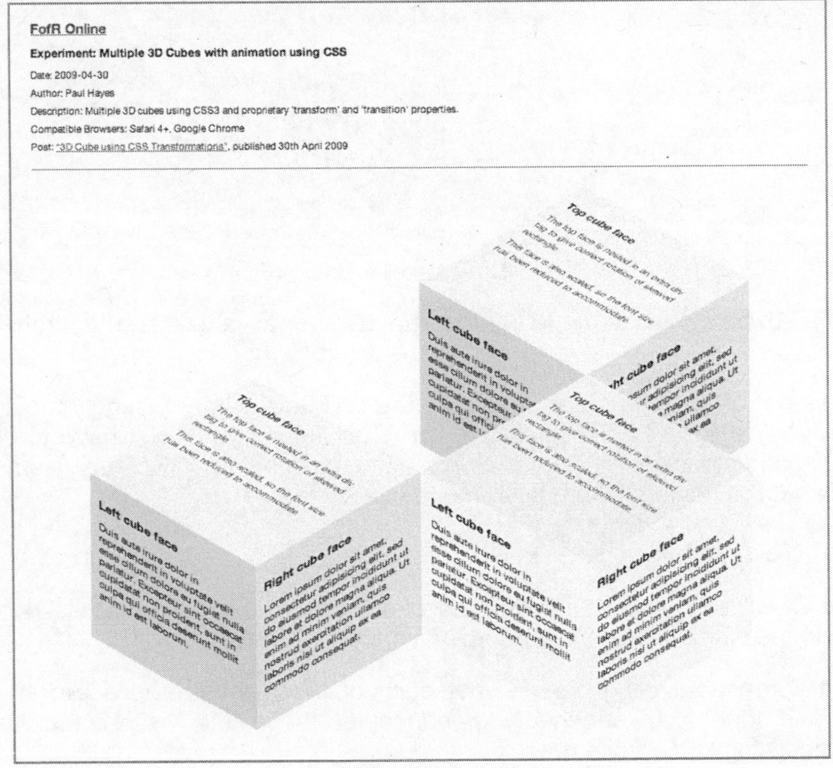

Diagram 14.9

To move an image in the photo gallery from its initial position upon **:hover**, use *translate* with the current transition in place, that movement will be smoothly animated.

Here's the syntax for moving the image 20 pixels to the right and 40 pixels from the top of its original location as shown in diagram 14.10.

```
ul.gallery li a:hover img {
-webkit-transform: scale(1.5) translate(20px, 40px);
-moz-transform: scale(1.5) translate(20px, 40px);
-o-transform: scale(1.5) translate(20px, 40px);
transform: scale(1.5) translate(20px, 40px);
}
```

Diagram 14.10

If the image had to be moved to the left and/or top, use negative values, e.g., translate (-20px, -40px).

Translate does not disturb the other images in the HTML document, simply moving a specific image explicitly to wherever it is required to go. That means you don't have to be concerned with margins, padding, clearing floats, or absolute positioning. Give any element translate coordinates in a CSS3 style rule and it will move exactly there.

Harmless Degradation

Like all other CSS3 style rule examples, the photo gallery example discussed earlier in this chapter, is harmless for Browsers that do not yet support CSS3 styling.

In the end, the important thing here is that each of these images is a clickable link. What happens beyond that is an enriched experience for those site visitors that use Browsers capable of processing CSS3 style rules.

Self Review Questions

Fill In The Blanks

1. CSS based transforms were also initially developed by the _________Browser engine team.
2. *____________ Transforms allow elements rendered by CSS to be transformed in two-dimensional space.*
3. A ___________ transform is being added to make a photo larger when a site visitor hovers their mouse cursor on the picture.
4. One can also optionally set a ___________ that dictates where the transform scaling will expand from: *top*, *bottom*, *center*, or a *percentage*.
5. The syntax for ___________ requires Browser vendor prefixes in order to work in *Safari*, *Chrome*, and *Firefox*.
6. ___________ and ___________ support the non-prefixed box-shadow.
7. The drop shadow effect is often ___________ by web designers.

True Or False

8. The property being transitioned is the transform:scale, hence appropriate Browser vendor prefixes are in place for both *transition* and *transform* CSS3 properties.
9. Scale transforms are not supported in *Safari*, *Chrome*, *Firefox*, and *Opera*.
10. Skew transform takes only the x coordinates.
11. Translate disturbs the other images in the HTML document.
12. In addition to *scale*, there are three other transforms available for *rotating*, *skewing*, and *translating* elements.
13. *CSS 2D Transforms allow elements rendered by CSS to be transformed in four-dimensional space.*
14. A scale transform is being added to make a photo larger when a site visitor hovers their mouse cursor on the picture.

Hands-on Exercise

1. Create a row with the Latest Products, using images given in the CD. Each image should have its own shadow effect. On mouse over of each image rotate the images. The first and third images should rotate towards the right. The second and fourth images should rotate towards the left. The rotation transformation should be very slow.

   Output of this exercise is shown in diagram 14.11

   Please use all the CSS3 elements that have been learned in this chapter.

Diagram 14.11

15. CSS3 - In Conclusion

In the above CSS3 chapters a lot of wonderful ways to use CSS3 right now in daily *web page / website / portal / web application* creation work was covered.

By demonstrating just how these CSS3 techniques can enhance site visitor experience in Browsers that support them, while gracefully degrading in Browsers that do not, hopefully inspires you to begin to use CSS3 styling rules today regardless of the project being worked on.

The real promise of CSS3 is that it enables web developers to solve common design problems more efficiently, with less code and greater flexibility when compared to using Flash or JavaScript.

Hence, as long as *clients* and *bosses* can accept that *web page / website / portal / web applications* may look and be experienced differently in Browsers that are CSS3 compliant and work perfectly well in Browsers that do not support CSS3, then the sky's the limit, Jump right in and being to experience the power of CSS3.

I often hear web designers and coders say they cannot wait to use CSS3 when it's fully supported across a plethora of Browsers. My goal in writing this book was to prove that web designers and coders do not need to wait until that happens.

They must start experimenting with CSS3 now. Begin using CSS3 for non-critical visual events in *web page / website / portal / web applications* designs.

Then armed with what knowledge and experience, importantly — how CSS3 styling rules degrade gracefully where they do not, you can comfortably achieve what previously took more time and code, with only a few lines of CSS in today work.

What About Clients And Bosses Who Just Don't Get CSS3?

Another question I've often encountered from fellow web designer and coders when talking about CSS3 is whether to use it in client work or not.

How do you educate clients on the benefits of using CSS3 over other solutions? It's the education that's most helpful. Do show your clients how much less code and how many fewer images are used to get exactly the same effect / styling job done.

Show them how the site visitor experience differs in Browsers that do not yet support CSS3. Explain the tradeoffs to them. If this sounds like too much work, then just buckle down and *do it.*

Start adding CSS3 style rules to daily work and let clients and bosses happily discover this. The truth is, many of the examples I've demonstrated in this book are discoverable while experiencing any *web page / website / portal / web application* i.e. hovering, focusing, interacting, and so on.

That's intentional of course. Often, with my own client work, I'll add a specific CSS3 style based site visitor experience enhancement into the project without saying a word about it, surprising and delighting the client when they stumble on it. More importantly, surprising and delighting the client's site visitors when they stumble upon it.

Well if a client demands that CSS3 type styling behaviors must work in every browser imaginable? Well, that costs extra does it not?.

Looking Ahead

What about the future? The whole of CSS3 styling elements is much, much more than can be covered in this material.

I wanted to focus very squarely on what's practically usable in CSS3 styling today, avoiding what's still being discussed at W3C and perhaps do not have widespread implementation across modern Browsers.

Having said that, Browser vendor support for CSS3 properties is growing strongly. New CSS3 property support is being added in almost every new iteration of WebKit, Mozilla, and Opera.

Rapid adoption using Browser vendor specific prefixing is what is driving innovation. Keeping tabs on what's new, and watching for a tipping point in Browser implementation among forward thinking browsers is what can educate real world use of CSS3 properties.

There are exciting times ahead by way of IE9 Beta. More and more CSS3 support is being added to Internet Explorer, and that means good things.

Eventually, CSS3 would be relied upon not only for site visitor delight, but also for those critical visual concepts as well (*web page layout being a primary example*).

It's been a seemingly slow path to get there, but that's necessary for things to unfold correctly. While on that slow path, don't hesitate to grab hold and use what works in the present. You, your clients, and the web's citizens will all benefit.

Answers To Self Review Questions

10. Using CSS Today

Fill In The Blanks

1 *-webkit-border-radius*

2 box-shadow

3 modular

4 *float*

5 border-radius

6 text-shadow

7 1, 0

8 *box-shadow*

9 opaque

10 CSS3 property

True Or False

11 False

12 True

13 *False*

14 True

15 True

16 True

17 *False*

18 *False*

19 *False*

20 True

11. Understanding CSS Transitions

Fill In The Blanks

1 JavaScript

2 WebKit

3 W3C

4 Opera, Firefox

5 triggering

6 :hover

7 duplication

8 pseudo-classes

9 *all*

10 jQuery, Prototype, script.aculo.us

11 sensibility

True Or False

12 False

13 False

14 True

15 True

16 False

17 True

18 True

19 False

12. Hover Crafting With CSS

Fill In The Blanks

1 Hovering
2 RGBA
3 *all*
4 *last*
5 flexibility
6 *opacity*
7 Microsoft filter

True Or False

8 True
9 False
10 True
11 False

13. Using CSS Today

Fill In The Blanks

1 Web forms
2 CSS3
3 *:last-child*
4 gradients
5 images
6 *Safari 4+*, *Chrome 2+*, *Firefox 3.6+*
7 flexible
8 stylesheet
9 Safari's, Firefox
10 –webkit, –moz
11 *background-image*
12 <Input type="button">

True Or False

13 False
14 True
15 True
16 False
17 True
18 False
19 True
20 False
21 True
22 True

14. Transforming The Message

Fill In The Blanks

1 WebKit
2 *CSS 2D*
3 scale
4 *transform-origin*
5 box-shadow
6 Opera 10+, IE9 Beta
7 overused

True Or False

8 True
9 *False*
10 False
11 *False*
12 True
13 *False*
14 True

Solutions To Hands On Exercises

Chapter 11 - Understanding CSS Transitions

1)

index.html

```
<!doctype html>
<html lang="en">
<head>
    <meta charset="utf-8" />
    <title>CSS 2 - Understanding CSS Transitions - Hands-On-Exercise</title>
    <link rel="stylesheet" href="css/styles.css" type="text/css" media="screen" />
</head>
<body>
<!-- divIeHack STARTS -->
<div id="divIeHack">
    <!-- divWrapper STARTS -->
    <div id="divWrapper">
        <!-- headerName STARTS -->
        <header id="headerName">
            <hgroup>
                <div id="divName">
                    <h1>Lorem Ipsum</h1>
                    <h2>Come learn how to use lorem ipsum</h2>
                </div>
```

```
            <div id="divLogo">
                <img src="images/logo1.gif" alt="Logo" width="150" height="107" align="right"
/>
            </div>
        </hgroup>
    </header><!-- headerName ENDS -->
    <!-- divMainSec STARTS -->
    <section id="divMainSec">
        <aside id="sidebar"><!-- sidebar -->
            <div id="divLeftMenu">
                <h3>Menu Section</h3>
                <nav><!-- top nav -->
                    <ul class="menu">
                        <li><a href="#">Home</a></li>
                        <li><a href="#">About Us</a></li>
                        <li><a href="#">Products</a></li>
                        <li><a href="#">Forum</a></li>
                        <li><a href="#">Contact Us</a></li>
                    </ul>
                </nav><!-- end of top nav -->
            </div><!-- divLeftMenu ENDS -->
        </aside><!-- end of sidebar -->
        <section id="content"><!-- #content -->
            <article>
                <h3><a href="#">Lorem Ipsum </a></h3>
                <p>Lorem Ipsum is simply dummy text of the printing and typesetting industry.
Lorem Ipsum has been the industry's standard dummy text ever since the 1500s, when an
unknown printer took a galley of type and scrambled it to make a type specimen book. It has
survived not only five centuries, but also the leap into electronic typesetting, remaining
essentially unchanged. It was popularised in the 1960s with the release of Letraset sheets
containing Lorem Ipsum passages, and more recently with desktop publishing software like
Aldus PageMaker including versions of Lorem Ipsum.</p>
```

```
                <p>Contrary to popular belief, Lorem Ipsum is not simply random text. It has roots in a piece of classical Latin literature from 45 BC, making it over 2000 years old. Richard McClintock, a Latin professor at Hampden-Sydney College in Virginia, looked up one of the more obscure Latin words, consectetur, from a Lorem Ipsum passage, and going through the cites of the word in classical literature, discovered the undoubtable source. Lorem Ipsum comes from sections 1.10.32 and 1.10.33 of "de Finibus Bonorum et Malorum" (The Extremes of Good and Evil) by Cicero, written in 45 BC. This book is a treatise on the theory of ethics, very popular during the Renaissance. The first line of Lorem Ipsum, "Lorem ipsum dolor sit amet..", comes from a line in section 1.10.32.</p>

            </article>
        </section><!-- end of #content -->

    </section><!-- divMainSec ENDS -->

    <footer id="footer-area">

        <section id="footer-outer-block">
                <aside class="footer-segment">
                    <h4>Socail Networking</h4>
                    <ul>
                        <li><a href="#">Twitter</a></li>
                        <li><a href="#">Facebook</a></li>
                        <li><a href="#">Skype</a></li>
                    </ul>
                </aside><!-- end of #first footer segment -->

                <aside class="footer-segment">
                    <h4>Awesome Stuff</h4>
                        <ul>
                            <li><a href="#">one linkylink</a></li>
                            <li><a href="#">two linkylinks</a></li>
                            <li><a href="#">three linkylinks</a></li>
                        </ul>
                </aside><!-- end of #second footer segment -->
```

```
                <aside class="footer-segment">
                    <h4>Coolness</h4>
                        <ul>
                            <li><a href="#">one linkylink</a></li>
                            <li><a href="#">two linkylinks</a></li>
                            <li><a href="#">three linkylinks</a></li>
                        </ul>
                </aside><!-- end of #third footer segment -->

                <aside class="footer-segment">
                        <h4>Blahdyblah</h4>
                        <p>Integer nec odio. Praesent libero. Sed cursus ante dapibus diam.</p>
                </aside><!-- end of #fourth footer segment -->

            </section><!-- end of footer-outer-block -->

    </footer><!-- end of footer-area -->

    </div><!-- divWrapper ENDS -->

</div><!-- divIeHack ENDS -->

</body>
</html>
```

css/styles.css

```
/* Styling HTML Tags */
body {
    line-height: 1;
    background: #5B250B;
    font-family:Tahoma, Arial, Helvetica, sans-serif;
    color: #666;
    font-size: 14px;
```

```
    line-height: 18px;
}
h1, h2, h3, h4, h5, h6
{
    font-weight: bold;
    clear: both;
}
a:link, a:visited
{
    color:#946c4e;
    text-decoration: none;
}
a:hover, a:active
{
    color: #7e5b30;
}
p
{
    margin-bottom: 18px;
}
li
{
    padding-left: 5px;
}
/* Styling User Defined Tags */
/* layout */
#divIeHack
{
    float:left;
    width:100%;
    height:150px;
}
```

```
#divWrapper
{
    width: 940px;
    margin: 0 auto;
}
    #headerName
    {
        float:left;
        width:100%;
        min-height:85px;
        background-color:#8C540C;
    }
        #headerName hgroup
        {
            float:left;
            width:95.8%;
            padding-left:40px;

            color: #EDE6DD;
            clear:both;
        }
            #divName
            {
                float:left;
                width:60%;
                height:auto;
            }
            #divLogo
            {
                float:left;
                width:40%;
                height:auto;
            }
```

```
        #divName h2
        {
            font-size:10pt;
            color:#FFFFFF;
        }
#divMainSec
{
    float:left;
    width: 940px;
    height:auto;

    padding: 15px 0 10px 0;
    background: #ede6dd;
}
    #sidebar
    {
        float: left;
        width: 28%;
        height:auto;

        padding-left: 20px;
        /*background: #990000;*/
    }
        #divLeftMenu
        {
            float:left;
            width:100%;
            height:auto;

            padding-top:30px;
            background-color:#8C540C;
        }
```

```
    #divLeftMenu h3
    {
        margin-left:28px;
        color:#FFFFFF;
    }
#content
{
    float: right;
    width: 67%;
    height:auto;

    margin-right: 10px;
    padding: 5px 5px;
    /*background-color:#FFFFCC;*/
}
/* ARTICLES */
article img {
    border: none;
    -webkit-box-shadow: 3px 3px 7px #777;
    -moz-box-shadow: 3px 3px 7px #777;
}
#content p, ul, ol, hr {
    margin-bottom: 24px;
}
#content ul ul, ol ol, ul ol, ol ul {
    margin-bottom: 0;
}
#content h2, h3, h4, h5, h6 {
    color: #333;
    margin: 0 0 20px 0;
    line-height: 1.5em;
}
```

```
/* Styling Top Menu STARTS */
nav .menu
{
    font-size: 14px;
    font-weight: bold;
}
nav .menu
{
    margin: 0px 0px;
    padding:0px 0px;
    list-style: none;
    line-height: normal;
}
nav .menu li
{
    margin: 0px 0px 20px 5px;
    list-style: none;
}
nav .menu a
{
    padding: 5px 15px;
    text-decoration: none;
    font-size: 11pt;
    text-decoration:none;
    -webkit-transition: all 5s ease;
    -moz-transition: all 5s ease;
    -o-transition: all 5s ease;
    transition: all 5s ease;
}
```

```
nav .menu a:hover,
nav .menu a:focus
{
    color: #fff;
    background: rgba(255, 255, 255, 0.15);
}
/* Styling Top Menu ENDS */
/* footer widget blocks - STARTS */
#footer-area
{
    float:left;
    width:100%;
    height:auto;
    padding: 18px 0;
    font-family: Trebuchet MS, serif;
    background-color:#8C540C;
    color: #ede6dd;
    font-size: 90%;
}
.footer-segment
{
    float: left;
    width: 190px;
    margin-right: 20px;
    margin-left: 20px;
}
footer aside h4
{
    color: #f5eee5;
    font-size: 16px;
    line-height: 1.5em;
}
```

```
            footer a:link,
            footer a:visited
            {
                color: #f5eee5;
            }
            /* footer widget blocks - STARTS */
/* Styling User Class Tags */
/* Styling For Product Images STARTS */
.productImg
{
    float:left;
    width:100%;
    height:auto;
    margin-bottom:10px;
}
.productImg a img
{
    border: none;
    opacity: 4;
    /* IE 8 hack */
    -ms-filter: "progid:DXImageTransform.Microsoft.Alpha(Opacity=25)";
    /* IE 5-7 hack */
    filter: alpha(opacity = 25);
}
.productImg a:hover img,
.productImg a:focus img
{
    opacity: 0.3;
    /* IE 8 hack */
    -ms-filter:"progid:DXImageTransform.Microsoft.Alpha(Opacity=60)";
    /* IE 5-7 hack */
    filter: alpha(opacity = 20);
}
/* Styling For Product Images ENDS */
```

Chapter 12 - Hover Crafting With CSS

1) Style the Left Menu of a Web page using CSS Transitions

index.html

```
<!doctype html>
<html lang="en">
<head>
    <meta charset="utf-8" />
    <title>CSS 12 - Understanding CSS Transitions - Hands-On-Exercise 1</title>
    <link rel="stylesheet" href="css/styles.css" type="text/css" media="screen" />
</head>
<body>
<!-- divIeHack STARTS -->
<div id="divIeHack">
    <!-- divWrapper STARTS -->
    <div id="divWrapper">
        <!-- headerName STARTS -->
        <header id="headerName">
            <hgroup>
                <div id="divName">
                    <h1>Lorem Ipsum</h1>
                    <h2>Come learn how to use lorem ipsum</h2>
                </div>
                <div id="divLogo">
                    <img src="images/logo1.gif" alt="Logo" width="150"
                    height="107" align="right" />
                </div>
            </hgroup>
        </header><!-- headerName ENDS -->
        <!-- divMainSec STARTS -->
        <section id="divMainSec">
```

```
        <aside id="sidebar"><!-- sidebar -->

            <div id="divLeftMenu">
                <nav><!-- top nav -->
                    <ul class="menu">
                        <li><a href="#">Home</a></li>
                        <li><a href="#">About Us</a></li>
                        <li><a href="#">Products</a></li>
                        <li><a href="#">Forum</a></li>
                        <li><a href="#">Contact Us</a></li>
                    </ul>
                </nav><!-- end of top nav -->
            </div>
        </aside><!-- end of sidebar -->

        <section id="content"><!-- #content -->

            <article>
                <h3><a href="#">Lorem Ipsum </a></h3>
                <p>Lorem Ipsum is simply dummy text of the printing
 and typesetting industry. Lorem Ipsum has been the industry's standard dummy text ever since the 1500s, when an unknown printer took a galley of type and scrambled it to make a type specimen book. It has survived not only five centuries, but also the leap into electronic typesetting, remaining essentially unchanged. It was popularised in the 1960s with the release of Letraset sheets containing Lorem Ipsum passages, and more recently with desktop publishing software like Aldus PageMaker including versions of Lorem Ipsum.</p>
                <p>Contrary to popular belief, Lorem Ipsum is not simply random text. It has roots in a piece of classical Latin literature from 45 BC, making it over 2000 years old. Richard McClintock, a Latin professor at Hampden-Sydney College in Virginia, looked up one of the more obscure Latin words, consectetur, from a Lorem Ipsum passage, and going through the cites of the word in classical literature, discovered the undoubtable source. Lorem Ipsum comes from sections 1.10.32 and 1.10.33 of "de Finibus Bonorum et Malorum" (The Extremes of Good and Evil) by Cicero, written in 45 BC. This book is a treatise on the theory of ethics, very popular during the Renaissance. The first line of Lorem Ipsum, "Lorem ipsum dolor sit amet..", comes from a line in section 1.10.32.</p>
            </article>

      </section><!-- divMainSec ENDS -->
```

```
<footer id="footer-area">
    <section id="footer-outer-block">
            <aside class="footer-segment">
                <h4>Friends</h4>
                    <ul>
                        <li><a href="#">one
                            linkylink</a></li>
                        <li><a href="#">two
                            linkylinks</a></li>
                        <li><a href="#">three
                            linkylinks</a></li>
                    </ul>
            </aside><!-- end of #first footer segment -->
            <aside class="footer-segment">
                <h4>Socail Networking</h4>
                    <ul>
                    <li><a href="#">Twitter</a></li>
                    <li><a href="#">Facebook</a></li>
                    <li><a href="#">Skype</a></li>
                    </ul>
            </aside><!-- end of #second footer segment -->
            <aside class="footer-segment">
                <h4>Coolness</h4>
                    <ul>
                        <li><a href="#">one
                        linkylink</a></li>
                        <li><a href="#">two
                        linkylinks</a></li>
                        <li><a href="#">three
                        linkylinks</a></li>
                    </ul>
            </aside><!-- end of #third footer segment -->
```

```
                <aside class="footer-segment">
                    <h4>Blahdyblah</h4>
                    <p>The standard chunk of Lorem Ipsum
                    used since the 1500s is reproduced
                    below for those interested.</p>
                </aside><!-- end of #fourth footer segment -->

            </section><!-- end of footer-outer-block -->

    </footer><!-- end of footer-area -->

    </div><!-- divWrapper ENDS -->

</div><!-- divIeHack ENDS -->
</body>
</html>
```

css/style.css

```
/* Styling HTML Tags */
body {
    line-height: 1;
    background: #5B250B;
    font-family:Tahoma, Arial, Helvetica, sans-serif;
    color: #666;
    font-size: 14px;
    line-height: 18px;
}
h1, h2, h3, h4, h5, h6
{
    font-weight: bold;
    clear: both;
}
a:link, a:visited
{
    color:#946c4e;
    text-decoration: none;
}
```

```
a:hover, a:active
{
    color: #7e5b30;
}
p
{
    margin-bottom: 18px;
}
li
{
    padding-left: 5px;
}
/* Styling User Defined Tags */
/* layout */
#divIeHack
{
    float:left;
    width:100%;
    height:150px;
}
    #divWrapper
    {
        width: 940px;
        margin: 0 auto;
    }
        #headerName
        {
            float:left;
            width:100%;
            min-height:85px;
            background-color:#8C540C;
        }
```

```
        #headerName hgroup
        {
            float:left;
            width:95.8%;
            padding-left:40px;
            color: #EDE6DD;
            clear:both;
        }
            #divName
            {
                float:left;
                width:60%;
                height:auto;
            }
            #divLogo
            {
                float:left;
                width:40%;
                height:auto;
            }
        #divName h2
        {
            font-size:10pt;
            color:#FFFFFF;
        }
    #divMainSec
    {
        float:left;
        width: 940px;
        height:auto;

        padding: 15px 0 10px 0;
        background: #ede6dd;
    }
```

```
#sidebar
{
    float: left;
    width: 28%;
    height:auto;

    padding-left: 20px;
    /*background: #990000;*/
}
    #divLeftMenu
    {
        float:left;
        width:100%;
        height:auto;
        margin-bottom:60%;
        /*background-color:#FFCCFF;*/
    }
    #content
    {
        float: right;
        width: 67%;
        height:auto;

        margin-right: 10px;
        padding: 5px 5px;
        /*background-color:#FFFFCC;*/
    }
    /* ARTICLES */
    article img {
        border: none;
        -webkit-box-shadow: 3px 3px 7px #777;
        -moz-box-shadow: 3px 3px 7px #777;
    }
```

```
#content p, ul, ol, hr
 {
    margin-bottom: 24px;
}
#content ul ul, ol ol, ul ol, ol ul {
    margin-bottom: 0;
}
#content h2, h3, h4, h5, h6 {
    color: #333;
    margin: 0 0 20px 0;
    line-height: 1.5em;
}
/* Styling Top Menu STARTS */
nav .menu
{
    font-size: 14px;
    font-weight: bold;
}
nav .menu
{
    margin: 0px 0px;
    padding:0px 0px;
    list-style: none;
    line-height: normal;
}
nav .menu li
{
    margin: 0px 0px 20px 5px;
    list-style: none;
}
```

```
nav .menu a
{
    padding: 5px 15px;
    text-decoration: none;
    font-size: 11pt;
    color: #5B250B;
    color: rgb(91, 37, 11);
    text-shadow: 0 1px 1px rgba(91, 37, 11);
    -webkit-border-radius: 14px;
    -moz-border-radius: 14px;
    border-radius: 14px;
    -webkit-transition: all 1s ease-in-out;
    -moz-transition: all 1s ease-in-out;
    -o-transition: all 1s ease-in-out;
    transition: all 1s ease-in-out;
}
nav .menu a:hover,
nav .menu a:focus
{
    color: #fff;
    background: rgba(255, 255, 255, 0.15);
}
/* Styling Top Menu ENDS */
/* footer widget blocks - STARTS */
#footer-area
{
    float:left;
    width:100%;
    height:auto;
    padding: 18px 0;
    font-family: Trebuchet MS, serif;
```

```
    background-color:#8C540C;
    color: #ede6dd;
    font-size: 90%;
}
.footer-segment
{
    float: left;
    width: 190px;
    margin-right: 20px;
    margin-left: 20px;
}
footer aside h4
{
    color: #f5eee5;
    font-size: 16px;
    line-height: 1.5em;
}
footer a:link,
footer a:visited
{
    color: #f5eee5;
}
/* footer widget blocks - STARTS */
```

2) Create a row with the Popular Products

index.html

```
<!doctype html>
<html lang="en">
<head>
    <meta charset="utf-8" />
    <title>CSS 12 - Understanding CSS Transitions - Hands-On-Exercise 2</title>
    <link rel="stylesheet" href="css/styles.css" type="text/css" media="screen" />
</head>
<body>
<!-- divIeHack STARTS -->
<div id="divIeHack">
    <!-- divWrapper STARTS -->
    <div id="divWrapper">
        <!-- headerName STARTS -->
        <header id="headerName">
            <hgroup>
                <div id="divName">
                    <h1>Lorem Ipsum</h1>
                    <h2>Come learn how to use lorem ipsum</h2>
                </div>
                <div id="divLogo">
                    <img src="images/logo1.gif" alt="Logo" width="150"
                    height="107" align="right" />
                </div>
            </hgroup>
        </header><!-- headerName ENDS -->
        <!-- divMainSec STARTS -->
        <section id="divMainSec">
```

```
<aside id="sidebar"><!-- sidebar -->

    <div id="divLeftMenu">
        <nav><!-- top nav -->
            <ul class="menu">
                <li><a href="#">Home</a></li>
                <li><a href="#">About Us</a></li>
                <li><a href="#">Products</a></li>
                <li><a href="#">Forum</a></li>
                <li><a href="#">Contact Us</a></li>
            </ul>
        </nav><!-- end of top nav -->
    </div>
</aside><!-- end of sidebar -->

<section id="content"><!-- #content -->

    <article>
        <h3><a href="#">Lorem Ipsum </a></h3>
        <p>Lorem Ipsum is simply dummy text of the printing
and typesetting industry. Lorem Ipsum has been the industry's standard dummy text ever since the 1500s, when an unknown printer took a galley of type and scrambled it to make a type specimen book. It has survived not only five centuries, but also the leap into electronic typesetting, remaining essentially unchanged. It was popularised in the 1960s with the release of Letraset sheets containing Lorem Ipsum passages, and more recently with desktop publishing software like Aldus PageMaker including versions of Lorem Ipsum.</p>
        <p>Contrary to popular belief, Lorem Ipsum is not simply random text. It has roots in a piece of classical Latin literature from 45 BC, making it over 2000 years old. Richard McClintock, a Latin professor at Hampden-Sydney College in Virginia, looked up one of the more obscure Latin words, consectetur, from a Lorem Ipsum passage, and going through the cites of the word in classical literature, discovered the undoubtable source. Lorem Ipsum comes from sections 1.10.32 and 1.10.33 of "de Finibus Bonorum et Malorum" (The Extremes of Good and Evil) by Cicero, written in 45 BC. This book is a treatise on the theory of ethics, very popular during the Renaissance. The first line of Lorem Ipsum, "Lorem ipsum dolor sit amet..", comes from a line in section 1.10.32.</p>
    </article>

    <article class="productImg">
        <h3><a href="#">Popular Product</a></h3>
```

```
            <a href="#">
            <img src="images/popularproducts/apple.gif"
            alt="Apple Laptop" width="125" height="125" />
            </a>
            <a href="#">
            <img src="images/popularproducts/dell.gif"
            alt="Dell Laptop" width="125" height="125" /></a>
            <a href="#">
            <img src="images/popularproducts/vaio_laptop.gif"
            alt="Vaio Laptop" width="125" height="125" /> </a>
            <a href="#">
            <img src="images/popularproducts/hplaptops.gif"
            alt="HP Laptops" width="125" height="125" />
            </a><br /><br />
        </article>
    </section><!-- end of #content -->
</section><!-- divMainSec ENDS -->
<footer id="footer-area">
    <section id="footer-outer-block">
            <aside class="footer-segment">
                <h4>Friends</h4>
                    <ul>
                        <li><a href="#">one
                            linkylink</a></li>
                        <li><a href="#">two
                            linkylinks</a></li>
                        <li><a href="#">three
                            linkylinks</a></li>
                    </ul>
            </aside><!-- end of #first footer segment -->
```

```
            <aside class="footer-segment">
                <h4>Socail Networking</h4>
                    <ul>
                    <li><a href="#">Twitter</a></li>
                    <li><a href="#">Facebook</a></li>
                    <li><a href="#">Skype</a></li>
                    </ul>
            </aside><!-- end of #second footer segment -->

            <aside class="footer-segment">
                <h4>Coolness</h4>
                    <ul>
                        <li><a href="#">one
                        linkylink</a></li>
                        <li><a href="#">two
                        linkylinks</a></li>
                        <li><a href="#">three
                        linkylinks</a></li>
                    </ul>
            </aside><!-- end of #third footer segment -->

            <aside class="footer-segment">
                    <h4>Blahdyblah</h4>
                    <p>The standard chunk of Lorem Ipsum
                    used since the 1500s is reproduced
                    below for those interested.</p>
            </aside><!-- end of #fourth footer segment -->

        </section><!-- end of footer-outer-block -->

    </footer><!-- end of footer-area -->

    </div><!-- divWrapper ENDS -->

</div><!-- divIeHack ENDS -->
</body>
</html>
```

css/style.css

```
/* Styling HTML Tags */
body {
    line-height: 1;
    background: #5B250B;
    font-family: Tahoma, Arial, Helvetica, sans-serif;
    color: #666;
    font-size: 14px;
    line-height: 18px;
}
h1, h2, h3, h4, h5, h6
{
    font-weight: bold;
    clear: both;
}
a:link, a:visited
{
    color:#946c4e;
    text-decoration: none;
}
a:hover, a:active
{
    color: #7e5b30;
}
p
{
    margin-bottom: 18px;
}
li
{
    padding-left: 5px;
}
```

```
/* Styling User Defined Tags */
/* layout */
#divIeHack
{
    float:left;
    width:100%;
    height:150px;
}
    #divWrapper
    {
        width: 940px;
        margin: 0 auto;
    }
        #headerName
        {
            float:left;
            width:100%;
            min-height:85px;
            background-color:#8C540C;
        }
            #headerName hgroup
            {
                float:left;
                width:95.8%;
                padding-left:40px;
                color: #EDE6DD;
                clear:both;
            }
                #divName
                {
                    float:left;
                    width:60%;
                    height:auto;
                }
```

```
            #divLogo
            {
                float:left;
                width:40%;
                height:auto;
            }
        #divName h2
        {
            font-size:10pt;
            color:#FFFFFF;
        }
#divMainSec
{
    float:left;
    width: 940px;
    height:auto;

    padding: 15px 0 10px 0;
    background: #ede6dd;
}
    #sidebar
    {
        float: left;
        width: 28%;
        height:auto;

        padding-left: 20px;
        /*background: #990000;*/
    }
        #divLeftMenu
        {
            float:left;
            width:100%;
            height:auto;
```

```
    margin-bottom:60%;
    /*background-color:#FFCCFF;*/
}
#content
{
    float: right;
    width: 67%;
    height:auto;

    margin-right: 10px;
    padding: 5px 5px;
    /*background-color:#FFFFCC;*/
}
/* ARTICLES */
article img {
    border: none;
    -webkit-box-shadow: 3px 3px 7px #777;
    -moz-box-shadow: 3px 3px 7px #777;
}
#content p, ul, ol, hr {
    margin-bottom: 24px;
}
#content ul ul, ol ol, ul ol, ol ul {
    margin-bottom: 0;
}
#content h2, h3, h4, h5, h6 {
    color: #333;
    margin: 0 0 20px 0;
    line-height: 1.5em;
}
```

```
/* Styling Top Menu STARTS */
nav .menu
{
    font-size: 14px;
    font-weight: bold;
}
nav .menu
{
    margin: 0px 0px;
    padding:0px 0px;
    list-style: none;
    line-height: normal;
}
nav .menu li
{
    margin: 0px 0px 20px 5px;
    list-style: none;
}
nav .menu a
{
    padding: 5px 15px;
    text-decoration: none;
    font-size: 11pt;
    color: #5B250B;
    color: rgb(91, 37, 11);
    text-shadow: 0 1px 1px rgba(91, 37, 11);
    -webkit-border-radius: 14px;
    -moz-border-radius: 14px;
    border-radius: 14px;
    -webkit-transition: all 1s ease-in-out;
    -moz-transition: all 1s ease-in-out;
    -o-transition: all 1s ease-in-out;
```

```
    transition: all 1s ease-in-out;
}
nav .menu a:hover,
nav .menu a:focus
{
    color: #fff;
    background: rgba(255, 255, 255, 0.15);
}
/* Styling Top Menu ENDS */
/* footer widget blocks - STARTS */
#footer-area
{
    float:left;
    width:100%;
    height:auto;
    padding: 18px 0;
    font-family: Trebuchet MS, serif;
    background-color:#8C540C;
    color: #ede6dd;
    font-size: 90%;
}
.footer-segment
{
    float: left;
    width: 190px;
    margin-right: 20px;
    margin-left: 20px;
}
```

```
        footer aside h4
        {
            color: #f5eee5;
            font-size: 16px;
            line-height: 1.5em;
        }
        footer a:link,
        footer a:visited
        {
            color: #f5eee5;
        }
        /* footer widget blocks - STARTS */
/* Styling For Product Images STARTS */
.productImg
{
    float:left;
    width:100%;
    height:auto;

    margin-bottom:10px;
}
.productImg a img
{
    border: none;
    opacity: 4;
    /* IE 8 hack */
    -ms-filter: "progid:DXImageTransform.Microsoft.Alpha(Opacity=25)";
    /* IE 5-7 hack */
    filter: alpha(opacity = 25);
}
```

```
.productImg a:hover img,
.productImg a:focus img
{
    opacity: 0.3;
    /* IE 8 hack */
    -ms-filter:"progid:DXImageTransform.Microsoft.Alpha(Opacity=60)";
    /* IE 5-7 hack */
    filter: alpha(opacity = 20);
}
/* Styling For Product Images ENDS */
```

Chapter 13 – Create an Register Form

2)
index.html

```
<!DOCTYPE html>
<html lang="en">
<head>
    <meta charset="utf-8" />
    <title>Chapter 13 - Enriching Forms Using CSS3 Properties - Registration Form</title>
    <link rel="stylesheet" type="text/css" href="css/styles.css" />
</head>
<body>
<div id="divRegister">
    <h3 class="alerts">Register</h3>
    <form action="/" id="registerAlerts">
        <fieldset>
            <label for="alertsFName">First Name:</label>
            <input type="text" id="alertsFName" />
        </fieldset>
```

```
        <fieldset>
            <label for="alertsLName">Last Name:</label>
            <input type="text" id="alertsLName"  />
        </fieldset>
        <fieldset>
            <label for="alertsEmailId">Email ID:</label>
            <input type="text" id="alertsEmailId" />
        </fieldset>
        <fieldset>
            <label for="alertsPassword">Password:</label>
            <input type="text" id="alertsPassword" />
        </fieldset>
        <fieldset>
            <label for="alertsConfirmPassword">Confirm Password:</label>
            <input type="text" id="alertsConfirmPassword" />
        </fieldset>
        <fieldset>
            <input type="submit" value="Register Now!!!" />
        </fieldset>
    </form>
</div> <!-- divLogin ENDS -->
</body>
</html>
```

styles.css

```
body {
    font-family: "Helvetica Neue", Helvetica, Arial, sans-serif;
    color: #222;
    background-color:#CCC;
}
a img
{
```

```
    border: none;
}
/* links */
a:link, a:visited
{
    text-decoration: none;
    font-weight: bold;
    color: #1e638d;
    outline: none;
}
a:hover
{
    color: #39c;
}
#divRegister
{
    float:left;
    width:auto;
    height:auto;
    margin:15px 15px;
    padding: 20px;
    border:2px solid #000000;
    -webkit-border-radius: 6px;
    -moz-border-radius: 6px;
    border-radius: 6px;
    border-top-left-radius: 6px 6px;
    border-top-right-radius: 6px 6px;
    border-bottom-right-radius: 6px 6px;
    border-bottom-left-radius: 6px 6px;
}
```

```
#divRegister p
{
    line-height: 1.5;
}
#divRegister h3
{
    margin: 0 0 10px 10px;
    background-color:#0033CC;
    background: url(../images/register_icon.png) left top no-repeat;
    font-size: 24pt;
    font-weight: bold;
    text-transform: uppercase;
    line-height: 1;
    text-shadow: 0 1px 0px #990000;
    color: #333333;
}
#divRegister h3.alerts
{
    padding: 3px 0 3px 36px;
}
#registerAlerts fieldset
{
    margin: 0 0 10px 0;
    border:none;
}
#registerAlerts label
{
    display: block;
    font-weight: bold;
    line-height: 1.4;
    color: #666;
    color: rgba(0, 0, 0, 0.6);
```

```
    text-shadow: 0 1px 1px #fff;
}
#registerAlerts fieldset:last-child
{
    margin: 0;
}
#registerAlerts fieldset input[type="text"]
{
    width: 215px;
    padding: 5px 8px;
    font-size: 1.2em;
    color: #666;
    border: none;
    background-image: -webkit-gradient(linear, 0% 0%, 0% 12%, from(#999), to(#fff));
    background-image: -moz-linear-gradient(0% 12% 90deg, #fff, #999);
    background-color: #fff;
    -webkit-border-radius: 4px;
    -moz-border-radius: 4px;
    -o-border-radius: 4px;
    border-radius: 4px;
}
#registerAlerts input[type="submit"]
{
    padding: 8px 15px;
    font-family: Helvetica, Arial, sans-serif;
    font-weight: bold;
    line-height: 1;
    color: #444;
    border: none;
    text-shadow: 0 1px 1px rgba(255, 255, 255, 0.85);
    background-image: -webkit-gradient(linear, 0% 0%, 0% 100%, from(#fff), to(#bbb));
```

```
    background-image: -moz-linear-gradient(0% 100% 90deg, #bbb, #fff);
    background-color: #fff;
    -webkit-border-radius: 23px;
    -moz-border-radius: 23px;
    -o-border-radius: 23px;
    border-radius: 23px;
    -webkit-box-shadow: 0 1px 2px rgba(0, 0, 0, 0.5);
    -moz-box-shadow: 0 1px 2px rgba(0, 0, 0, 0.5);
    box-shadow: 0 1px 2px rgba(0, 0, 0, 0.5);
}
@-webkit-keyframes pulse
{
    0%
    {
        -webkit-box-shadow: 0 0 12px rgba(255, 51, 0, 0.2);
    }
    50%
    {
        -webkit-box-shadow: 0 0 12px rgba(255, 51, 0, 0.9);
    }
    100%
    {
        -webkit-box-shadow: 0 0 12px rgba(255, 51, 0, 0.2);
    }
}
#registerAlerts input[type="text"]:focus
{
    -webkit-animation-name: pulse;
    -webkit-animation-duration: 1.5s;
    -webkit-animation-iteration-count: infinite;
    -webkit-animation-timing-function: ease-in-out;
}
```

```
#registerAlerts input[type="submit"]:hover,
#registerAlerts input[type="submit"]:focus
{
    -webkit-animation: pulse 2s infinite ease-in-out;
    cursor:pointer;
}
```

Chapter 14 - Enriching Forms Using CSS3 Properties

1) Create a row with the Latest Products

```
<!doctype html>
<html lang="en">
<head>
    <meta charset="utf-8" />
    <title>CSS3 Chap 14 - Transforming The Message - Hands-On-Exercise</title>
    <link rel="stylesheet" href="css/styles.css" type="text/css" media="screen" />
</head>
<body>
<!-- divIeHack STARTS -->
<div id="divIeHack">
    <!-- divWrapper STARTS -->
    <div id="divWrapper">
        <!-- headerName STARTS -->
        <header id="headerName">
            <hgroup>
                <div id="divName">
                    <h1>Lorem Ipsum</h1>
                    <h2>Come learn how to use lorem ipsum</h2>
                </div>
```

```
            <div id="divLogo">
                <img src="images/logo1.gif" alt="Logo" width="150"
                height="107" align="right" />
            </div>

        </hgroup>

    </header><!-- headerName ENDS -->
    <!-- divMainSec STARTS -->
    <section id="divMainSec">

        <aside id="sidebar"><!-- sidebar -->

            <div id="divLeftMenu">
                <nav><!-- top nav -->
                    <ul class="menu">
                        <li><a href="#">Home</a></li>
                        <li><a href="#">About Us</a></li>
                        <li><a href="#">Products</a></li>
                        <li><a href="#">Forum</a></li>
                        <li><a href="#">Contact Us</a></li>
                    </ul>
                </nav><!-- end of top nav -->
            </div>

        </aside><!-- end of sidebar -->

        <section id="content"><!-- #content -->

            <article>
                <h3><a href="#">Lorem Ipsum </a></h3>
                <p>Lorem Ipsum is simply dummy text of the printing and typesetting industry. Lorem Ipsum has been the industry's standard dummy text ever since the 1500s, when an unknown printer took a galley of type and scrambled it to make a type specimen book. It has survived not only five centuries, but also the leap into electronic typesetting, remaining essentially unchanged. It was popularised in the 1960s with the release of Letraset sheets containing Lorem Ipsum passages, and more recently with desktop publishing software like Aldus PageMaker including versions of Lorem Ipsum.</p>
            </article>
```

```
<article>
    <h3><a href="#">Latest Products</a></h3>
    <ul class="latestProd">
        <li class="img1"><a href="#">
        <img src="images/multi-touch-consumer.gif"
         alt="Multi Touch Consumer" width="125"
        height="125" /> </a></li>

    <li class="img2"><a href="#">
    <img src="images/ hp.gif" alt="HP Laptop" width="125"
    height="125" /> </a></li>
    <li class="img1"><a href="#">
    <img src="images/mac-apple-tablet1.gif" alt="MAC
    Apple Tablet" width="125" height="125" /> </a> </li>
    <li class="img2"><a href="#">
    <img src="images/appleinsider.gif"
    alt="MAC Apple Laptop" width="125" height="125" />
    </a></li>
    </ul>
</article>

</section><!-- end of #content -->

</section><!-- divMainSec ENDS -->

<div class="divClear"></div>

<footer id="footer-area">
    <section id="footer-outer-block">
        <aside class="footer-segment">
            <h4>Social Networking</h4>
            <ul>
                <li><a href="#">Twitter</a></li>
                <li><a href="#">Facebook</a></li>
                <li><a href="#">Skype</a></li>
            </ul>
        </aside><!-- end of #first footer segment -->
```

```
            <aside class="footer-segment">
                <h4>Awesome Stuff</h4>
                    <ul>
                        <li><a href="#">one
                        linkylink</a></li>
                        <li><a href="#">two
                        linkylinks</a></li>
                        <li><a href="#">three
                        linkylinks</a></li>
                    </ul>
            </aside><!-- end of #second footer segment -->
            <aside class="footer-segment">
                <h4>Coolness</h4>
                    <ul>
                        <li><a href="#">one
                        linkylink</a></li>
                        <li><a href="#">two
                        linkylinks</a></li>
                        <li><a href="#">three
                        linkylinks</a></li>
                    </ul>
            </aside><!-- end of #third footer segment -->
            <aside class="footer-segment">
                    <h4>Blahdyblah</h4>
                    <p>Integer nec odio. Praesent libero.
                    Sed cursus ante dapibus diam.</p>
            </aside><!-- end of #fourth footer segment -->
        </section><!-- end of footer-outer-block -->
    </footer><!-- end of footer-area -->
    <div class="divClear"></div>
</div><!-- divWrapper ENDS -->
```

```
    <div class="divClear"></div>

</div><!-- divIeHack ENDS -->
</body>
</html>
```

css/styles.css

```
/* Styling HTML Tags */
body {
    line-height: 1;
    background: #5B250B;
    font-family:Tahoma, Arial, Helvetica, sans-serif;
    color: #666;
    font-size: 14px;
    line-height: 18px;
}
h1, h2, h3, h4, h5, h6
{
    font-weight: bold;
    clear: both;
}
a:link, a:visited
{
    color:#946c4e;
    text-decoration: none;
}
a:hover, a:active
{
    color: #7e5b30;
}
p
{
    margin-bottom: 18px;
}
```

```
li
{
    padding-left: 5px;
}
/* Styling User Defined Tags */
/* layout */
#divIeHack
{
    float:left;
    width:100%;
    height:auto;
}
    #divWrapper
    {
        width: 940px;
        margin: 0 auto;
        background-color:#EDE6DD;
    }
        #headerName
        {
            float:left;
            width:100%;
            min-height:85px;
            background-color:#8C540C;
        }
            #headerName hgroup
            {
                float:left;
                width:95.8%;
                padding-left:40px;

                color: #EDE6DD;
                clear:both;
            }
```

```
            #divName
            {
                float:left;
                width:60%;
                height:auto;
            }
            #divLogo
            {
                float:left;
                width:40%;
                height:auto;
            }
        #divName h2
        {
            font-size:10pt;
            color:#FFFFFF;
        }
#divMainSec
{
    float:left;
    width: 940px;
    height:auto;

    padding: 15px 0 10px 0;
    background: #ede6dd;
}
    #sidebar
    {
        float: left;
        width: 28%;
        height:auto;

        padding-left: 20px;
    }
```

```
#divLeftMenu
{
    float:left;
    width:100%;
    height:auto;
}
#content
{
    float: right;
    width: 67%;
    height:auto;

    margin-right: 10px;
    padding: 5px 5px;
}
/* ARTICLES */
article img {
    border: none;
    -webkit-box-shadow: 3px 3px 7px #777;
    -moz-box-shadow: 3px 3px 7px #777;
}
#content p, ul, ol, hr {
    margin-bottom: 24px;
}
#content ul ul, ol ol, ul ol, ol ul {
    margin-bottom: 0;
}
#content h2, h3, h4, h5, h6 {
    color: #333;
    margin: 0 0 20px 0;
    line-height: 1.5em;
}
```

```
/* Styling Top Menu STARTS */
nav .menu
{
    font-size: 14px;
    font-weight: bold;
}
nav .menu
{
    margin: 0px 0px;
    padding:0px 0px;
    list-style: none;
    line-height: normal;
}
nav .menu li
{
    margin: 0px 0px 20px 5px;
    list-style: none;
}
nav .menu a
{
    padding: 5px 15px;
    text-decoration: none;
    font-size: 11pt;
    color: #5B250B;
    color: rgb(91, 37, 11);
    text-shadow: 0 1px 1px rgba(91, 37, 11);
    -webkit-border-radius: 14px;
    -moz-border-radius: 14px;
    border-radius: 14px;
    -webkit-transition: all 1s ease-in-out;
    -moz-transition: all 1s ease-in-out;
```

```
    -o-transition: all 1s ease-in-out;
    transition: all 1s ease-in-out;
}
nav .menu a:hover,
nav .menu a:focus
{
    color: #fff;
    background: rgba(255, 255, 255, 0.15);
}
/* Styling Top Menu ENDS */
/* footer widget blocks - STARTS */
#footer-area
{
    float:left;
    width:100%;
    height:auto;
    padding: 18px 0;
    font-family: Trebuchet MS, serif;
    background-color:#8C540C;
    color: #ede6dd;
    font-size: 90%;
}
.footer-segment
{
    float: left;
    width: 190px;
    margin-right: 20px;
    margin-left: 20px;
}
```

```
        footer aside h4
        {
            color: #f5eee5;
            font-size: 16px;
            line-height: 1.5em;
        }
        footer a:link,
        footer a:visited
        {
            color: #f5eee5;
        }
        /* footer widget blocks - STARTS */
/* Styling User Class Tags */
.divClear
{
    clear:both;
}
/* Styling User Class Tags */
/* Styling For Latest Product Images STARTS */
ul.latestProd li
{
    float: left;
    margin: 0 10px;
    padding: 0px;
    border: 1px solid #ddd;
    list-style: none;
}
ul.latestProd li a img
{
    float: left;
    width: 100px;
```

```
    -webkit-transition: -webkit-transform 5s ease-in-out;
    -moz-transition: -moz-transform 5s ease-in-out;
    transition: transform 5s ease-in-out;
}
ul.latestProd li.img1 a:hover img {
    -webkit-transform: scale(1.5) rotate(20deg);
    -moz-transform: scale(1.5) rotate(20deg);
    -o-transform: scale(1.5) rotate(20deg);
    transform: scale(1.5) rotate(20deg);
    -webkit-box-shadow: 4px 4px 10px rgba(0, 0, 0, 0.5);
    -moz-box-shadow: 4px 4px 10px rgba(0, 0, 0, 0.5);
    box-shadow: 4px 4px 10px rgba(0, 0, 0, 0.5);
}
ul.latestProd li.img2 a:hover img {
    -webkit-transform: scale(1.5) rotate(-20deg);
    -moz-transform: scale(1.5) rotate(-20deg);
    -o-transform: scale(1.5) rotate(-20deg);
    transform: scale(1.5) rotate(-20deg);
    -webkit-box-shadow: 4px 4px 10px rgba(0, 0, 0, 0.5);
    -moz-box-shadow: 4px 4px 10px rgba(0, 0, 0, 0.5);
    box-shadow: 4px 4px 10px rgba(0, 0, 0, 0.5);
}
/* Styling For Latest Product Images ENDS */
```

Index

OTHER TITLES OF INTEREST

Cybersecurity Fundamentals
ISBN: 9789390684731

Cyber Forensics Up and Running
ISBN: 9789355517180

Mastering Network Forensics
ISBN: 9789355516916

Practical Digital Forensics
ISBN: 9789355511454

Modern Cybersecurity Strategies for Enterprises
ISBN: 9789355513137

Modern Cybersecurity Practices
ISBN: 9789389328257

Python for **Cybersecurity** Cookbook
ISBN: 9789355513809

Fundamentals of **Information Security**
ISBN: 9789389328400

Cybercrime and Preventive Measures
ISBN: 9789390684526

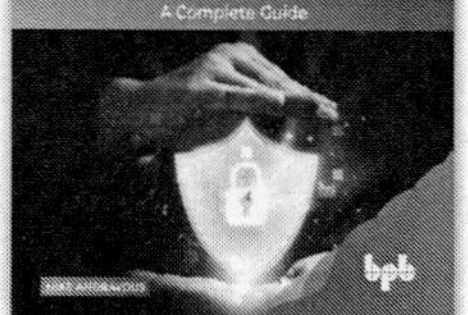

Zero Trust Security
ISBN: 9789355512512

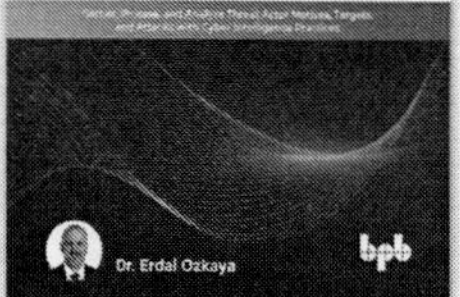

Practical Cyber Threat Intelligence
ISBN: 9789355510297

Cyber Safety for Everyone
ISBN: 9789391392567

AWS All-in-one Security Guide
ISBN: 9789355510327

Cryptography and **Network Security**
ISBN: 9789389328660

Secure Chains
ISBN: 9789389328653

My Data My Privacy My Choice
ISBN: 9789389845181